Business Law

Fourth edition

J. D. De Freitas LLM, MA, FABE, Solicitor

Senior Lecturer in Law - South Bank Business School

Castlevale Limited, London

First Published by Castlevale Ltd., 1987
Second Edition 1991
Third Edition 1994
Fourth Edition 1999

William House
14 Worple Road
Wimbledon
London SW 19

ISBN 0 907235 07 7

To the memory of Joseph Ivan De Freitas

Contents

Preface

Changes in the law have continued unabated since the publication of the third edition of this book, mainly in the consumer field, and in employment. This edition has been substantially re-written and updated to take account of those changes and at the same time to achieve a greater coherence in presentation of material. Several new cases have been mentioned including Re Selectmove Ltd, Steveson & Anor v. Rogers, Thomas Witter Ltd v. TBP Industries Ltd, and White v. Jones. Of equal importance and also dealt with is the effect of the Unfair Terms in Consumer Contracts Regulations 1994, the Sale and Supply of Goods Act 1994 and the Employment Rights Act 1996.

The text is self-contained and covers the syllabus requirements of the Chartered Association of Certified Accountants, the Chartered Institute of Management Accountants, the Institute of Chartered Secretaries and Administrators, and the Association of Business Executives. It will also be useful to students preparing for Law Degrees, the Common Professional Examination and the Legal Practice Course.

Students should read each chapter once through, and then go over it again, this time making notes in a file or notebook. Research suggests that the act of writing and collating notes aid learning and recall. To assist students with examination preparation, the book includes a chapter on 'Examination Technique' and a selection of examination questions with suggested answers from professional examinations.

The author would like to thank the following professional bodies for permission to use their past examination questions:

Chartered Association of Certified Accountants
Chartered Institute of Management Accountants
Institute of Chartered Secretaries and Administrators

In addition, thanks are due to Michelle Ramsammy for her invaluable contribution in the form of the chapter of 'Law of Tort', to Ralph Gharibi for technical help and advice, and to Nick Richards (Head of Undergraduate Studies, South Bank Business School) for his support and encouragement in ensuring that the necessary research was undertaken. Finally, the author wishes to record his gratitude to South Bank University for making available its research facilities without which this edition would not have been possible.

Jerry De Freitas
South Bank University
May 1999

Chapter 1

Nature and Sources of Law

Introduction

It is far easier to describe law than to define it. Various attempts at a definition have been made by learned jurists. Thus, Austin defined it as 'a command issued by a superior (the state) to an inferior (an individual);' and Salmond as 'the body of principles recognised and applied by the state for the administration of justice.' The weaknesses of these definitions and definitions of other jurists, notably the Greek philosophers, are within the sphere of jurisprudence and outside the scope of this book. A useful description of law is to say that it embodies rules of conduct recognised by the state and enforced by the courts. Law differs from morality in that the latter is based on rules which are voluntarily adhered to by virtue of their intrinsic rightness. Law serves various functions. It is used to enforce the accepted values of society, to determine rights and to settle disputes.

The most important characteristic of English law is its continuity. English law has continued to grow since medieval times, without the need to import foreign legal systems. Another important characteristic is its lack of codification. While in continental countries, most of the law has been reduced to written codes, English law remains, by and large, unwritten. Also the practice of following previous judicial decisions (i.e. the doctrine of precedent) is a distinctive feature of the English system. An English court is bound by a previous judgement of a superior court and, subject to exceptions, a court of equal standing when it has to deal with a similar case.

This is in sharp contrast with the Continental civil law system which does not treat case law as actually binding in later cases. English law is enforced in the courts through the accusatorial procedure, whereby the courts remain aloof and leave it to the parties' advisers to take the initiative and present their arguments. Continental judiciaries use the inquisitorial procedure, whereby the courts play a more active part by questioning the parties and their witnesses.

A major classification of law is the division between criminal and civil law. Criminal law is concerned with rules of conduct imposed on individuals by the state and its object is punishment of the wrongdoer. Proceedings are instituted by the state and brought in a criminal court. Civil law regulates disputed rights and obligations between individuals in a civil court; and its object is to provide compensation to the wronged party.

The phrase 'sources of law' is also not so easy to define, since it can be used in different senses. It can be used to mean the *historical sources* which indicate how the law originated and which are regarded generally as common law and equity; or the *legal sources* which indicate the means by which the law is presently brought into existence and which are regarded generally as legislation, judicial precedent and European Union law; or the *literary sources* which identify the materials in which the legal sources are recorded and which include the various publications of statutes (notably the Queen's Printer's Copy), the law reports (with respect to precedent), the Official Journal of the European Union (with respect to EU law) and certain authoritative textbooks (an indirect source of all the legal sources); or the *subsidiary sources*, a portmanteau for minor historical, legal and literary sources (e.g. the law merchant, canon law, local customs, textbooks and the law commission).

I Common Law

The term 'Common Law' can be used in different senses. It is sometimes used to described all the unwritten laws of the land (e.g. common law, equity and local customs) in the sense that they have not been enacted, but are contained in innumerable recorded decisions of the judges. It is also used to distinguish the English legal system from other systems, such as the Continental civil law system. The former is relatively free of Roman influence. However, the narrow meaning of the term 'common law' refers to the historical source of English law in relation to the law which was administered in the Royal Courts before the passing of the Judicature Acts 1873 and 1875. This law originated from local customs and dated back to the Norman Conquest in 1066.

Prior to 1066, there was no unified system of law in the country. England was divided into Saxon kingdoms, each with its own laws based on local customs and administered in local courts. After the Norman Conquest, a central system of Royal Courts was established to administer the law with the result that the law became unified.

The process of unification was slow and took over three centuries to complete. The Norman Conquest saw the administration of justice and ownership of land concentrated in Norman hands. Norman landowners established their own courts, the feudal courts, to which the local courts had to transfer their land jurisdiction. Both the local courts and feudal courts were subject to control by the King's Council (the Curia Regis) which initially exercised administrative, legislative and judicial functions. From the King's Council evolved three Royal Courts, namely, the Court of Exchequer which dealt principally with revenue matters involving subjects and the Crown, the Court of Common Pleas which dealt with disputes between subjects in which the Crown had no interest, and the Court of King's Bench which dealt with 'Pleas of the Crown'. (i.e. criminal matters and civil disputes, involving a breach of the King's peace or some other royal interest). These Royal Courts sat at Westminster though, subsequently, Royal Justices from the courts were sent to travel the country to hold 'Assizes'.

The feudal courts lost their land jurisdiction to the Royal Courts when the latter removed proceedings from the former, such as by the writ of Pone which fictitiously alleged a defect in proceedings in the feudal courts. The local courts' jurisdiction in personal actions diminished in importance after the Royal Judges used the Statute of Gloucester 1278 to require personal actions in excess of forty shillings to be dealt with in the Royal Courts.

The administration of the law in the Royal Courts was accompanied by the creation of individual writs by the Chancery. These writs recognised specific rights and allowed litigants to commence proceedings in the Royal Courts only if the facts alleged fell within the scope of an existing writ. In this way, the law became common throughout the land.

II Equity

The concept of equity is based on justice and fair play. As an historical source of English law, it refers to the body of rules formulated and administered by the Court of Chancery before the passing of the Judicature Acts. These rules were introduced to fill in the gaps let by common law.

The ability of the common law to grow rapidly after the reign of Henry III in the thirteenth century was hindered both by precedent and by the Provisions of Oxford 1258 which prevented the Chancellor from issuing new writs on his own initiative; and while the Statute of Westminster 1285 (also known as *In consimili casu*) allowed variations of existing writs to be issued, justice could not be done in every case Injustices resulted either because of the very strict common law requirement of proof, or because the facts alleged did not fall within the scope of an existing writ.

An individual who suffered an injustice under the common law would petition the king to obtain redress by direct royal intervention. The king would pass on the petition to his chief minister, the Lord Chancellor, who acted initially in the king's name. But in 1474, a decree was made by the Lord Chancellor on his own authority and this practice continued with the result that the Lord Chancellor was able to set up his own court, the Court of Chancery, independent of the Royal Courts, and which developed its own type of laws based on 'conscience' and 'fair play', called equity.

Equity as administered by the Court of Chancery supplemented the common law and corrected its deficiencies in three ways. With its ***concurrent jurisdiction,*** the Court of Chancery introduced remedies which the common law failed to provide (e.g. the specific performance of a contract, and an injunction to refrain or continue the doing of an act). These remedies were very useful as an alternative to common law damages. With its ***exclusive jurisdiction***, it recognised rights which the common law failed to enforce (e.g. trusts, and equitable rights resulting from proprietary estoppel). With its ***auxiliary jurisdiction,*** it introduced new procedures to supplement those of common law. For example, unlike the common law, it could compel the defendant to appear before the courts, and could require him to prepare accounts. Also while a common law action could only be commenced by an established writ, an action in equity could commence by petition which did not require any particular formality as long as it disclosed some reason for the Lord Chancellor's intervention.

As a result of the introduction of precedent in the Court of Chancery, equity became as rigid as the common law by the early nineteenth century. It thus operated as a separate system of law which often ran into conflict with the common law. A number of reforming statutes were passed, but it was left to the Judicature Acts to cure the anomalies. These Acts abolished the Royal Courts and the Court of Chancery and replaced them with a unified system of courts, called the Supreme Court of Judicature which administered both the common law and equity. The Acts also simplified court procedure (e.g. by providing a standard writ) and declared that whenever there was a conflict between common law and equity, the latter was to prevail.

III Legislation

This is law enacted by Parliament (parliamentary legislation) or by a subordinate body under Parliament's control (delegated legislation). Parliament comprised the House of Commons, the House of Lords and the Queen.

Legislation has become necessary for several reasons. Common law and equity, because of the doctrine of precedent, are fairly inflexible and can only be developed to meet new conditions by varying and extending the application of existing principles. Legislation provides a more rapid and efficient means of effecting such legal changes. This reforming function of legislation is particularly useful where an unpopular House of Lords decision exists. Legislation is also useful to simplify the law (e.g. by consolidating and codifying the law); to raise revenue for the government (e.g. the Finance Acts) and to regulate the day to day running of the welfare state.

(i) Parliamentary legislation. The process by which this enacted law is made is by the passing of 'bills' which, on receiving the Royal Assent, become Acts of Parliament or Statutes. A bill has to pass through five stages in each House before receiving the Royal Assent. These stages are: the First Reading (an informal stage where only the title of the bill is read), the Second Reading (where the principles of the bill are debated), the Committee Stage (where the details of the bill are considered), the Report Stage (where amendments made at the Committee Stage are considered by the whole House), and the Third Reading (where only minor amendments are made).

Once a bill receives the Royal Assent, it becomes law and remains so until repealed by a subsequent Act of Parliament. Moreover, the courts have no common law power to question its regularity. This supremacy of Parliament is sometimes called 'the Sovereignty of Parliament'. The European Communities Act 1972 which effected the changes to the English legal system, so that the United Kingdom could obtain membership of the European Union from 1st January 1993, has given the courts statutory power to prevent national law from being enacted, if it would conflict with EU provisions. As Lord Denning observed in **Macarthys Ltd v. Smith (1979)** '...if on close investigation, it should appear that our legislation is deficient, or is inconsistent with Community law, by some oversight of our draughtsman, then it is our bounded duty to give priority to Community law. Such is the result of Section 2 (1) and (4) of the European Communities Act...' In **Factortame Ltd v. Secretary of State for Transport (No.2) (1991),** the UK Parliament passed the Merchant Shipping Act 1988 which required that 75% of the directors and shareholders of a company had to be British before the company could obtain a fishing licence to fish in British waters. A UK company controlled by Spanish fishermen challenged the validity of the Act on the ground that it was incompatible with the relevant articles of the EEC treaty relating to the common fisheries policy of the European Union. The relevant articles of the Treaty were referred to the European Court of Justice for interpretation, in particular to see whether they had direct effect. In the meantime, the House of Lords granted an injunction to prevent the British Government from implementing the provisions of the Merchant Shipping Act until final judgement.

(ii) Delegated legislation. As a result of the lengthy process of making statue law, Parliament does not have time to pass all the necessary legislation. Thus it is usual for it to delegate its legislative powers to subordinate bodies. Such bodies include the Privy Council which can then make laws by issuing orders-in-council; government departments which may issue statutory instruments, and local authorities which may make by-laws. The power to make laws is then said to be 'delegated' and the laws that are made in this way are termed 'delegated legislation.' A vast amount of law is made by subordinate bodies, the main feature which distinguished delegated legislation from Acts of Parliament is that while Parliament is sovereign (at least where domestic legislation are concerned), these subordinate bodies are not.

One reason for the increasing use of delegated legislation is that it eases the pressure on parliamentary time available to deal with other important and pressing matters. Another reason is that the subject matter requiring regulation may be too technical for ordinary Members of Parliament to deal with. Also, as parliamentary procedure is slow and cumbersome, it may be necessary to delegate power to some other body when immediate action is required, especially in times of national crisis. Such powers are exercised frequently by orders-in-council.

Despite its obvious advantages, various arguments have been raised against delegated legislation. Too much power is given to subordinate bodies who, in many instances, are non-elected bodies removed by a considerable distance from Parliament (e.g. the five-tier authority of the Emergency Powers Act 1939). Since delegated legislation is so easy to make (e.g. many statutory instruments take effect once placed before Parliament) it can lead to uncertainty in the law. Moreover, it can lead to an abuse of power as its sheer volume makes it difficult for Parliament to control.

Two types of control exist over delegated legislation - parliamentary control and judicial control. Parliamentary control is exercised mainly by the scrutinising of statutory instruments by the Select Committee on Statutory Instruments set up under the Statutory Instruments Act 1946. This committee is made up of MPs and its function is to check all statutory instruments laid before Parliament to ensure that government departments do not exceed their powers. The Act also requires publicity of such instruments and states that it is a defence for any person charged with contravening the provisions of a statutory instrument to show that the instrument had not been issued by Her Majesty's Stationery Office at the date of the alleged contravention, unless other reasonable steps had been taken to bring the instrument to the notice of the public. The Local Government Act 1972 requires by-laws to be confirmed by the appropriate minister before they can come into force and for public notice to be given both before and after confirmation.

Judicial control is exercised by the courts which have power to declare any form of delegated legislation *ultra vires* and void. Statutory instruments have been declared invalid because ministers have exceeded their powers, or have failed to follow set procedures laid down by Parliament. By-laws may be challenged on the grounds that they are unreasonable (e.g. they unfairly favour particular interests in the community).

(iii) The Courts and legislation. It is the duty of the courts to enforce the law declared in statutes and delegated legislation. Where the law is drafted in very broad terms, as is the continental practice, the courts have full scope to develop the relevant applications of the principles and to adapt them to new situations as they arise, so that the general problem of interpretation is minimised. However, with the English practice of having detailed legislation, legal interpretation is much more of a problem, especially as the meaning of an enactment is often far form clear. The English courts may have regard to the title and preamble of the Act and, since **Pepper v. Hart (1993),** to Hansard and other Parliamentary materials as aid of construction. However, parliamentary materials can be looked at only if the following conditions are satisfied: (a) the words of the Act are ambiguous, obscure or absurd. Words are ambiguous, if they are capable of two or more different meaning; they are obscure if they have no clear meaning at all; they are absurd if they have a clear meaning , but the meaning renders the Act self-contradictory or undermines a fundamental legal principle; (b) the materials consist of extracts by the sponsor of the bill, and (c) the statements relied on are clear.

The courts have also developed rules of construction and presumptions as external aids. The main rules of construction are:-

(a) The Literal Rule. This states that the words of an enactment should be given their ordinary and popular meaning. In **Gammans v. Ekins (1950),** the Court of Appeal was called upon to construe the word 'family' under the Rent Restrictions Acts in order to decide whether, on the death of a statutory tenant, her live-in partner who had adopted her name and posed as her husband for some 20 years, was entitled to protection by succession as being a 'member of the tenant's family'. The court held that 'family' should be given its ordinary and popular meaning and , on the facts, the defendant was not a member of the family.

(b) The Golden Rule. This states that if in using the literal rule, this would lead to absurdity or some repugnancy with the rest of the enactment, then the ordinary sense of the word should be modified so as to avoid that absurdity. In **Adler v. George (1964),** the defendant was charged with obstructing members of the air force on their RAF base. It was an offence under Official Secrets Act 1920 to obstruct HM Forces in the vicinity of a prohibited place. The defendant argued that he had not committed an offence under the Act because 'in the vicinity' means 'surrounding' the base and not 'in' the base. However, Lord Parker CJ said 'in the vicinity' should not be read literally, but should be used to include 'in' the prohibited place itself as it would lead otherwise to absurdity.

(c) The Contextual Rule. This states that a word in isolation has no absolute meaning. Its meaning is relative to the context in which it is used.

(d) The *Eiusdem Generis* Rule. This states that where general words follow specific words, the general words should be taken as referring to those things of the same class as specifically mentioned. In **Powell v. Kempton Park Racecourse Co (1899)**, the Betting Act 1853 prohibited the keeping of a 'house, office, room or other place' for betting with persons resorting thereto. The court held that 'other place' did not apply to an uncovered enclosure adjacent to the racecourse.

For the *Eiusdem Generis* rule to apply, there has to be two specific words to create a genus . Thus, in **Allen v. Emmerson (1944)** where a statute referred to 'theatres and other places of amusement', it was held that a funfair was within the Act even though not within the same class as 'theatres'.

(e) The Mischief Rule. This states that if the words of the statute are ambiguous, then to find out the true meaning of the enactment, the courts must consider the defects of the old law and the mischief which the statute was intended to prevent.

Presumptions. Apart from rules, the courts also make certain assumptions unless the contrary is stated. These include the presumption that legislation is not intended to bind the Crown, the presumption that legislation does not have retrospective effect, the presumption against imposition of criminal liability without fault, the presumption against alteration of the law, and the presumption that proprietary rights are not to be taken away without compensation.

IV Judicial Precedent

This means a judgement for later courts to follow when similar facts come before them for a solution. The doctrine of precedent has its origins in the reign of William I who wanted to preserve Anglo-Saxon laws. Judges were required to declare the law either by example or analogy, or because it was declared before by a competent court and therefore had to be followed. So whenever a dispute comes before the courts today the judges are required to listen to the evidence submitted by the parties and then settle the dispute by arriving at a decision which is binding on the parties (known as *res judicata*) and by establishing a legal principle which will bind all future cases with similar facts (known as *ratio decidendi*). The doctrine of precedent therefore depends on two factors (a) the standing of the courts in a particular hierarchy, and (b) the existence of a legal principle established by the courts as to what the law is.

Under the English common law system, lower courts are obliged to follow a judgement of a superior court as long as that judgement has not been reversed on appealed or overruled (a judgement is overruled where a superior court states at a later date that the legal principle established in the judgement must not be followed). Even a previous judgement of a court of equal standing has to be followed on occasions. Thus the Court of Appeal must follow its previous judgement and can only depart from it where the judgement was made in ignorance of an existing statute or earlier precedent of the House of Lords (**Young v. Bristol Aeroplane Corp Ltd (1944)**), or where the previous judgement conflicted with a later House of Lords judgement (i.e. the House of Lords overruled it), or where there are two conflicting Court of Appeal judgements on the same matter, or where in a criminal case to follow the previous judgement would lead to injustice (**R v Gould (1968)**). The House of Lords need not follow its previous judgement if it would lead to injustice. The High Court is not bound by the judgement of a single High Court judge.

Where later courts **must** follow the previous judgement the precedent is called a ***binding precedent*** (or *stare decisis*). Where the courts **may** follow the previous judgement the precedent is called a ***persuasive precedent***. Examples of persuasive precedent are foreign judgements, *ratio decidendi* of inferior courts and the *obiter dicta* (see below) of a judgement.

***Ratio decidendi* and *obiter dicta*.** *Ratio decidendi* (literally: the reason for the decision) may be defined as the statement of law applied by the courts to the legal problem raised by the material facts upon which the judgement is based. The 'statement of law' established by the courts is the judges' opinion as to the principle of common law or equity relevant to the problem. Occasionally, the courts will anticipate variation of the material facts and will state the legal principles which would then apply. This is known as *obiter dicta* and is only of persuasive authority. An example of *obiter dicta,* is Denning J's judgement in **Central London Property Trust v. High Trees House (1947)** on promissory estoppel. In that case, the plaintiffs voluntarily agreed to take a reduced rent for a fixed period, and when the period expired, they asked for a return of the original rent. The judge allowed them to enforce future rent at the contract rate, but stated that had they asked for the arrears of rent, they would not have succeeded because of their promise to take a reduced rent for a limited period. *Obiter dicta* may be used also to mean statements of law in support of dissenting judgements.

Where there is no precedent and legislation does not provide for a certain problem, the courts will resolve that problem by reference to analogous principles. For example, the principle of law imposing liability for negligent **acts** causing injury to person or physical damage to property was extended by the House of Lords in **Hedley Byrne & Co Ltd v. Heller & Partners Ltd (1964)** to cover negligent **statements** causing economic or financial loss. On the other hand, if the courts feel that a principle of law established in an earlier judgement is far too wide, they may limit the application of that judgement (**Caparo Industries plc v. Dickman & Others (1990)**).

Where statements of law are expounded and developed in the course of a judgement, the law extracted from the case is called 'case law.'

Advantages and disadvantages of precedent. Precedent makes the law certain and predictable. If the legal problem raised had been solved before, then persons who contemplate litigation will know the possible outcome of the case. Precedent allows the law to grow and develop according to the changing needs of society. The law can be altered comparatively easily without requiring lengthy parliamentary proceedings. Precedent is more practical in so far as there exists no legal rule for which there cannot be found practical solutions.

The obvious disadvantages are its rigidity, bulk and complexity. It is rigid in the sense that the courts are bound to follow a legal principle even though it is thought to be wrong and this in turn can lead to hardship. Sometimes the courts make illogical distinctions in order to avoid following precedent. Also too many laws are made by precedent with the result that basic principles tend to be obscure.

IV European Law

This is the law of the European Union (formerly the European Community). The European Union was set up in 1957 by the Treaty of Rome. Originally only six countries (France, Germany, Italy, Belgium, Holland and Luxembourg) comprised the Union but this number is gradually being extended (e.g. the United Kingdom, Ireland and Denmark joined in 1973 as a result of signing the First Treaty of Accession 1972; Greece joined in 1981 by signing the Second Treaty of Accession 1979; Portugal and Spain in 1986 by signing the Third Treaty of Accession 1985.

The principal institutions of the European Union are the Council of Ministers, the European Commission, the European Parliament, and European Court of Justice and (although not formally created) the European Council.

The Council of Ministers comprises one government minister from each member state. When general external matters are being discussed, the foreign minister of each member state will sit on the Council; otherwise the ministers whose portfolio relates to the matters under discussion will sit. The office of president of the Council rotates among member states for six-month terms. The Council exercises all the powers conferred by the Treaties. For example, Article 145 of the EEC Treaty gives the Council power to legislate (by making regulations, taking decisions and issuing directives) usually acting upon a proposal from the Commission. Voting on the Council can be by simple majority (for procedural questions), qualified majority i.e. weighted votes based on the relative population of member states (for most proposals to achieve the Single Market), or unanimity (for new policies, or if the Council wishes to amend a Commission's proposal without the Commission's consent).

The European Commission consists of Commissioners appointed on grounds of their general competence from among nationals of member states. Each member state has a national on the Commission; but by practice the larger states (the UK, France, Germany, Italy and Spain) have two. The Commission is the executive of the European Union. It ensures that the EU's policies are observed, it initiates legislation by making proposals (after consultation with interested parties) for the Council to act on. It also represents the European Union in negotiations with non-member states and is responsible for the administration of the European Union funds.

The European Parliament comprises MEPs appointed for five years by direct elections. The structure of the Parliament is dual-based : political groupings and parliamentary committees. The European Parliament has no general law making power and cannot raise taxes like a national parliament. However, as a result of the Treaty of the European Union 1992 (i.e. the Maastricht Treaty) it is actively involved in the framing of EU legislation through co-operation and joint decision -making. Under the co-operation procedure, the Commission initiates legislation by sending its proposal to the Parliament for its opinion (this constitutes the first reading of the proposal). The Council of Ministers adopts a common position on the Commission's proposal, and the common position is sent to Parliament for a second reading. If the Parliament rejects the common position by an absolute majority, the Council can only adopt it by unanimity. In other areas of the EU treaties (e.g. Article 49 which deals with the free movement of workers), the Council can only legislate with the consent of the Parliament. Under this joint decision -making procedure, if after the second reading, Parliament and the Council cannot agree on a common position (even after the intervention of a Conciliation Committee comprising of an equal number of members of the Council and representatives of the Parliament), the Council cannot act on the proposal even by unanimous vote. Proposed treaties of a financial or political nature between the European Union and third countries also require the approval of the

European Parliament by absolute majority before they can become binding.

The European Parliament has a supervisory function in that it can require answers from the Council and the Commission on the day to day activities of the European Union; and it can remove the whole Commission from office by a motion of censure. However, such a motion has to be moved by a political grouping or by one-tenth of the MEPs, there must be a three-day 'reflection time' between the time the motion is tabled and the actual vote, a majority of the total representatives of the Parliament must have voted, and the motion must be passed by a two-thirds majority. Finally, the European Parliament participates in the budgetary procedure of the European Union.

The European Court of Justice has judges and Advocate does not participate in the discussions that lead to the Court's decision, but rather prepares in open court for the judges a 'reasoned submission' of the law and justice in the context of the treaties relevant to the case.

The Court of Justice hears actions in connection with European law by virtue of specific articles in the treaties. Article 169 allows the Commission (and Article 170, a member state) to institute proceedings in the Court of Justice for an alleged failure of a member state to fulfil a treaty obligation. Article 173 enables a member state, the Commission or the Council of Ministers to apply to the Court of Justice for a review of the legality of binding acts of the Commission, the Council and the Parliament. An individual can only apply for an annulment order under Article 173 if the act of the institution was specifically directed at him (as in the case of certain decisions). Article 175 allows a member state or any EU institution (including the European Parliament) to apply for a declaration by the Court of Justice that the failure of an EU institution to carry out a binding act was an infringement of an EU obligation. An individual can use Article 175 only if the institution had failed to act on a Decision for which he was the beneficiary.

The Court of Justice also has jurisdiction to hear actions brought against EU institutions by a member state or by an individual for compensation for damage caused by the institution **(Art. 178)** and to give preliminary rulings at the request of national courts and tribunals **(Art.177).** Article 177 provides that whenever an undecided point of European law comes up in a national court from which there is no appeal (e.g. the House of Lords) such court *must* suspend the case concerned and refer the question to the Court of Justice for a decision called a preliminary ruling. The Court of Justice decides the point on European law and sends the answer back to the national court which then decides how the case should be decided in the light of the answer. In **CILFIT v. Ministro della Sanita (1983),** the Court of Justice said that there is no need to refer the issue for a preliminary ruling if (a) the answer to the question will not influence the outcome of the case, (b) there was a previous ruling of the European Court on the same question , or (c) the correct application of EU law is so obvious as to leave no room for reasonable doubt. Even if the decision of the national court is not final, the national court *may* still refer the European issue to the Court of Justice. In **H.P. Bulmer Ltd v. J. Bollinger SA (1974),** Lord Denning MR said that the discretion whether to refer an issue to the Court of Justice belongs to the English court and it should not ask the Court of Justice to give guidelines as to how the discretion should be exercised. Moreover, in view of the expenditure in time and costs which would arise if a reference is made to the Court of Justice, the English court should try and interpret the matter if it is not too difficult; and in any event no reference should be made unless the ruling is necessary to enable the English court to give judgement.

Attached to the Court of Justice is a Court of First Instance set up under a power conferred by the Single European Act

1986. This court has judges but no Advocate General. It hears disputes between EU institutions and its employees, and also actions against the Commission by individuals for annulment or failure to act in relation to the implementation of EU competition rules. Appeals go to the Court of Justice.

The European Council was given recognition by the Single European Act and consists of Heads of States or governments, together with their foreign ministers. It meets at least twice a year to issue broad policy outlines which the Council and the Commission will then act on.

European law consists of primary laws and secondary laws. Primary laws are all the laws contained in the treaties and they are automatically incorporated in each member state's legal system. Some of the articles of the treaties are specific and detailed; others are in general outline leaving the details to the Council of Ministers and the Commission. The laws made by the Council and the Commission are called secondary laws (like delegated legislation) and they may take the form of ***regulations, decisions,*** and ***directives.***

Regulations are of general application, binding in 'their entirety' and 'directly applicable' in each member state **(Art.189).** 'Directly applicable' means that they have automatic and binding effect on national law without the need for the state to implement them. Where the requirements of a regulation are breached it is the Commission, rather than an individual, which must take steps to enforce it. An individual can sue in a national court only if the regulation has direct effect. 'Direct effect' means conferring rights and imposing obligations on individuals without the need for an act of implementation by the state. To have direct effect, a regulation must impose a clear, precise and unconditional obligation on the state and private individuals must be the beneficiaries of the rights or obligations.

Decisions are similar to regulations in that they are binding in their entirety; but they differ in that they are not of general application. They are binding only on identified addressees who may be states , individuals or corporations.

Directives require a stated objective to be achieved, but leave the means by which this is done for each state to decide. Directives are addressed to states, not individuals, and they become law only when they are implemented by the states. States are usually given a time limit to implement a directive. Where a state fails to implement a directive, the following consequences may arise: (a) the Commission will take action against the offending state in the Court of Justice which will then make a declaration that the state has failed to implement the directive; (b) an individual who suffers loss at the hands of another individual because of the state's failure to implement the directive can apply to the Court of Justice for damages. In **Francovich (1991),** the Court of Justice said that the state is liable in damages only if the result prescribed by the directive conferred rights on the individual who suffered the loss, the directive had 'direct effect' in the sense of being sufficiently precise and unconditional, and the loss would not have occurred had the state fulfilled its European obligation to implement the directive; (c) an individual who is the beneficiary of rights conferred on him by a directive which has direct effect can enforce those rights in a national court where the state or an arm of the state (e.g. a local authority or a nationalised industry) has breached those rights. In **Marshall v. Southampton and South -West Hampshire Area Health Authority (1986),** the plaintiff was employed by the defendants and she was forced to retire at the age of 60 while male colleagues were allowed to work until 65. The Equal Treatment Directive required states to alter their national law to ensure that men and women were treated equally at the workplace; but this directive had not yet been implemented by the UK government. The English courts awarded the plaintiff damages against her employers for unfair dismissal. If the plaintiff was employed by a private sector employer her claim would have failed because 'direct effect' in a directive (unlike other types of European laws) does not impose obligations on individuals, only on states.

VI Customs

A local custom is treated as law for a particular locality subject to the following conditions being satisfied: it must be reasonable and for the benefit of a specified class of persons, it must have existed from time immemorial (i.e.1189), it must be in existence continuously, it must be certain and clearly defined, and it must have been obtained neither by force, secrecy nor by permission.

VII Law Reports

They record important decisions of the courts together with the reasons for the decisions as given in judgements and they have played an important part in the development of precedent. Among the best known are the Law Reports and the All England Reports.

VIII Codes of Practice

A code of practice is similar to delegated legislation in that the power to issue a code is conferred on a specified body. For example, ACAS is given power under the Employment Rights Act 1996 to issue codes of practice containing 'such practical guidance as the service thinks fit for the purpose of promoting the improvement of industrial relations.' However, unlike delegated legislation, it is not legally binding but only admissible evidence in legal proceedings.

IX The Law Commission

This body was established by the Law Commission Act 1965, and its function is to review the law as a whole and to prepare propos be codified (i.e. bringing together the case law and statutory provisions on a particular topic in one statute) or consolidated (i.e. bringing together the statutory provisions on a particular topic in one statute). In particular, the Commission is concerned with the modernisation of the law and to ensure that it develops systematically.

Chapter 2

The Courts of Law

Introduction

The courts are an institution independent of the state and their function is to administer the law. They will resolve disputes by applying the law in a way that would do justice to the parties. If a court makes a mistake, when trying a dispute for the first time, the law allows the party dissatisfied with the outcome of the case to appeal to a higher court. Courts which try cases for the first time are called 'Courts of First Instance', and the courts to which the dissatisfied party can go, when the trial court makes a mistake, are called 'Appeal Courts'.

The jurisdiction of the courts depends on the type of law they administer. Thus, civil law is administered by the civil courts and criminal law is administered by the criminal courts, although some courts may administer both. Civil courts are presided over by a judge without a jury (except in the case of fraud, defamation and false imprisonment); criminal courts are, generally, presided over by a judge and jury. The procedure in civil courts differs from the procedure in criminal courts, and the rules of evidence are much more relaxed in civil courts.

This chapter examines the structure of the courts, and looks briefly at the alternative methods of dispute resolution.

I Civil Courts

(i) County Courts. These are governed by the County Courts Act 1984 (as amended) and presided over by a Circuit Judge, sitting without a jury (unless the action relates to fraud or to a defamation action transferred from a High Court, in which case there is a jury of 8). Each court has a 'District Judge' (formerly Registrar of the County Court or High Court) who is a lawyer of seven years advocacy experience, acting as clerk of the court. The District Judge deals with pre-trial issues; hears undefended cases and cases where the value of the claim does not exceed £5,000; and administers the arbitration procedure for small claims not exceeding £3,000.

(a) Jurisdiction. This is a civil jurisdiction and it has been extended considerably by the High Court and County Courts Jurisdiction Order 1991, which gives the County Court concurrent jurisdiction with the High Court in contract and tort. Since County Court proceedings are less formal and cheaper, most actions in contract and tort are likely to *commence* in the County Court. However, whether the action will be *heard* in the County Court, or whether it will be transferred to the High Court will depend on the following criteria: the financial substance of the action (if under £25,000, it will be dealt with usually in the County Court, but if over £50,000 it should be dealt with in the High Court); whether the action raises questions of importance to persons other than the litigants themselves; the complexity of the action; and whether the transfer is more likely to result in a speedy trial. Personal injury actions, where the plaintiff would be expected to recover more than £50,000 must be commenced in the High Court and not in the County Court.

The County Court also has jurisdiction to hear claims of an equitable character and probate matters where the net value of the estate does not exceed £50,000; and actions concerning the title of land and the recovery of possession of land where the capital value of the land, or the interest in the land does not exceed £30,000. Some County Courts can deal with bankruptcy matters without any limit (although, in the case of the winding up of a company, jurisdiction depends on the company's paid up capital) and certain family matters, such as undefended divorces.

As a rule, the plaintiff can commence proceedings in any County Court, but where the claim is for a liquidated sum, and the defendant states that he intends to contest it, the action will be transferred automatically to the defendant's home court for a hearing. An action involving land has to be brought in the County Court in which the land is situated.

(b) Procedure. It varies between a fixed date action (i.e. a claim for a remedy, other than a money remedy) and a default action (i.e. a claim for damages), but in both cases, proceedings are commenced by the plaintiff completing a request for a summons form and preparing a 'Particulars of Claim'. If the action is for an unliquidated sum, the Particulars of Claim must include a statement of value to the effect that the amount claimed is in excess of £5,000, otherwise the action will be heard by the District Judge and the plaintiff may be liable for wasted costs, if during the hearing the judge has to transfer the claim to the Circuit Judge for trial, because of lack of jurisdiction. If it is a personal injuries action, the Particulars of Claim must also include a statement of special damages giving full particulars of expenses and losses, including an estimate of future losses (e.g. loss of earnings); and a medical report must be filed substantiating the alleged injuries as stated in the Particulars of Claim.

The request for summons and the Particulars of Claim have to be filed at the County Court, and appropriate fee paid. Court staff will enter a case number (formerly called a plaint note number) in the court record and, for a fixed date action, fix a return date when the Court will look at the documents in the presence of the parties for the first time. The summons and the Particulars of Claim (and, if relevant, the return date and a copy of the medical report) will be served by an official of the Court on the defendant. Alternatively, if it is a personal injuries action, the plaintiff's solicitors may prepare the summons and have it sealed by the Court which will then hand it back to the solicitors for them to serve on the defendant.

Enclosed with the summons and other documents is a form of admission, defence and counter-claim which the defendant must return to the Court within 14 days. Failure to file a defence in a default action will give the plaintiff the right (on submission of the appropriate form) to have judgement entered against the defendant immediately. If the defendant in a default action submits a defence in the prescribed form, the Court may fix a day for a pre-trial review. Automatic directions will then apply, provided this is done before the pleadings are deemed to be closed. In a fixed date action the defendant can file a defence at any time before the return day, but if it is outside the 14 days' period, he will have to meet the costs resulting from the delay. The filing of a defence/counter-claim will result in the Court forwarding a copy to the plaintiff.

If the Court does not require a pre-trial review then, on the close of pleadings, which is 14 days after the defence is filed, or 28 days after the last pleading, the Court will issue automatic directions including the disclosure of expert reports by the parties to each other within 10 weeks, discovery within 28 days and inspection 7 days thereafter. Discovery is by exchanging lists. The list will state all those relevant documents which a party has in his possession and is willing to produce for inspection and those which he has, but is not willing to produce (e.g. on grounds of privilege). The right to inspect includes the right to take copies. Within 6 months after the close of pleadings, the plaintiff must request the Court to fix a hearing and must give an estimate of the likely length of the trial. The Court will give all parties 21 days notice of the trial date.

(ii) The High Court of Justice. This court has three divisions, namely, the Queen's Bench Division, the Chancery Division and the Family Division and has both first instance jurisdiction (where a single High Court judge sits alone dealing almost exclusively with civil matters) and an appellate jurisdiction (where two or more judges sit as a divisional court hearing appeals from magistrates Courts, Special Commissioners of Income Tax, and from Provisional Bankruptcy Courts).

(a) Queen's Bench Division. This division is presided over by the Lord Chief Justice who is assisted by Puisne Judges, who are appointed from among barristers of at least 10 years standing. The Division deals mainly with common law matters, such as contract and tort. In addition, it has a further jurisdiction over commercial and admiralty matters, which are dealt with by two specialised courts, the Commercial Court and the Admiralty Court. It can grant *Mareva* injunctions and *Anton Piller* injunctions. A *Mareva* injunction is an interlocutory injunction and it prevents the defendant from removing specific assets out of the jurisdiction until the outcome of the case. The court will grant such an injunction only if the plaintiff is likely to recover judgement, and there is a likelihood that the defendant may remove assets from the jurisdiction in order to avoid meeting the judgement. An *Anton Piller* injunction is an *ex parte* injunction (i.e. it is granted to one party in the absence of the other), and it authorises the applicant's solicitor to inspect, photograph, to take away documents or property with a view to safeguard evidence.

As a divisional court, the Queen's Bench Division has a supervisory jurisdiction and can issue a writ of *habeas corpus* (requiring a person who has been wrongly detained to be released); an order of *mandamus* (requiring a public body to carry out its duty); and an order of *prohibition* (preventing a court or tribunal from exceeding its jurisdiction). It can order a judicial review of any proceedings by a tribunal, inferior court, national or local government department or even individuals.

The criminal jurisdiction of the High Court is exercised by the Queen's Bench Division which hears appeals by way of case stated from Magistrates Courts and Crown Courts.

(b) Chancery Division. The Lord Chancellor is historically head of this division but, in practice, it is presided over by the Vice-Chancellor and Puisne Judges. It deals mainly with equity matters (e.g. trusts and mortgages). It also deals with the winding up of companies, bankruptcy, revenue matters and contentious probate matters. It hears appeals from decisions of the Special Commissioners of Income Tax, and from Bankruptcy Courts.

(c) Family Division. This division is presided over by the president of the Family Division and Puisne Judges. It has exclusive jurisdiction over matrimonial disputes and proceedings relating to children (e.g. wardship, guardianship, adoption etc). In addition, it deals with non-contentious probate matters. It hears appeals on matrimonial matters dealt with in Magistrates Courts.

(iii) The Restrictive Practices Court. This has the same status as the High Court and consists of five High Court judges and ten non-judicial members who have expert knowledge in commerce, industry and public affairs. Cases are normally heard by one judge and two non-judicial members. It investigates agreements under the Restrictive Trade Practices Act 1976 and the Resale Prices Act 1976 to ensure that they are not against the public interest. It can also prohibit commercial practices which are deemed prejudicial to consumers under the Fair Trading Act 1973.

(iv) Court of Appeal (Civil Division). This court is presided over by the Master of the Rolls and 16 Lord Justices of Appeal. The quorum of the court is three. It hears appeals from the High Court, County Court, the Restrictive Practices Court and various specialised tribunals. It may uphold or reverse a lower court's decision, or substitute its own decision and can order a new trial.

(v) House of Lords. This is presided over by the Lord Chancellor and assisted by Law Lords. A quorum of three is necessary, but usually five members sit. It hears appeals from the Court of Appeal, but the appellant must obtain leave of the Court of Appeal or the House of Lords. Leave will be granted only if a point of law of public importance is involved. The Lords also hears appeals directly from the High Court by means of the 'leap-frog' procedure. This procedure will apply if the trial judge grants a certificate that the case involves a point of law of public importance, both parties to the action consent and the House of Lords agrees to hear the appeal.

II Criminal Courts

(i) Magistrates' Courts. These are presided over by either Stipendiary (i.e. salaried) Magistrates who are legally qualified, or by Lay Magistrates who are unpaid and serve on a part-time basis. A Stipendiary Magistrate sits alone; but two or more Lay Magistrates are necessary to constitute a court and they are advised by a magistrates' clerk who is a qualified lawyer.

Magistrates' Courts deal mainly with criminal matters. They have power to try offences (***summary offences***) but if, on conviction, they wish to impose penalties in excess of six months' imprisonment or fines in excess of £5,000, they must commit the accused to a Crown Court for sentence. They also act as courts of preliminary hearings for more serious offences which can only be tried by judge and jury (***indictable offences***). Magistrates' Courts also constitute the Youth Courts where magistrates deal exclusively with offences committed by children (aged 10 to 13) and young persons (aged 14 to 17).

Magistrates' Courts have limited civil jurisdiction to deal with such matters as custody and maintenance of children, separation and maintenance orders, licensing and the enforcement of council taxes.

(ii) The Crown Court. This was set up by the Courts Act 1971, and is presided over by High Court Judges, Circuit Judges and Recorders. The Crown Court hears all indictable offences (i.e. serious offences such as treason, murder, manslaughter or rape) with a jury. It also has an appellate jurisdiction hearing appeals from Magistrates' Courts against conviction or sentence. When hearing appeals from Magistrates' Courts, the Crown Court will comprise a judge sitting with two or four lay magistrates. Appeals take the form of a complete re-hearing of the case in the Crown Court.

(iii) Court of Appeal (Criminal Division). This is presided over by the Lord Chief Justice, assisted by Lord Justices of Appeal. The quorum of the court is three judges. It hears appeals against sentence or convictions in the Crown Court, when the latter is acting as a Court of First Instance. Appeals against sentence can only be made with leave of the Court of

Appeal. Appeals against conviction based exclusively on a question of law do not require permission.

(v) House of Lords. This hears appeals from the Court of Appeal (Criminal Division) and from the Division Court of the Queen's Bench Division on points of law.

(vi) Privy Council. In its judicial capacity, it is presided over by the Lord President of the Council, assisted by Law Lords. It acts as a final court of appeal for certain Commonwealth countries; and in this respect it has both civil and criminal jurisdiction. It also hears appeals form English ecclesiastical courts.

III Other Judicial Bodies.

(i) Administrative Tribunals. These are bodies outside the hierarchy of the courts, with judicial or quasi-judicial powers. They are normally set up by statute to ease the pressure on the courts and deal with disputes arising in certain areas of the law affecting government policies (e.g. rent, social security and conditions of work) Although lawyers may sit on them, in practice, they are staffed by laymen with special knowledge of the matter with which each tribunal is dealing. However, ***Industrial Tribunals***, which deal with employment disputes are staffed by lawyers and representatives of employers' associations and trade unions. The quorum for an industrial tribunal is three. Appeals from industrial tribunals go to the

Employment Appeal Tribunal, which is staffed by High Court judges, and then on a point of law to the Court of Appeal.

As a method of settling disputes, Administrative Tribunals are relatively cheaper than the courts and, since they deal with only one type of dispute (e.g. social security), disputes are resolved relatively quicker than in the courts which deal with all types of disputes. Proceedings in tribunals are not too formal and matters such as social conditions which normally carry less weight in the ordinary courts, are taken into consideration by tribunals in arriving at their decisions. The rules of evidence in tribunals are relaxed, thus encouraging the parties to present their own case, rather than being forced to obtain legal representation.

The decisions of statutory tribunals are subject to the supervision of the High Court.

(ii) Domestic Tribunals. These are special bodies set up by professional accosiations (e.g. the General Medical Council and the Football Association) to deal with allegations of misconduct and breach of membership obligations. Thier decisions are subject also to the supervision of the High Court.

(iii) Arbitration. This is the reference of a matter in dispute to the decision of one or more person called arbitrators andis an alternative to settling disputes, especially those of a commercial nature by litigation in the courts. It can arise by contract (called voluntary arbitration) or by statute, or by order of the Courts.

(a) Voluntary Arbitration. The parties may include a clause in their contract with each other that disputes arising out of the contract should be resolved by arbitration. Such a clause is known as an arbitration clause and, if a party breaches it by taking the dispute to court, the other party may be granted a stay of proceedings as long as he has not taken any steps in the court proceedings (e.g. by filing a defence). The arbitration clause may go even further and make an arbitration award a conditional precedent to the right to sue in court. This type of arbitration clause is known as a **Scott v. Avery Clause** and its effect is to ensure that no court proceedings can be brought on the contract until an award is made first by the arbitrator. Nevertheless, the courts may ignore such a clause and will allow court proceedings, if the dispute relates to a point of law, or if the arbitrator was not impartial, or if the party seeking a stay of proceedings was guilty of fraud. Also the Consumer Arbitration Agreements Act 1988 states that an arbitration clause in a consumer contract not exceeding £1,000 is not binding on a non-consenting consumer.

Voluntary arbitration is cheaper than court proceedings because the parties are encouraged to plead their case in person since the winning party is not usually entitled to recover his legal costs from the losing party. Moreover, although the normal judicial procedure (including the rules of evidence) applies to arbitration, in practice, the parties dispense with this, thus ensuring that the proceedings do not become too formal and legalistic. By having control of the arbitration the parties are able to keep the proceedings private and so their business affairs are not published in the press. The main disadvantages of arbitration are that there is generally no rights of appeal against an award, and that arbitration is not suitable for legally complicated matters of dispute.

(b) Compulsory Arbitration. It may arise as a result of statute; and the courts themselves may order arbitration (e.g. the High Court may do so because of the technical nature of the case). The County Court has its own arbitration procedure where claims not exceeding £3,000 can be referred by the District Judge to arbitration even if one party does not agree.

Chapter 3

Making a Contract

Introduction

Making a contract is not only a vital element in business but is a characteristic feature of every day life. A person is entering into contracts all the time, eg., when buying food, travelling by public transport or renting a flat. It is the legal mechanism for providing goods and services and ensures justice is done if things go wrong.

Modern contract law has its origin in the nineteenth century and reflects the predominant value of that era - freedom, self-government and equality. It was assumed that the parties to a contract entered into it freely in pursuit of their own goals and that the terms of the contract were fair and reasonable if both parties were to be in agreement. This idea has become embodied in the philosophy known as freedom of contract and continues to the present day, although in recent years parliament has placed some restrictions on contractual freedom to prevent the weaker party to the contract being taken advantage of by the economically stronger.

Nature of a Contract

There are many definitions of a contract but a useful as well as a brief one is :

> " *A contract is an agreement which binds the parties*".

This definition requires some elaboration.

(a) 'Agreement'. Two points need to be made.

(1) **The objective test.** In most cases 'agreement' means that the parties have understood that they are making a contract; but in the final analysis it is what a reasonable person in the parties' position would have inferred from their words or conduct. In **Upton RDC v. Powell (1942)**, the defendant whose house was on fire, telephoned the police and asked for the fire brigade. Instead of the police informing the defendant's local fire brigade of the fire in which case the service would be free, they contacted the fire brigade of another district which responded to the call in the belief that it was rendering gratuitous service in its own area. The court held that the fire brigade was entitled contractually to payment for its service even though it was not aware that by responding to the defendant's call it was accepting an offer. Here, acceptance was the objective inference from the fire brigade's conduct in responding to the call, just as the offer was the objective inference from the defendant's conduct in calling the fire brigade.

(2) **Standard form contract.** It is a familiar feature of business that one party to a contract will produce a written document containing the terms on which he will contract with the other party on a "take it or leave it" basis. The other party only has to sign the document or agree to it to be bound by it. An agreement cannot be reached through negotiation, and any attempt by the other party to alter its terms is discouraged or refused.
Finance companies, manufacturers, suppliers and nationalised industries inevitably utilise this method of contracting since it reduces performance of the contract to a standard operation and minimises costs. The Unfair Terms in Consumer Contracts Regulations 1994 now governs such contracts. It requires all

terms to be drafted in plain and intelligible language and for the terms to be fair. It states that a term will be unfair if contrary to the requirement of good faith it causes a significant imbalance in the parties' rights and obligations under the contract to the detriment of the consumer. The Regulations contains a list of terms which are *presumed* to be unfair. However, this list is not exhaustive and it is up to the consumer to show that other terms are unfair, although he is not allowed to challenge the fairness or otherwise of any term which simply defines the main subject matter of the contract or which concerns the adequacy of the price to be paid for the goods or services. Unfair terms are not binding on the consumer.

(b) **"Binds".** If one party fails to carry out his part of the agreement or his performance is defective, then he is liable at law to pay monetary compensation known as *damages.*Only in exceptional circumstances will he be made to perform the contract by means of an order known as *specific performance.* Another court order, known as an *injunction*,may sometimes indirectly achieve the same result as specific performance. These remedies available for failure to perform are examined in greater detail in Chapter 7.

Form of contract. Generally a contract does not have to take any prescribed form. It can be made quite informally; by word of mouth, in writing or may even arise by conduct. Occasionally, some contracts (such as contracts of guarantee) must be supported by written evidence; some (such as land contracts and consumer credit agreements) must be in writing; and others (such as leases for more than three years)must be under seal. Contracts not made under seal are called **simple contracts.** Where a contract is made under seal an action for breach can be brought within twelve years after the breach has occurred. However, a six year limitation is imposed on simple contracts.

Requirements for Contractual Formation.

As a result of the relative freedom in making contracts and the absence of any general requirement for them to be in writing , the question that has troubled many people is: when does a conversation become a contract ? The answer lies in case law which prescribes three minimum requirements to be satisfied in order for a contract to exist. These requirements are**:**

(I) An Offer and Acceptance (11) Consideration

(III) An intention to create legal relations.

Of these three requirements consideration, the element of bargain, is arguably the most important.

I Offer and Acceptance

A contract is the result of an agreement. In determining whether an agreement has been reached , the courts will inquire whether an **Offer** has been made by one party (the offeror) and whether there has been **Acceptance** of that offer by the other party (the offeree). Most contractual negotiations, whether short and simple or long and complicated, conform to this formula. Occasionally, however, the cases do not fit into the conventional analysis of "offer and acceptance" so the courts must take account of the conduct of the parties. In **Clarke v. Dunraven (1897)**, the court held that two competitors who had entered their boats in a club race had on the basis of the club rules formulated a contract between themselves, either when they entered for the race or at the latest when they actually sailed. Nevertheless the courts are reluctant to depart from the traditional "offer and acceptance" approach (as was evidenced in **Gibson v. Manchester City Council (1979)** where the

House of Lords in overruling the Court of Appeal, disagreed with Lord Denning who said "there is no need to look for a strict offer and acceptance. You should look at the correspondence as a whole and the conduct of the parties ").

(i) Offer. This is an expression of willingness by the offeror to be bound by stated terms if those terms are accepted by the offeree. There is an offer whenever as a result of the objective inference a person by his words or conduct shows a clear intention to be bound without further negotiations by the terms he is proposing. In **Gibson v. Manchester City Council,** a local authority wrote to a council tenant stating that it "may be prepared" to sell him his council flat at a certain price and that he should make a formal application if he wished to purchase it. It was held that the local authority had not made an offer and was not liable in damages when it changed its mind about selling, after the tenant sent in his application to purchase.

(a) Identifying offers. An offer needs to be distinguished from an invitation to treat and a supply of information since the last two cannot be accepted to form a contract.

An invitation to treat. This is an expression of willingness to negotiate over stated terms. Most of the cases in this area are well documented. A window display of a shop is not an offer to sell but is simply inviting offers from customers **(Fisher v. Bell (1961)).** Similarly, the display of goods on the shelves of a supermarket is merely an invitation to treat. The offer is made by the customer and it is accepted by the shop, usually at the cash desk where the contract is therefore made **(Pharmaceutical Society of Great Britain v. Boots Cash Chemist (1953)).** An advertisement for the sale of goods is not generally an offer, but simply an invitation to treat. So in **Partridge v. Crittenden (1968),** an attempt to prosecute a dealer under the Protection of Birds Act 1954 for unlawfully offering a wild bird in a newspaper advertisement failed. However, if the advertisement is couched in very firm words (e.g., it states "the first reader to reply positively will get the goods") it will constitute an offer. Thus an advertisement for a reward will invariably be an offer and not just an invitation to treat. In **Carlill v. Carbolic Smokeball Co. (1893),** the defendants placed an advertisement in a newspaper offering a "reward" of £100 to anyone who caught influenza after using their smokeball in accordance with the instructions. The advertisement was held to be an offer and so Mrs Carlill who had bought the smokeball and used it as prescribed, but still caught influenza was able to recover £100 from the defendants.

The rules on auction sales are similar to retail sales and advertisements. In **British Car Auctions v. Wright (1972),** an auctioneer in inviting bids was not "offering for sale an unroadworthy car ". The highest bidder makes the offer which the auctioneer can then accept or reject. In accordance with this the Sale of Goods Act 1979 provides that until the auctioneer signifies his acceptance in the customary manner, such as by the fall of the hammer, the bidder may withdraw his bid. Likewise, a statement that an auction will be held on a certain day is not an offer to hold it **(Harris v. Nickerson (1873)**) . However, it was said obiter in **Warlow v. Harrison (1859)** that if the statement indicates that the auction will be held "without reserve ", it constitutes an offer to bidders that the sale will not be subject to a reserve price, so that the auctioneer himself (as opposed to the owner of the item) will be liable in damages to the highest bidder if, at the auction, he withdraws the item on auction after the highest bid is made.

A request for tenders is not generally an offer, so the party requesting the tenders is not bound to sell to (or buy from) the party submitting the highest (or lowest) tender. In **Spencer v. Harding (1870),** the defendants issued a circular stating that they were instructed "to offer to the wholesale trade for sale by tender "certain stock. The plaintiffs who submitted the highest tender sued for breach of contract when they were not given the stock. The court held that the circular was not an offer as it was not a reasonable inference that the defendants intended to bind themselves to the highest bidder, however low the bid might be. In some cases, the request for tender will be an offer either to accept the tender submitted or to consider it. If the request for tender expressly states that the highest tender to buy (or as the case may be, the lowest tender to sell) will be accepted then the tradesman submitting the appropriate tender has a right to have his tender accepted **(William Lacey Ltd. v. Davis (1957)).** On the other hand, if an elaborate and formal tendering machinery had been adopted by the person requesting the tender, then the request for tender may constitute an offer to consider (though not to accept) the tender submitted. In **Blackpool & Fylde Aero Club v. Blackpool Borough Council (1990),** the Council invited tenders from seven selected companies for a concession to run pleasure flights from its local airport. The invitation to tender required the tenders to be submitted in envelopes provided by the Council, which were to bear no identifying marks and stated that tenders submitted after the specified deadline would not be considered. The plaintiffs' tender was submitted before the deadline but due to an oversight by Council employees it was never considered. The Court of Appeal held that the request for tender implied that a person who submitted his tender in accordance with its strict rules of compliance would have a right to have his tender considered along with others. The plaintiffs were therefore entitled to damages for loss of chance to be the successful bidder.

A request for tender for goods or services to be supplied 'as and when required' or in 'such quantities (not exceeding a stated amount) as you may order' will result in the person submitting the tender to make a *standing offer* rather than an offer. Acceptance of the standing offer by the offeree does not constitute acceptance in the legal sense to produce a binding contract. Each requisition by the offeree is an individual act of acceptance and creates a separate contract which the tenderer must fulfil. In **Great Northern Rail Co. v. Witham (1873),** the defendant submitted a tender to supply such quantity of goods as the plaintiffs "may order from time to time". The plaintiffs accepted the tender by letter and subsequently made various orders which were met. However, the defendant failed to supply a delivery after a particular order was placed by the plaintiffs. The plaintiffs successfully sued for breach of contract. A tender which amounts to a standing offer can be revoked and the tenderer will not be liable for future deliveries **(Offord v. Davies** (1962) **),** unless he had bound himself to meet any such orders.

The mere supply of information. This includes statements of intention and statements of price. In **Harvey v. Facey (1893),** the plaintiff asked the defendants to state the lowest price at which they would be prepared to sell their farm 'Bumper Hall Pen'; the defendants replied that their lowest price would be £900. The plaintiff unsuccessfully argued that the defendants' statement constituted an offer which they accepted. Here, the defendants' reply was merely a statement of the lowest price in the event of a decision to sell.

(b) **Communication of offers .** As the **Carlill** case shows an offer need not be directed at a specific person (the newspaper advertisement was addressed to the readers of the newspaper) but it must be communicated to the offeree before he can accept it. If services are rendered which fulfil the terms of an offer but are given in ignorance of the words or conduct which constitute the offer, those services cannot be relied on to constitute acceptance of the offer. In **R. v. Clarke (1927),** an accomplice gave information about the identity of some murderers 'to save his skin' and had forgotten that a reward had been offered for such information. The High Court of Australia held that he could not claim the reward because he had forgotten it when he supplied the information.

As long as the offeree is aware of the words or conduct which constitute the offer, his motive for accepting it is irrelevant. In **Williams v. Carwardine (1833),** a reward of £20 was offered for information leading to the arrest and conviction of the murderer of Walter Carwardine. The plaintiff knew of the reward but provided the information to ease her conscience as she felt that she did not have long to live. The court held that she was still entitled to the reward.

The rule that an offer must be communicated before it can be effective also accounts for the view that cross offers in identical terms cannot create an agreement **(Tin v. Hoffman (1873)).** Thus, if two persons send identical offers to each other in the post, neither knowing of the other's offer when he makes his own, there is no contract if no further communication takes place.

(ii) Acceptance. "This is the unconditional assent to all the terms of the offer, communicated to the offeror by the offeree." Difficulties may arise here because people seldom adopt the simple "I accept your offer" formula. Spoken words, writing and the parties' conduct, all play their part in determining whether there has been acceptance of an offer. Mere silence, however, is not sufficient to constitute acceptance.

For acceptance to be effective, the following rules need to be observed:

(a) Unconditional acceptance. The acceptance must be close to, if not identical, to the terms of the offer. If while purporting to accept, the offeree introduces a new term that is more favourable to him (a *counter-offer*), the offer automatically terminates and is replaced by the new proposal (an offer from the offeree) which the offeror may then accept or reject. In **Hyde v. Wrench (1840)** , the defendant offered a farm to the plaintiff for £1000. The plaintiff said he would accept it for £950. The defendant refused this and the plaintiff then said he would pay him the original asking price of £1000; but by this time the defendant had changed his mind about selling. The court held that the original offer of £1000 had been terminated by the counter-offer, so that it no longer could be accepted. However, if the offeree is only making a request for information before making up his mind as to acceptance, this will not terminate the offer. In **Stevenson v. McLean (1880),** the defendant offered to sell iron to the plaintiffs. The plaintiffs asked whether delivery could be made over four months. The court held that this was not a counter-offer, but a request for information and did not prevent the plaintiffs from subsequently accepting the offer.

Modern commercial practice frequently presents the counter-offer analysis in a 'battle of forms' where the parties contract on their own standard terms which may conflict. In **Butler Machine Tool Ltd. v. Ex-Cello Crop (1979),** the sellers offered to sell a machine tool for £75,535 to the buyers on their own terms which were to prevail over the buyers' terms. The sellers' standard conditions of sale included a price variation clause which entitled them to claim any extra costs incurred up to the date of delivery. The buyers placed an order on their own standard conditions of purchase which did not include a price variation clause. The order included a tear-off slip with the words "We accept your order on your terms" for the sellers to sign and acknowledge. The sellers signed the slip and returned it with a covering letter stating that "Your order is entered in accordance with our (original) quotation". When the tool was delivered, the sellers claimed an additional £2,892 for an increase in costs. Their claim failed. The Court of Appeal held that the buyers' order did not amount to an acceptance but rather a counter-offer which terminated the sellers' original offer. The sellers had accepted the counter-offer when they acknowledged the buyers' order on the tear-off slip. Their accompanying letter did not qualify their acceptance but simply confirmed the price and quality of the machine. If neither party accepts the other's terms and the goods are accepted by the buyer, then the seller is entitled to a *quantum meruit* payment i.e. a fair sum **(British Steel Corp. v. Cleveland Bridge and Engineering Co. Ltd. (1984)).**

Frequently met with in the case of buying land is the phrase 'subject to contract'. Unless there is firm evidence to the contrary the courts will assume that the parties still have other terms to be negotiated before they are willing to bind themselves to the agreement (**Chillingworth v. Esche (1924)**). However, if all the terms have been finalised and the agreement satisfies the requirements of the Law of Property (Miscellaneous Provisions) Act 1989 the parties will be bound by the agreement notwithstanding the phrase 'subject to contract'. In **Alpenstow Ltd. v. Regalian Properties plc (1985),** the court found that on the true construction of letters for the sale of land sent by the parties to each other, there was no further terms to be negotiated and held an agreement 'subject to contract' binding on the parties.

(b) Method of acceptance. The offeror may prescribe a particular method of acceptance by which the offeree must comply for acceptance to be effective. If the offeree adopts some other equally efficacious method, acceptance will still be effective unless the offeror has made it clear that no other method than the method prescribed will suffice **(Manchester Diocesan Council of Education v. Commercial and General Investments Ltd. (1970)).** The offeror is however limited in one respect. He cannot insist that silence will amount to acceptance since this would force an offeree who did not want to be bound by an offer always to notify the offeror of his rejection of the offer. In **Felthouse v. Bindley (1862),** the plaintiff offered to buy a horse from his nephew stating "If I hear no more about him, I shall consider the horse mine at the price." The nephew who had a number of horses for sale at the auction told the auctioneer not to sell the horse but the auctioneer sold the horse by mistake. The uncle sued the auctioneer in conversion (a tort alleging wrongful disposal of the plaintiff's property by the defendant), but the action failed as the court held that there had been no acceptance of the uncle's offer. To have agreed with the uncle's argument would be greatly in favour of 'inertia sellers' who would then be able to force their own products on consumers. The rule in **Felthouse** is intended for the protection of the offeree, not the offeror. So it will not apply where the offeree clearly shows his intention to accept the offer.

Reinforcing **Felthouse,** statutes like the Unsolicited Goods and Services Act 1971 make it a criminal offence to demand payment for the goods where the seller is a dealer. In addition , the 1971 Act confers title on the recipient of unsolicited goods unless the seller collects them within six months (30 days if the recipient of the goods sends notice to the seller to collect the goods and the seller fails to do so) .

(c) Communication of acceptance. The general rule is that the contract is only created when acceptance is brought to the attention of the offeror. This is the position of the so-called instantaneous contracts (i.e. those face to face or by telephone). For instance, if the telephone line goes dead after acceptance is spoken into the telephone but before it is heard by the offeror, acceptance is not complete and there is no contract until the offeror actually receives knowledge of the acceptance. The Court of Appeal in **Entores v. Miles Far East Corp. (1955),** held that where the parties were using the telex to deal with each other at the same time or virtually the same time the telex messages would also be another form of instantaneous communication, and this was confirmed by the House of Lords in **Brinkibon Ltd. v. Stahag Stahl Gmbh (1983).** In **Brinkibon,** the plaintiffs' action against the defendants for breach of contract failed, as the contract had been made outside the English courts' jurisdiction. Success in this case depended on showing that the contract had been made in the United Kingdom. Acceptance, however, was telexed from the United Kingdom and was only complete when received at the defendants' place of business in Vienna where therefore the contract was made. According to **The Brimnes (1975),** communication is effective as soon as the message is printed out on the recipient's (offeror's) telex machine during office hours.

In the case of non-instantaneous contracts (i.e. those where the mode of communication is such that acceptance will reach the offeror at a later time as with the telephone, fax, e-mail and the telex where acceptance is sent outside business hours or by night knowing that it will take a while to reach the offeror) it is an open question as to the time communication becomes effective. There are various possibilities. It could be that the contract is created from the moment acceptance is sent by the offeree, or when it is received by the offeror's machine or by some other person, or received by the offeror himself, or when the offeree could reasonably expect the offeror to know of it. In **Brinkibon,** Lord Wilberforce said that no universal rule could be laid down to cover such cases. The courts would have to look at the intention of the parties, sound business practice and in some cases by a judgement as to where the risk should lie.

If acceptance is conveyed to the offeror by a third party, the third party must have authority from the offeree to do so before a contract can exist. It is not enough to show that the third party is a reliable source. In **Powell v. Lee (1908),** the plaintiff applied for the post of headmaster at a school . After the interviews the committee decided to appoint the plaintiff as headmaster, and a committee member without authority unofficially told him of the committee's decision . The committee subsequently changed its decision to appoint the plaintiff. The plaintiff sued the committee for breach of contract. It was held that no contract existed between the plaintiff and the committee because the committee member, though a reliable source, was not authorised by the committee to inform the plaintiff of his appointment.

There are four exceptions where a contract will be created even though acceptance is not communicated to the offeror.

1. Conduct of the offeror. If it is the offeror's own fault that acceptance is not communicated to him, then acceptance is nevertheless complete and a contract is created. **The Brimnes** was a case not concerned with acceptance but rather with notice of withdrawal from an existing contract. The court held that a telexed notice of withdrawal took effect when it was received during office hours, even though it was not read until at a later date as a result of office staff neglecting to read it when received by the recipient's machine.

2. Communication to agent. As soon as acceptance is communicated to the offeror's agent who has authority to receive it a contract will be created (**Henthorn v. Fraser** (1892) **).** If the agent only has authority to transmit acceptance to the offeror, the contract is created when the offeror receives it.

3. Waiver of communication. If the offeror waives the need for communication of acceptance, a contract is created notwithstanding that the offeror is unaware that his offer has been accepted. The waiver may be express or may be implied from the circumstances. In the classic case of **Carlill v. Carbolic Smokeball Co.,** an offer implied that acceptance would be complete as soon as a reader of the advertisement went to the chemist, purchased a smoke ball and used it in accordance with the instructions. Despite strenuous arguments to the contrary , the court held that Mrs. Carlill was not obliged to notify the defendants that she had accepted their offer before there could be a binding contract.

4. Acceptance by post. Where acceptance is conveyed by letter and it is "within the contemplation of the parties that, according to the ordinary usage of mankind, the post might be used......acceptance is complete as soon as it (the letter of acceptance) is posted " (Lord Herschell in **Henthorn v. Fraser).** Thus the postal rule provides that a contract is created as soon as the letter of acceptance is posted regardless of whether or not it is actually received by the offeror **(Household Fire Insurance Co. v. Grant (1879)).**

The postal rule will not apply if it would lead to inconvenience or absurdity. So if negotiations are conducted entirely by telephone and it is clear that the offeror expects a reply by telephone and the offeree communicates his acceptance by letter, a contract is created only when the letter is delivered to the offeror. In **Holwell Securities Ltd. v. Hughes (1974)**, the defendant made an offer to sell a house to the plaintiffs and stated that acceptance must be made "by notice in writing to the intended vendor ". The plaintiffs posted a letter accepting the offer but it was never received by the defendant. The Court of Appeal refused to apply the postal rule because it was clear that the defendant had expected to be notified of acceptance before there could be a contract binding the parties.

The postal rule will not apply if the letter is not correctly addressed, stamped and actually posted. A letter is posted when it is in the control of the Post Office or one of its employees authorised to receive letters. So handing the letter to a postman who is only authorised to deliver letters is not posting (**Re London and Northern Bank (1900)**).

The postal rule also applies to telegrams and telemessages (which have replaced inland telegrams in the UK); but not to the telex, fax machines and e-mail used by individuals other than the Post Office.

(iii) Termination of Offers. As long as an offer has no yet been accepted, it may be terminated without the offeror incurring any liability. An offer may come to an end in the following ways:

(a) Revocation by offeror. According to **Dickenson v. Dodds (1876),** the offeror may withdraw his offer providing the offeree is notified of it before he accepts. The notification need not come directly from the offeror himself as long as the source of information is reliable. This was the case in **Dickenson** where the plaintiff purported to accept the defendant's offer within the time limit but had already learnt indirectly from a third party that the house on offer had just been sold. **Dickenson** is also authority for the proposition that a promise not to withdraw an offer for a certain period of time is not binding on the offeror unless it is made under seal or some payment is made to keep the offer open.

Revocation raises difficulty with regard to the so-called *unilateral contracts*. These are contracts of which **Carlill** is an example, where the performance of an act is demanded in return for the other party's promise. Here, only one party is promising to do something; the other party is free to perform or not perform the act and so in this sense the contract is '*unilateral'*. It is in contrast to a *bilateral contract* where each party is undertaking an obligation. With a *unilateral contract,* the promise does not become binding until the act is performed , thus leaving the promisor free to withdraw at any time before performance it completed. So, if **X** is promised £2,000 if he completes the London Marathon, it will be possible for this promise to be withdrawn when **X** is only a few yards from the finishing line! Several solutions have been suggested to avoid this result, all of which prevent the offeror from withdrawing his offer once the other party has embarked upon performance unless the offeror expressly reserves the right to revoke. These solutions are supported by **Errington v. Errington (1952),** a case where a father promised to make a house the property of his son and daughter-in-law when they had completed mortgage payment. It was held that the father could not withdraw his promise while payments continued to be made. The Court of Appeal in **Daulia Ltd. v. Four Milbank Nominees Ltd. (1979)** also favours this solution.

The need to notify revocation of an offer makes for potential conflict with the postal rule. The conflict arose in **Byrne v. Van Tienhoven (1880),** where the defendants posted an offer on October 1; on October 8 they posted a letter revoking that offer. Meanwhile, the plaintiffs having received the offer telegraphed their acceptance on October 11; the defendants' letter of revocation did not reach the plaintiffs until October 20. The court held that a contract existed on October 11 when the plaintiffs' telegram of acceptance was sent, as at that time the letter of revocation had not been received.

(b) Rejection. This includes not only outright refusal of the offer by the offeree, but also the **Hyde v. Wrench** situation dealt with earlier, where Hyde's counter-offer amounted to a rejection of the original offer.

(c) Lapse of time. An offer which is open for a fixed period terminates once the time limit expires. If no time limit is imposed the offer lapses after a reasonable length of time. What is a reasonable length of time will depend on the nature of the subject matter, the volatility of the market and what can be implied from the offer itself. In **Ramgate Victoria**

Hotel Co. v. Monteflore (1866), it was held that an offer to buy shares in the plaintiff company had lapsed after five months. An offer sent by telegram or telemessage lapses after a very short time, so if acceptance is sent by post it will be too late (**Quenerduaine v. Cole** (**1883**)).

(d) Death. The effect of this event will depend on whether it is the offeror or the offeree who has died and the type of contract contemplated. If the offeror has died and the offeree knows of this before he accepts, the offer lapses **(Re Whelan** (**1897**)). If the offeree is unaware of the offeror's death before acceptance, then according to **Bradbury v. Morgan (1862)** acceptance is valid unless the contract is one which involves personal services of the offeror. If it is the offeree who has died, a Canadian case **Re Irvine (1928),** points to the conclusion that the offer lapses.

(e) Non-occurrence of a condition. Where an offer is made subject to an express or implied condition , it will terminate if the condition is not met. In **Financing Ltd. v. Stimson (1962),** the defendant made an offer to purchase a car on hire-purchase terms. By the time the finance company accepted his offer, the car (whilst still with the dealers) had become badly damaged as a result of a theft. The court held that the defendant was not bound to take the car as there was an implied condition in the defendant's offer that the car would be in substantially the same condition when the offer was accepted as when it was made.

Certainty of Terms

Despite the satisfaction of the offer and acceptance formula, a contract may fail for uncertainty about what has been agreed. In **Scammell v. Ouston (1941),** the House of Lords held that an agreement to acquire goods ' on hire purchase ' was too vague, there being many types of hire purchase agreements with different terms so that it was not possible to spell out the exact terms on which the parties had agreed. A similar conclusion was reached in **Lee-Parker v. Izzet (1972)** in relation to an agreement 'subject to the purchaser obtaining a satisfactory mortgage'.

In general, the courts are unwilling to find uncertainty, wanting to uphold bargains wherever possible. As Lord Wright explained in **Hillas & Co. Ltd. v. Arcos Ltd. (1932)** "Businessmen often record the most important agreements in crude and summary fashion; modes of expression sufficient and clear to them in the course of their business may appear to those unfamiliar with the business, far from complete or precise. It is accordingly the duty of the court to construe such documents fairly and broadly, without being too astute or subtle in finding defects..."

Generally, the courts approach such cases along the following lines:

(a) Effect will be given to a contractual clause which seeks to resolve any uncertainty. In **Foley v. Classique Coaches Ltd. (1934),** Foley owned a petrol station and adjacent land. He sold the land to the defendants on condition that they agree to buy petrol for their coach business exclusively from him "at a price to be agreed by the parties from time to time". The agreement also contained an arbitration clause which was construed to apply to any failure to agree on the price. The agreement was broken by the defendants. They were sued , and it was argued by them that the agreement was incomplete because the price for the petrol was uncertain. The Court of Appeal rejected this argument and resolved the matter by reference to the arbitration clause; the defendants being required to pay a reasonable price for the petrol.

(b) Trade customs or previous dealings between the parties can be used to clarify vague terms. In **Hillas & Co. Ltd. v. Arcos Ltd.,** an option to buy timber without the mention of detailed terms was held binding because the terms could be settled by reference to those agreed in previous dealings between the parties and to the normal course of trade.

(c) The courts will ignore meaningless phrases wherever possible. For instance, in **Nicolene Ltd. v. Simmonds (1953)** steel bars were bought on clear terms apart from a clause which stated that the sale was subject to "the usual conditions of acceptance". In fact, there were no such conditions and it was held that the phrase could be ignored .

II Consideration

English contract law is concerned with bargains, not mere promises. To constitute a bargain each party must contribute something of value towards the agreement. What they contribute is known as 'consideration'. Consideration is therefore essential to the formation of a contract. Only a person who has given consideration can enforce a promise not under seal. Hence the maxim 'consideration must move from the promisee'.

There are various definitions of consideration; but the shortest as well as the most expressive is Pollock's "The price for which a promise is bought". The definition of consideration in terms of 'price', apart from being easily understood, also stresses the commercial character of the doctrine.

Consideration can be either:

(a) **Executed**, where the price is paid (or required to be paid) by one party at the time the agreement is made in return for the other's promise (e.g., where a tenant pays rent in advance in return for the landlord's promise to give him possession of a flat), or

(b) Executory, where one party promises to pay at a later date in return for the other's promise which is to be performed first (e.g., where a buyer promises to pay 'cash on delivery'. Here, the buyer will be entitled to sue on the seller's promise to deliver if delivery fails to take place).

Provided one party to the agreement has supplied consideration, he can take action against the other party if the latter fails to honour his promise. However:

(*i*) *The consideration must not be past.* It is not possible to use a previous act done for the benefit of another as the price paid for a later promise made by the other party. The consideration has to be given as part of the agreement and not before the agreement was contemplated. In **Re McArdle (1951),** a woman paid for repairs to a house owned by her relatives. After the repairs had been carried out the relatives promised to reimburse her for the cost of repairs, but they failed to do so. Her action failed as there was no consideration for the relatives' promise other than the act of paying for the repairs; but that was past consideration.
To this somewhat harsh rule, there are exceptions:

(i) The performance of an act by **A** at the request of **B** may enable **A** to enforce a subsequent promise made by **B** to pay for the act. Such a promise is only enforceable if it was reasonable for **A** to expect payment for the act. In **Lampleigh v. Braithwait (1615),** a lawyer who acted in consequence of a desperate plea by a convicted murderer was able to recover £100 promised by the murderer after the lawyer had secured his release from prison.

(2) Past consideration can create liability on a negotiable instrument such as a cheque **(S.27 Bills of Exchange Act 1882).**

(*3*) The Limitation Act 1980 states that if after a debt becomes statute barred (i.e., six years have lapsed since the date repayment was due) the debtor simply acknowledges in writing that he owes the money, then the debt will again become enforceable by the creditor. The debt, although past consideration, is sufficient to enforce the written acknowledgement.

(*ii*) *The consideration must be real or sufficient.* Consideration must have some value in the eyes of the law. There are two threads of meaning to this:

(a) It can mean any **act** or **promise** which has 'economic' value as opposed to 'moral' or 'sentimental' value. Most commercial transactions involve money paid or promised for goods and services, so the economic value of the consideration is apparent. However, where the transaction involves a non-money payment the economic value may not be apparent. In **White v. Bluett (1853),** the court held that a son's promise not to bore his father with complaints had no economic value and so could not be relied on as sufficient consideration to enforce the father's promise not to sue him on a promissory note.

(b) It can mean any **act or promise** which is not legally due from the promisee, either under

(1) a duty owed at law, or
(2) a duty owed under an existing contract.

(1) A duty owed at law. The performance of an existing duty owed at law will not be sufficient consideration or a 'real price'. In **Collins v. Godefroy (1831),** the plaintiff was under a legal duty by subpoena to attend court to give evidence for the defendant. It was held that he could not enforce the defendant's promise to pay him six guineas for his loss of time, as he was bound under the general law to be a witness (because this is the effect of a subpoena) and so his court attendance did not constitute any 'real'consideration for the defendant's promise.

In **Glasbrook Bros. Ltd. v. Glamorgan County Council (1925),** mine owners requested extra police protection at their colliery during a strike and promised to pay £2,200 for the extra protection, even though the police maintained that a mobile force was adequate. The House of Lords held that the services provided by the police exceeded their statutory duty and was sufficient consideration to enforce the promise of £2,200.

(2) **A duty owed under an existing contract.** The performance (or the promise to perform)by one party of an existing contractual duty which he already owes the other contracting party is not sufficient consideration to enforce a later promise by the other to pay extra for it. This principle was firmly established in **Stilk v. Myrick (1809),** where two members of a crew deserted the ship and the remaining eight members of the crew were promised extra wages by the captain if they completed the voyage. On arrival, the captain refused to pay the extra wages. It was held that the captain's promise was not enforceable as the remaining members of the crew were simply doing what they were already bound to do. However in **Hartley v. Ponsonby (1856),** a similar claim succeeded. In this case, half the crew deserted the ship and only a few of the remaining crew were able seamen. The court held that the captain's promise to pay extra wages could be enforced as the voyage had become extra hazardous, and its completion by the seamen was new consideration.

The principle in **Stilk v. Myrick** has been modified further by **Williams v. Roffey Bros. & Nichols (Contractors) Ltd. (1991)** where the Court of Appeal decided that in contracts for the provision of goods or services, a promise by one party to perform an existing contractual obligation owed to the other party will be sufficient consideration for the other's promise to pay extra for the performance if (x) the promise to pay 'extra' was made freely, and not extracted by threat, and (xx) the other party obtained some practical commercial benefit from the performance. In **Williams v. Roffey Bros.,** the defendant builders had a contract to refurbish a block of flats. They subcontracted the carpentry work to the plaintiff for £20,000. However, before the plaintiff could complete the work he found himself on the verge of bankruptcy, partly because he had underpriced the job. The defendants, knowing that they would incur penalties to the flat owners for any delay in completing the work on time, freely promised to make extra payments to the plaintiff if the work was completed on time. It was held that the defendants' promise was binding because the plaintiff had provided consideration to support the promise in the form of the completion of the work on time, which in turn was beneficial to the defendants by their avoidance of the penalties, and the cost and inconvenience of finding another contractor to finish the work.

The exact status of **Williams v. Roffey Bros.** is still unclear. In **Re Selectmove Ltd. (1995),** the Court of Appeal refused to extend it to contracts for the payment of debts whereby a creditor willingly agrees to accept a smaller sum in discharge of the debt or to accept repayment by instalment or over time and the agreement is of some practical benefit to the creditor.

The performance of an existing contractual obligation (as opposed to a legal obligation) owed to a third party can qualify as real consideration. In **Shadwell v. Shadwell (1860),** a nephew who was already engaged to a young lady was able to enforce his uncle's promise to support him at the Bar if he married the young lady (an engagement to marry was a binding contract then).

(iii) *The consideration need not be adequate.* While the courts will only enforce promises for which some value has been given, in general they do not ask whether adequate value had been given. Payment of 'too much' or 'too little'may be evidence of fraud or mistake but it does not directly affect the formation of a contract. In **Thomas v. Thomas (1842),** the court held that payment by the plaintiff of £1 per annum rent was consideration for the defendant's promise to grant her the lease of a house. In **Chappell & Co. Ltd. v. Nestle Ltd. (1966),** the defendants offered for sale gramophone records which could be obtained for 1s. 6d with three wrappers from their 6d chocolate bars. The court held that even though the wrappers were of no value to the defendants (because they threw them away) , they still formed part of the consideration for the purchase of the gramophone records. It would appear to follow that the wrappers alone may have constituted the whole consideration for the records.

(iv) *Part payment of a debt is not consideration for a promise to discharge the debt.* This is known as the rule in **Pinnel's Case (1602)**, and it was applied in **Foakes v. Beer (1882)** where the court held that Mrs. Beer who had promised Dr. Foakes that she would forego the interest in a judgement debt for £2,000 if he paid off the sum by instalments, could still sue him for the interest because he had not given her any consideration for her promise.

There are a number of exceptions to this harsh common law rule. In **Pinnel's Case,** the following were spelt out:

a) Early payment of a smaller sum.

b) Part payment on the due date but at a different place for the convenience of the creditor.

c) Delivery of a chattel of a lower value rather than money (e.g. a pen).

Until **D & C Builders Ltd. v. Rees (1966),** part payment by cheque was also good consideration for the creditor's promise to give up his right to payment of a debt by cash. However in **D & C Builders Ltd. v. Rees** the Court of Appeal decided that there was no longer any real distinction between the two modes of payment ; therefore part payment by cheque can no longer discharge a debt.

In addition, there are two common law exceptions to the rule in **Pinnel's Case**.

d) Composition agreements. If a debtor agrees with his creditors that they will accept part payment in full settlement of his debts, the debts are effectively discharged **(Woods v. Roberts (1818)).**

e) Part payment of a debt by a third party **(Hirachand Punamchand v. Temple (1911)).**

The final exception arises in equity:

f) The doctrine of promissory estoppel. Apart from the above common law exceptions, it was believed that there was nothing to stop the creditor from going back on his promise to release the debtor from payment of the full debt. Then in **Central London Property Trust Ltd. v. High Trees House Ltd. (1947),** Denning J. indicated that equity could be utilised to offer some relief to the debtor. In **High Trees** a block of flats was let on a long lease in 1937 by the plaintiffs to the defendants for a rent of £2,500. The defendants sublet the flats , but in 1940, because of the war, many of the flats were empty and the defendants were unable to meet the rent. The plaintiffs agreed to accept half the rent which was paid during the war years. After the war, the plaintiffs withdrew their promise to accept a reduced rent and demanded a return to the full rent. It was held that they were free to do so for the future because no consideration had been given for their promise. However, Denning J. also said that the plaintiffs would not have been able to recover the full rent during the war years, had they attempted to do so, because the defendants had relied on their promise.

The High Trees principle is also known as the doctrine of **Promissory Estoppel** or waiver and has since been endorsed by the House of Lords in **Tools Metal Manufacturing Co. Ltd. v. Tungsten Electrical Co. Ltd. (1955),** although the exact status and scope of the doctrine remains unclear. However, the main structure and requirements of the doctrine are as follows :

1) There must be a clear representation by the promisor that he would not enforce his strict contractual rights **(Scandi navian Trading Ltd. v. Flota Petroleva Ltd. (1983)).**

2) The promisee must have acted in reliance on the promise. It remains unclear whether the promisee must have acted to his detriment or simply have altered his position.

3) **D & C Builders Ltd. v. Rees** makes it clear that the doctrine will apply only if it would be inequitable for the promisor to go back on his promise. In **D & C Builders**, the plaintiffs who were building contractors agreed to accept £300 in full settlement of a debt of £482 which was owed to them. The plaintiffs acceptance of the smaller sum by cheque was induced only when the defendant's wife threatened to withhold payment altogether. The plaintiffs subsequently sued for the balance and obtained judgement against the defendant.

Winn LJ. applying **Foakes v. Beer** stated that the defendant had not provided any consideration for the plaintiffs' promise to forego the balance. Denning LJ. said that since the promise was extracted by threats and not given freely, the defendants could not rely on promissory estoppel.

4) The doctrine will not allow the promisee to use the promise to bring an action against the promisor. It will only allows him to use the promise as a defence if the promisor goes back on his promise and attempts to enforce his contractual rights **(Combe v. Combe** (1951) **).**

5) The effect of the doctrine is generally suspensory, not extinctive. The promisor can resume his contractual rights on giving reasonable notice of his intention to do so **(Tool Metal Manufacturing Co. Ltd. v. Tungsten Electrical Co.).** According to Lord Hodson in **Ajayi v. Briscoe Ltd. (1969)** and Lord Denning in **Alan v. El Nasr (1972)**, only if the promisor is unable to resume his original rights do the rights become extinctive (as in the case of a continuing obligation to make periodical payments such as rent under a long lease or instalments under a hire purchase agreement).

III An Intention to Create Legal Relations

An agreement will be legally enforceable only if it is of a contractual nature. This will depend on whether or not the parties intended to create legal relations. The courts make the assumption that not all agreements are intended to be binding and in order to separate mere agreements from contracts two presumptions operate:

1) Where the agreement is of a domestic, family or social nature it is presumed that the parties do not intend legal relations to follow. The leading case on domestic agreements is **Balfour v. Balfour (1919),** where a husband promised to pay his wife £30 a month and was not bound to pay. Similarly, in **Jones v. Padavatton (1969)** a promise by a mother to support her daughter if she gave up her job and studied law was held not binding; and in **Buckpitt v. Oates (1968)** the plaintiff failed to convince the court that his contribution towards the cost of petrol when given a lift in the defendant's car amounted to anything more than a 'friendly agreement'.

The presumption will not apply , however, where a husband and wife are living apart at the time the agreement is made (**Merritt v. Merrit** (1970)), or where the agreement expressly states that it is intended to have legal consequences. The test in such cases is whether a reasonable person would conclude that the parties intended legal consequences to flow from the agreement. In **Simpkins v. Pays (1955)**, three ladies living in the same house agreed to share the winnings of a newspaper competition. The court held that the agreement was binding.

2) Where the agreement is of a business or commercial nature, there is a very strong presumption that legal consequences are intended. Only firm evidence to the contrary will convince the courts otherwise. In **Rose & Frank v. Crompton Bros. Ltd. (1925),** an agreement to sell carbon paper provided "this arrangement is not entered into ..... as the form of legal agreement and shall not be subject to legal jurisdiction in the Law Courts". The court held that the agreement was not legally binding. The football pools cases **Jones v. Vernon's Pools (1938)** and **Appleson v. Littlewoods Ltd. (1939)** underline this approach by concluding that pools coupons containing a 'binding in honour only' clause prevented plaintiffs claiming that the pools companies had committed a breach of contract by not paying out winnings.

Although the parties are free to declare their agreement not to be a contract, the courts will not accept any form of words which seek to oust their jurisdiction and will declare clauses of this type illegal and void on grounds of public policy. In **Baker v. Jones (1954),** the rules of the British Amateur Weightlifters' Association provided that the council of the association should be the sole interpreter of its rules and that its decision in all cases should be final. A member of the association questioned whether the use of the association's funds for a certain purpose was lawful and took the matter to court. The court held that the clause which gave the council the sole right of interpretation of its rules was void on grounds of public policy and that the courts had jurisdiction to entertain the action. It is always a question of construction as to whether a clause is intended to oust the courts' jurisdiction or simply intended to make an agreement legally unenforceable.

Chapter 4

The Contents of a Contract

Introduction

Every contract creates rights and obligations marking out the promised commitments of the parties. The extent of such rights and obligations can be discovered by examining the **terms** of the contract. The terms embody all those statements agreed by the parties as forming part of their contract (called **express terms**) as well as provisions incorporated in the contract by custom, in fact, and at common law or by legislation (called **implied terms**).

1 Express Terms

The express terms of a contract are those made by word of mouth, in writing or a combination of both. If written, they need not be set out in any formal document. In such a case however, one of the courts' function is to settle whether documentation is contractual or not. For example, in **D'Mello v. Loughborough College of Technology (1970),** the court held that a college prospectus containing an outline of the syllabus of a course of study formed part of a contract between a college and a student.

Most everyday transactions are made by word of mouth and present no problem, often this is because the contract is performed at the instant it is made. If difficulties arise with such contracts, a major problem is providing evidence of the terms agreed. Almost inevitably there will be disagreements about what was promised and how serious a promise was meant to be.

With written contracts, the problem of evidence is minimised. This is because of the old legal rule, called the **parol evidence** rule, which states that where a contract is in writing the parties cannot introduced extrinsic evidence to 'add to, vary or contradict' the written instrument. The rule will not apply if the purpose of the extrinsic evidence is (a) to prove a custom or trade usage (**Hutton v. Warren (1836)**); or (b) to prove a previous oral agreement to suspend the operation of the written contract until the occurrence of some event (as in **Pym v. Campbell (1856)** where a written agreement to buy an invention was subject to a prior oral agreement that the invention should be approved by a third party who in fact failed to approve); or (c) to prove that the contract is partly oral and partly written; or (d) to prove that the written contract was simply recording an oral agreement and in so doing inaccurately recorded its terms.

(i) Express Terms and Representations. Not all statements or promises made by the parties during the course of negotiations will form part of the contract. Some of these statements will be terms (*contractual statements*) , while others will be representations (*pre-contractual statements*). Where the statement is a term and it is broken the wronged party is in a stronger position than if the statement is a representation. Damages for breach of a term are awarded as of right, regardless of fault; and the contract may be set aside (rescinded) as long as the breach is sufficiently serious. On the other hand, damages for a representation which is false are awarded as of right only on proof of fault (fraud or negligence by the statement maker); and the contract may be rescinded only if restitution is possible and the courts do not exercise their discretion to award damages instead (see Chapter 5 on Misrepresentation).

Whether a statement is a term or a representation is a question to be determined by reference to the intention of the parties. In ascertaining the nature of the statement the courts will proceed by following certain guidelines as laid down in case law:

(a) A statement is likely to be a representation if the statement maker asks the other party to verify the truth of the statement for himself. In **Ecay v. Godefrey (1974),** the seller of a boat stated that it was sound but advised the buyer to have it surveyed independently. The buyer bought the boat without having it surveyed. The boat turned out to be unsound and the buyer sued the seller for warranting a sound boat. It was held that the seller's statement was a mere representation.

(b) A statement is likely to be a term if it is made with the intention of preventing the other party from discovering a flaw and in turn causes him to act in reliance upon the statement. In **Schawel v. Reade (1913),** the seller of a horse which the buyer was examining said "you need not look for anything; the horse is perfectly sound. If there is anything the matter with the horse, I would tell you". As a result of this confident assurance the buyer discontinued with the examination and purchased the horse. Later he discovered that the horse was unfit and sued the seller. The court held that the seller's statement was a term of the contract.

(c) If the recipient of the statement places great importance on the statement and would not have entered into the contract had it not been made, the statement is likely to be a term. In **Bannerman v. White (1861),** a prospective buyer of hops asked the seller if any sulphur had been used in the treatment of the hops, adding that if it had, he would not even bother to ask the price.The seller assured him that no sulphur had been used and the buyer bought the hops. Later the buyer discovered that sulphur had been used in the cultivation of some of the hops and refused to pay. In an action for the price, the court held that the seller's assurance was a term of the contract even though it was not included in the written contract.

(d) Where an oral agreement is reduced to a written document, statements not included in the document will be regarded as representations, unless there is firm evidence to the contrary.

(e) Where the statement maker has special knowledge or skill in relation to the subject-matter compared to the other party, the statement is likely to be a term of the contract. In **Dick Bentley Productions Ltd. v. Smith (Motors) Ltd. (1965),** the plaintiff bought a Bentley car from the defendant car dealers after they stated that the car had done only 20,000 miles. In fact, the car engine had done nearly 100,000 miles. The plaintiff claimed damages for breach of warranty. The Court of Appeal held that although the oral statement was not included in the written contract, it was nevertheless a term of the contract because the defendants were in the position of experts as compared to the plaintiff. Accordingly, the plaintiff was awarded damages for breach of contract.

On the other hand, if the parties possess equal knowledge or skill or the recipient of the statement possesses greater knowledge or skill than the statement maker, the statement is likely to be a representation. In **Oscar Chess Ltd. v. Williams (1957),** the defendant , a private car owner, traded in his Morris in part-exchange for another car to the plaintiff car dealers. He wrongly stated that it was a 1948 model, and received an allowance of £290. In fact, the car was a 1939 model and worth only £175. The statement was made quite innocently because the registration book had been falsified by the previous owner. It was held that the defendant's statement was a representation and as he believed it to be true, the plaintiff's claim for damages failed.

(ii) Collateral Contracts. Where a main contract is entered into as a result of a statement made by one party, the courts may hold the statement as a separate contract, thus creating two contracts: the main contract and the collateral contract based on the statement. This device may be used to overcome the term / representation conflict. In **Andrews v. Hopkinson (1959),** the defendant car dealer recommended a second-hand car to the plaintiff by stating : "It is a good little bus. I would stake my life on it." The plaintiff then took the car on hire purchase from a finance company. When the finance company delivered the car, the plaintiff signed a delivery note stating that he was 'satisfied as to its condition.' A week later the plaintiff was injured because of a steering fault and when he sued the car dealer on the basis of whose promise that it was ' a good little bus' that he agreed to buy the car, the court held that the statement was a collateral contract and the defendant was liable for damages.
For the collateral argument to work, consideration must be given for the statement. Consideration is usually found by showing that the wronged party entered into the main contract as a result of the statement. It does not matter that the main contract is void or illegal **(Strongman Ltd. v. Sincock (1955)).**

11 Implied Terms

These are terms not present in the contract as concluded but are added to it on a variety of grounds. They include terms implied by custom; terms implied as fact; terms implied at common law; and terms implied by statute.

(i) Terms Implied by Custom. The courts may admit evidence of known usage or custom. In **Hutton v. Warren (1836)** , a tenant claimed a local custom entitling him to a fair allowance for seed and labour in relation to arable land after his landlord had given him notice to quit. The court admitted the custom as an addition to the written lease.

(ii) Terms Implied as Fact. The courts may give effect to the presumed intention of the parties. Thus a term may be implied into a contract on the basis that even though it was not expressed by the parties, they must have intended its inclusion so as to give the contract business efficacy. This mode of implication is sometimes known as **The Doctrine of the Moorcock.** In **The Moorcock (1889),** the appellant wharfingers owned a wharf on the River Thames and agreed with the respondent owner of the *Moorcock* that he could unload his cargo at the wharf. It was known that the ship would ground at low water but when it did, the ship suffered damage because it settled on the ridge of hard ground underneath the mud. There was no express term that the ground was safe for the ship, but the Court of Appeal confirmed that in a business transaction the law would wish to ensure that such business efficacy is given to the contract as the parties must have intended. In this case this must have included an undertaking that the ground would be safe for the ship to rest at low water.

The **Doctrine of the Moorcock** is also expressed in the words of MacKinnon LJ in **Shirlaw v. Southern Foundries Ltd (1939)** as follows : '*prima facie* that which in any contract is left to be implied and need not be expressed is something so obvious that it goes without saying; so that if, while the parties were making their bargain, an officious bystander were to suggest some express provision for it in their agreement, they would testily suppress him with a common 'Oh, of course'. ' Although the officious bystander poses the question, the courts, not the parties, give the answer (per Lord Diplock in (**Pettitt v. Pettitt (1970)).**

For the courts to imply a term in question it must be obvious to both parties **(Spring v. N.A.S. & D.S. (1956)).** Also, it is not enough that it is reasonable to imply the term **(Liverpool City Council v.Irwin (1977)).** The term must be necessary to give the contract business efficacy. In **Bournemouth FC v. Manchester United FC (1980),** the court implied a term that a player transferred to Manchester United would be given a reasonable opportunity to score goals by being included in their first team to give efficacy to a contract which provided for the payment of £28,000, as part of the transfer fee, when the player scored twenty goals.

(iii) Terms Implied at Common Law. This category embraces all those contractual relationships which are of common occurrence (e.g. seller and buyer, employer and employee) so that where the courts imply a term for the first time in a particular type of contract, the same term will be implied in subsequent contracts, unless the parties otherwise exclude it. In disputes concerning contracts of common occurrence, the problem is solved not by asking what the parties intended but whether the law has already defined their obligations.

(iv) Terms Implied by Statute. In particular types of contracts (those of common occurrence) terms will be implied by statute. For example, in sale of goods contracts terms will be implied by virtue of sections 12 to 15 of the Sale of Goods Act 1979 (see Chapter 8).

A more recent illustration is provided by the Supply of Goods and Services Act 1982. This Act, in so far as it relates to contracts for the supply of goods, barter and contracts for work and materials, implies into such contracts terms similar to those covering sale of goods contracts. Thus, there is an implied condition that the transferor has title to the goods, and has a right to transfer them to the customer **(s.2);** the goods will correspond with their description if transferred by description **(s.3);** the goods will be of satisfactory quality and reasonably fit for their purpose if transferred in the course of a business **(s.4);** and the goods will correspond with the sample in quality if transferred by reference to a sample **(s.5).**

The 1982 Act also deals with contracts for the supply of services and covers two types of service contracts: (1) where the supplier provides goods and services; and (2) where the supplier provides a 'pure' service. The provision of goods and services is governed by sections 2 to 5 of the Act dealing with the supply of goods. The provision of 'pure' service is governed by sections 13 to 15 which imply similar terms to those previously implied at common law. Under section 13, there is an implied term that when acting in the course of a business, the service will be carried out with reasonable care and skill. This means that the customer must show that the supplier of the service was negligent , and is in contrast to the strict liability of the supplier in contracts for the supply of goods and also the sale of goods. Section 14 implies that where there is no fixed time in the contract for the carrying out of the service, it shall be carried out within a reasonable time. Section 15 implies that the charge for the service will be reasonable, if not already fixed by the contract.

111 The Relative Importance of Contractual Terms

As already said, a contract consists of rights and obligations;each side promises to perform his part of the transaction. However, not all the promises or terms of the contract are of equal importance. "There are some which go so directly to the substance of the contract....are so essential to its very nature that their non-performance may fairly be considered by the other party as a substantial failure to perform the contract at all. On the other hand, there are other obligations though they must be performed, are not so vital that a failure to perform them goes to the substance of the contract (per Fletcher Moulton LJ in **Wallace, Son & Wells v. Pratt & Haynes (1911)**)

The vital, fundamental or major term which goes to the root of the contract is known as a *condition;* its breach entitles the wronged party to repudiate the contract and to claim damages against the other party for breach of contract. Alternatively, the wronged party may elect to affirm the contract and claim damages only. The minor or subsidiary term which does not go to the root of the contract is known as a *warranty*; its breach only entitles the wronged party to claim damages, and he has to continue with the contract.

While this is the distinction, it is not always clear into which category a particular promise or term falls. The parties do not always set the value of the terms which they impose of each other. It is then the courts' task to infer and interpret their intention. Some statutes like the Sale of Goods Act 1979 sections 12 to 15 and the Supply of Goods and Services Act 1982 sections 2 to 5 and 7 to 10, specifically provide what implied terms are conditions and what are warranties. However, sections 13 to 15 of the 1982 Act only describe the implied duties as terms presumably leaving it to the courts to decide in the circumstances into which category the breach falls. This may be the result of the tendency in recent years to identify certain terms as *innominate* or *intermediate.*, the effect on the contract , if broken, will determine whether the wronged party has a right to repudiate the contract or be confined to an action for damages.

The courts' general approach is as follows :

(*I*). Once a term has been classified by the courts or by statute as a condition, it will be classified thereafter as a condition **(The Mihalis Angelos (1971)).**

(*ii*) If the nature of the term has not been previously classified by the courts or specified by statute, then the courts will attempt to ascertain the intention of the parties at the time the contract was made. If the parties clearly indicated that a breach of the term will give the wronged party a right to discharge the contract, the term will be regarded as a condition. If the parties clearly had no such intention, the term will be a warranty and a remedy will lie only in damages for its breach. The description given to the term by the parties in the contract is not conclusive of their intention since parties frequently misuse terminology. In **Schuler AG v. Wickman Machine Tools (1974),** it was described as a condition in a distribution agreement between the appellant and respondent that one of two representatives of the respondent should visit six named customers once every week. When this term was broken the appellant terminated the contract. The respondent successfully claimed damages for wrongful termination of the contract, the House of Lords holding that the parties could not have intended that a mere failure to make a visit would give rise to a right to terminate.

(*iii*) If it is not possible for the courts to assess the status of the term at the time the contract was made, then the term will be classified as 'innominate'and the exact nature of the term will be ascertained by looking at the **effect** of the breach on the wronged party. A breach that deprives the wronged party of a substantial benefit of the contract will give him the right to terminate the contract.

The so-called 'innominate' term , one which is neither a condition nor a warranty , is considered by Smith and Thomas in their 'Contract Casebook' not to have been a recent invention, but rather a concept being used by the courts long before **Hong Kong Fir Shipping Co. Ltd v. Kawasaki Kisen Kaisha Ltd (1961)** where the term was first identified. These authors have taken the classic cases illustrating conditions and warranties **Poussard v. Spiers (1876)** and **Bettini v. Gye (1876)** and have analysed them on the footing of the new orthodoxy as laid down in the **Hong Kong** case and interpreted in **Cehave NV v. Bremer Handelsgesellschaft mbH** (alias the **Hansa Nord (1976)**) and **Bunge Corp v. Tradax Exports SA (1982).**

In both **Poussard** and **Bettini,** the plaintiffs were singers, and in each case because of illness were unable to attend on the day their presence was first required. In consequence each defendant terminated the contract and the plaintiffs respectively claimed damages. In **Poussard,** the plaintiff became ill five days before the first performance. Her illness seemed serious and of uncertain duration and in the circumstances the defendant was held justified in terminating the contract. In **Bettini,** in contrast, the plaintiff was required to be present for rehearsals six days before the first performance but arrived in time only for the last two days prior to the opening of the production. His late arrival did not prevent the contract from being substantially carried out; the defendant was therefore not entitled to terminate the contract and so was liable in damages. In both cases, the courts looked at the effect of the breach at the time of the failure to perform and not when the contract was made. In **Poussard's** case and not **Bettini's,** non-availability was clearly crucial.

Hong Kong concerned an obligation of seaworthiness on the part of the plaintiff shipowners. The Court of Appeal held that the obligation was not a condition, breach of which would entitle the defendant charterers to terminate the contract, since breaches of seaworthiness might be extremely trivial (e.g. the omission of a nail) or extremely grave (e.g. a serious defect in the hull or the ship's engine). The courts decision was that on the facts it was impossible to ascribe to the obligation of seaworthiness in advance, the character of a condition. In the case, the defendants terminated the contract because of the state of the ship but this breach did not deprive them of a substantial part of the contract (the charter party still had twenty months of the two year period to run). In **Cehave,** essentially the decision was reached. Here, a German company sold 12,000 tons of citrus pulp pellets to a Dutch company for cattlefood, on standard terms requiring 'shipment in good condition'. On arrival, some of the pellets were found damaged by overheating. The buyer rejected the whole consignment but subsequently bought it at a reduced price when the cargo was sold under a court order, and used it for its original purpose. It was held that 'in good condition' was not a condition in the legal sense of the term so as to entitle the buyer to refuse delivery; and the pellets were of satisfactory quality under s. 14 (2) of the Sale of Goods Act 1979 since the buyer was ultimately happy to use them for the purpose envisaged.

Finally, in **Bunge Corp v. Tradax Exports SA** a contract for the sale of soya bean meal to be shipped through a US Gulf port nominated by the seller provided that the buyer should give the seller fifteen days' notice of the ship's readiness to load the goods. The buyer gave less than fifteen days notice and the seller repudiated the contract and claimed damages as the market price had dropped substantially. The House of Lords held that in mercantile contracts stipulations as to time were usually of the essence of the contract and in this case there was no exception; the seller was therefore entitled to repudiate the contract. In **Bunge,** while the parties did not expressly classify the term as a condition, it was apparent from the surrounding circumstances that a breach of the term was intended to give the wronged party a right to terminate the contract. This is in line with the courts' approach described above in (*ii*) where the House of Lords made it clear that this stage of their inquiry into the status of the term had not been superseded by the **Hong Kong** approach. Only if it is not possible to label a term a condition or a warranty, does the term become innominate and its effect then assessed on the basis of the seriousness of the breach.

The **Bunge** decision seems to have reconciled the more recent with the older decisions. An unbridled **Hong Kong** approach would have had the effect of requiring the wronged party to wait and see the consequences of the breach (i.e. the seriousness of the breach) before deciding if it was safe to terminate the contract. It would seem that as long as the parties clearly express that they regard a particular term as important or fundamental they will remain entitled to terminate the contract if the term is broken, even if the effect of the breach is not serious.

1V Exemption (Exclusion) Clauses

These are well-known , even notorious examples of an express term found in a contractor's standard trading terms. They seek to exclude or limit a person's or a business's liability for breach of contract or for negligence. Examples include:

(1) 'In the event of loss or damage to articles cleaned, the company limits its liability in respect of all claims to £50.'

(2) 'Vehicles are parked at owner's risk.'

Such clauses are regulated by common law and increasingly by legislation. Over time, the courts' attitude to these clauses has been ambivalent. The traditional approach has been to allow the clause to stand as long as the parties consented to it.The modern approach on the other hand, has placed emphasis not only on consent but on the fairness or otherwise of the clause, and on the use of judicial techniques of construction and interpretation to nullify the clause if it is considered unfair. However, the courts' attitude has not always been consistent which has largely led to parliamentary regulation mainly in the form of the Unfair Contract Terms Act 1977.

The Common Law or Judicial Approach

(i) Incorporation. To be effective at common law the exemption clause must be incorporated in the contract. Incorporation can be by signature, notice or course of dealing.

(a) *Signature*: where the plaintiff signs a document containing an exemption clause it will be extremely difficult for him to deny the contractual nature of the document and he will be bound by his signature whether or not he has read or understood the document. In **L'Estrange v. Graucob (1934),** a cafe proprietress who signed a 'sales agreement' for the purchase of a cigarette vending machine without bothering to read it, was bound by its contents which included in small print an exemption clause excluding 'any express or implied condition, statement or warranty.' However, the signer will not be bound by the exemption clause if its effect was misrepresented to him. In **Curtis v. Chemical Cleaning and Dyeing Co (1951)** , the plaintiff who left her wedding dress at the drycleaners for cleaning was wrongly told by the assistant that the document containing the exemption clause, which she was about to sign , only excluded the defendants' liability for damage to sequins and beads, when in fact it excluded the defendants from all liability. The court held that the exemption clause could not protect the drycleaners from liability when they damaged the wedding dress. In certain circumstances, the plaintiff may be able to avoid liability altogether on the document he signed by relying on the doctrine of *Non est factum* (see Chapter 5).

(b) *Notice*: where the exemption clause is an unsigned document, the plaintiff is only bound by it if the document is a contractual one and reasonable steps were taken to bring the clause to his attention. A document is contractual if the party to be bound knows that it is intended to have contractual force, or if it is delivered to him in such circumstances so as to give him reasonable notice that it contains contractual terms. In **Chapelton v. Barry UDC (1940)**, an exemption clause was present on the back of a ticket which authorised the use of a deck chair and showed that the hirer had paid the prescribed fee. It was held that the ticket was only a receipt in respect of the money paid since no reasonable person would have regarded it as containing contractual terms. However, the fact that a document is described as a receipt , is not conclusive as to its character **(Watkins v. Rymill (1883)).**

The following documents have been held to have contractual effect : a railway ticket **(Thompson v. LMS Rly (1930))** ; a car park ticket **(Thornton v. Shoe Lane Parking Ltd (1971)) ;** a prominently displayed colour notice displayed at the place where the contract was made **(White v. British Rail (1981)).**

Whether or not notice of the exemption clause is reasonable is a question of fact to be decided in each case. The courts will consider the legibility of the print and the manner in which the clause was displayed in the document. Notice of the exemption clause must be given before or at the time the contract is made and not after. In **Olley v. Marlborough Court Ltd (1949)** , the plaintiff succeeded in her claim for damages after furs were stolen from her hotel room as the exemption clause on the bedroom wall was brought to her attention after the contract was made, which was at the reception desk at the time the plaintiff 'booked in'.

(c) *Course of dealing* : notice of the exemption clause after the contract is made will be sufficient only if the parties have had a regular contractual relationship and the exemption clause was present in previous contracts. In **Spurling Ltd v. Bradshaw (1956)** , a warehouse firm was allowed to rely on an exemption clause in a document sent to the other contracting party several days after the contract was made, and so were not liable when some barrels of orange juice deposited with the firm were found empty on collection. The court held that although there had been insufficient notice of the exemption clause it was nevertheless incorporated because the parties had on previous occasions contracted on terms excluding the warehouse firm's liability for 'negligence, wrongful act or default'. For an exemption clause to be incorporated in this way the terms on which the previous dealings are based must be consistent (**McCutcheon v. MacBrayne (1964)**) and there must be more than just a few isolated transactions (e.g. three transactions a month for three years will qualify as in **Hardwick Game Farm v. Suffork Agricultural Assoc. (1969)**) ; but not three or four transactions in five years, as in **Hollier v. Rambler Motors Ltd (1972)).**

(ii) Construction. The exemption clause in its true construction must cover the type of loss or damage that has occurred. Here, the courts have the role of construing or interpreting exemption clauses. So even though the clause overcomes the hurdles mentioned above, it may still fail on the ground that it is not clear. There are two approaches to the courts' role of construction :

(a) The *contra proferentem rule.* In summary, if the meaning of the clause is ambiguous, it will be construed against the party who wishes to rely on it. So an exemption clause which excludes 'all conditions, warranties and liabilities implied by statute, common law or otherwise' does not cover an express condition that a car for sale is 'a new Singer car' (**Andrews v. Singer & Co (1934)**).

(b) The *main purpose rule.* In construing an exemption clause, there is a presumption that it is not intended to defeat or depart from the main purpose of the contract. The rule was approved by the House of Lords in **Suisse Atlantique Societe D'Armement Maritime SA v. Rotterdamsche Kolen Central (1967)** where it was said that it is a rebuttable presumption only if sufficiently clear words are used. It was given statutory force by section 3 of the Unfair Contract Terms Act 1977. **George Mitchell Ltd. v. Finney Lock Seeds (1983)** suggests that the rule may be utilised to perform a similar function to the discredited doctrine of fundamental obligation. The doctrine as promulgated in a series of Court of Appeal cases stated that as a rule of law no exemption clause could protect a party for breach of a fundamental obligation under a contract (in essence non-performance of the contract). However, the House of Lords in **Photo Production Ltd v. Securicor Transport Ltd (1980)** denied that such a rule of law existed and declared that it was always a question of construction as to whether an exemption clause covered the breach in question and was reasonable.

In **Photo Production Ltd,** the plaintiff factory owners, entered into a contract by which the defendants provided for a very modest charge a patrolman to keep watch on the factory so as to ensure that it was safe from intruders The patrolman set light to the factory and burnt it down. The plaintiffs were covered by a fire and theft insurance policy; the defendants were covered by an exemption clause in the contract which stated that 'under no circumstances were they to be responsible for an injurious act or default by any employee.... unless such act or default could have been foreseen and avoided by the exercise of due diligence'. The House of Lords held that even though the defendants were in breach of contract, they could rely on the exemption clause because it clearly covered the breach in question and was reasonable. The House of Lords also stressed that the doctrine of fundamental obligation was no longer applicable, it being replaced by the test of reasonableness. Therefore, on the facts, it was not unreasonable for the factory owners to bear the risk of loss as they were insured against fire and theft and were better able to estimate the protection needed, and as the defendants were only charging a modest fee for their service.

There are, however, cases where it could never be reasonable to use an exemption clause to avoid liability (eg. where the buyer buys one thing and the seller supplies something else).

(iii) Other limitations on exemption clauses.

(a) An oral undertaking overrides an exemption clause : where there is a conflict between an earlier oral promise and printed conditions the former will take precedence. Thus, if carriers verbally assure a customer that his goods will not be carried on deck, then should this undertaking be breached and the goods are damaged in consequence, no exemption clause in the contract of carriage can protect the carriers (**Evans & Son Ltd v. Andrea Morzario Ltd (1976)**).

(b) An exemption clause cannot benefit a third party : an exemption clause cannot protect a person who is not a party to the contract. In **Alder v. Dickson (1955),** P & O Steamers included an exemption clause in their passenger tickets stating 'passengers are carried at passengers' entire risk'. When the plaintiff was injured he sued not the company ,but the ship's master and boatswain. The court held that the company's employees could not claim protection under the clause because they were strangers to the contract.

Regulation of Exemption Clauses by Legislation.

The Unfair Contract Terms Act 1977 represents the most far reaching attempt to control exemption clauses. Most cases will be governed by the Act, though the common law approach to exemption clauses is not entirely excluded. Despite its name, the Act does not deal with all unfair terms; it only deals with exemption clauses in contracts, and with non-contractual notices which attempt to give protection against negligence liability.

The Act applies principally to business liability which is defined as liability arising from things done or to be done in the course of a business or from the occupation of premises used for business purposes **(s.1(3)).**

The Act gives the consumer special protection. A consumer is any person who does not make or hold himself out as making a contract in the course of a business, whereas the other party does make the contract in the course of business. In contracts for the sale or supply of goods, there is the additional requirement that the goods must be of a type ordinarily supplied for private use or consumption. In a sale by auction, the buyer is not a consumer **(s. 12).** However, a company can be a consumer as long as the particular contract is not of the type which forms part of its normal business activities. In **R and B Customs Brokers Ltd. v. UDT Finance Ltd. (1988),** the plaintiff company which carried on business as shipping brokers bought a second-hand car which was to be used for business purposes and partly for the private purposes of the two directors who were husband and wife. The Court of Appeal held that the plaintiff company was still dealing as a consumer since it was not in the business of buying cars.

The Act refers to two methods of control of exemption clauses: some exemption clauses are outlawed ; while others are valid if they are reasonable.

Exemption clauses which are ineffective under the Act include the following: (a) a contract term or a non-contractual notice cannot exclude or restrict business liability for death or personal injuries resulting from negligence **(s.2(1)).** This provision only operates as between the wrongdoer and the injured party. In **Thompson v. T. Lohan (Plant Hire) and Another (1987),** a business hired out an excavator and driver to a customer on terms that the customer should indemnify the business for any liability it might incur from the operation of the excavator by the driver. Through the driver's negligence the customer's husband was killed. The customer recovered damages from the business for the driver's negligence but was then held liable to indemnify the business for the amount recovered. The court held that section 2 did not affect arrangements between the wrongdoer and others as to the sharing of the burden of compensation; (b) a 'guarantee' (e.g., manufacturer's guarantee) of consumer goods cannot exclude or restrict liability for damage arising from defective goods while in consumer use where such damage is caused by the negligence of the person concerned in the manufacture or distribution of the goods **(s.5);** (c) the statutory implied term as to title in sale or the supply of goods contracts cannot be excluded etc. by reference to a contract term, and where the buyer is dealing as a consumer the statutory implied terms as to description, satisfactory quality and fitness for purpose cannot be excluded or restricted **(ss. 6 and 7).**

Exemption clauses which are valid if they are reasonable include (a) a contract term or a non-contractual notice excluding or restricting business liability for loss (other than personal injuries or death) caused by negligence **(s.2(2));** (b) a contract term in a standard form contract excluding etc. liability for breach of contract where the innocent party is a consumer **(s.3);** (c) an indemnity clause in a contract which requires the consumer to indemnify the business for its liability (to the consumer or to a third party) resulting from negligence or breach of contract **(s.4);** (d) a contract term excluding etc. the statutory implied terms (other than title) in sale or the supply of goods contracts where the buyer is a non-consumer **(ss.6 and 7).**

In deciding whether or not reliance on an exemption clause is reasonable , the courts will have regard to all the circumstances which were, or ought reasonably to have been, known to or in the contemplation of the parties when the contract was made **(s.11).** Guidelines for reasonableness are also laid down in Schedule 2 of the Act in relation to the sale or supply of goods, namely, :

(a) the strength of the bargaining position of the parties;

(b) whether the customer was induced into agreeing to the term (e.g. where there is a two-tier pricing system where the customer will pay a higher price for the goods together with his full statutory protection and a lower price with limited statutory protection and the customer chose the lower price in return for agreeing to the exemption clause);

(c) the customer's knowledge of the existence and extent of the term (e.g. is it 'in such small print that one can barely read it' ; is it so complex 'that one almost has to be an LLB to understand it' - Staughton J in **Stag Line v. Tyne Ship Repair Group (1984)**);

(d) the practicality of complying with a condition of the contract. In **R W Green Ltd. v. Cade Bros. Farm (1978),** a clause in a standard form contract for the sale of seed potatoes stated that unless the buyer notified the supplier of his rejection of defective seeds within three days after delivery, the buyer would forfeit his right to reject. The clause was held to be unreasonable as defective seeds would not be detected until they had germinated;

(e) whether the goods were manufactured, processed or adapted to the special order of the customer.

Failure to follow the Code of Practice of a trade association can also render an exemption clause unreasonable. In **Woodman v. Photo Trade Processing Ltd. (1981),** the defendants were sued for losing a reel of film given to them for processing . They sought to rely on an exemption clause which limited their liability to the cost of the film. The court held that the clause was unreasonable because the Code of Practice for the photographic industry, as approved by the Office of Fair Trading, clearly recognised the possibility of a two-tier pricing system which was not used by the defendants in their business. Additionally, the clause was too wide in that it attempted to give protection to the defendants for negligence as well as accident, and no insurance was offered to the plaintiff for the risk he was asked to undertake.

Section 11 (4) of the Act lays down two additional guidelines for determining the reasonableness of an exemption clause.Where a business seeks to limit its liability to a specific sum of money, the courts will consider : (i) the resources which the business can expect to have available to meet its liability ; and (ii) how far it is open for the business to cover itself by insurance without having to materially raise the price for the goods or services. In **George Mitchell Ltd. v. Finney Lock Seeds Ltd. (1983),** the plaintiffs ordered 30 lb. of the defendants' Late Cabbage Seed. The plaintiffs had dealt with the defendants for many years and knew that the contract was subject to certain conditions of sale including a clause limiting the defendants' liability for any loss or damage to the replacement value of the seed or a refund of the price. So a clause to this effect on the back of an invoice was validly incorporated through previous dealing. Owing to the defendants' negligence, the seed was not Late Cabbage Seed and was not of satisfactory quality, and when germinated was commercially useless. The seed cost £201.60, the plaintiffs' loss through missing the market was £61,000. The House of Lords held the exemption clause to be unreasonable. The fact that the defendants had in the past negotiated farmers' claims for damages in excess of the price if they felt that the claims were 'justified' was conclusive that the defendants recognised that reliance on the clause was not fair and reasonable. The House of Lords further concluded that the sellers of seed could insure against crop failure caused by supplying the wrong variety without significantly increasing the price of the seed.

Certain contracts are specifically excluded from some or all of the provisions of the Unfair Contract Terms Act and are contained in Schedule 1 (e.g. insurance contracts, land contracts, international supply of goods contracts and contracts for the carriage of goods by sea).

The Act does not apply to a clause which merely defines a contracting party's liability as opposed to excluding his liability (e.g. a clause that 'the horse is warranted sound except for hunting'). Such a clause is known as a *definition of liability clause* and as it is outside the scope of the Unfair Contract Terms Act it does not have to be reasonable before it could be effective. In **Overbrooke Estate Ltd. v. Glencombe Properties Ltd. (1974),** principals limited the ostensible authority of their agents, who were auctioneers, by a clause in the particulars of sale which stated that 'neither the auctioneers nor any person in the employment of the auctioneers has any authority to make or give any representation or warranty'. The court held it was not an exemption clause but a clause limiting the ostensible authority of the auctioneers, and since the purchasers of property had notice of the clause, they could not impose liability on the principals for the auctioneers' alleged representations.

It is always a question of fact whether a clause is a definition of liability clause or an exemption clause. The courts will look at the reality of the situation rather than the way in which the clause is drafted. In **Cremdean Properties Ltd. v. Nash (1977),** the Court of Appeal held that what was to be treated as a representation was to be approached in a broad and reasonable way, so that a clause that a statement shall not be a representation , when it would otherwise be classified as a representation will not do. This approach was also adopted by the House of Lords in **Smith v. Eric Bush (1990),** in relation to a disclaimer of liability for negligence. In this case, Mrs. Smith purchased a house with a loan from a building society. She did not have the house independently surveyed but relied on a valuation report (the cost of which she financed) prepared for the building society by a surveyor employed by them. Soon after Mrs. Smith had acquired the house, the chimney collapsed and caused substantial damage. She sued the surveyor for negligently surveying the house and he attempted to rely on a clause in the mortgage application form which stated that neither the building society nor the surveyor warranted the accuracy of the valuation report and that it was supplied without responsibility on their part. The House of Lords held that although the clause negated a duty of care towards Mrs Smith,in reality it was an exemption clause and, on the facts, the surveyor would have owed a duty of care at common law but for the clause. The clause was therefore subject to the reasonableness test under the 1977 Act which it failed to satisfy and was ineffective.

The Unfair Terms in Consumer Contracts Regulations 1994, discussed earlier in relation to unfair terms in standard form contracts (see Chapter 3), also provides the consumer with some protection against unfair exemption clauses. However, this protection is not as extensive as that given by the 1977 Act.

Instead of declaring any exemption clause invalid, the Regulations only sets out a list of exemption clauses which are *presumed* to be unfair, thus leaving it to the courts to conclude otherwise; and the burden of proving that other exemption clauses not on the list are unfair is on the consumer who must be a natural person rather than a company. The test of 'unfairness' is similar to the guidelines under the 1977 Act for the 'reasonableness' test.

An additional means of controlling exemption clauses is provided by the Fair Trading Act 1973. It gives the Secretary of State for Trade and Industry power to prohibit undesirable trade practices. For example, the Consumer Transactions (Restrictions on Statements) Order issued by the Secretary of State in 1976 makes it a criminal offence for a trader to display in his window or on his goods a 'no refund' notice or any other notice purporting to take away the rights conferred by consumer legislation.

Chapter 5

Defects in a Contract

Introduction

This chapter examines defects which may have an adverse effect on an apparently valid contract. Some defects (such as untrue statements which induce a contract, mistake about the type of contract made or about the person with whom it is made, and unfair pressure to contract) affect contractual consent. Personal flaws such as age and insanity, lie with the parties themselves. In addition, defects may exist in the contractual formalities (on the few occasions when required), or the agreement may infringe a legal rule.

The consequences for the parties vary, depending on the seriousness of the defect and are reflected in a range of legal terms employed to differentiate the gravity of the defect. Such terms range from 'voidable' and 'void' and 'unenforceable' to 'illegality'. As might be expected, equity makes an important contribution in this area of the law..

This chapter therefore considers the nature and quality that the defect must possess before it can jeopardise a contract. The nature and effect of a misrepresentation is dealt with first.

1 Misrepresentation

In the previous chapter it was seen that the promises contained in a contract are called terms. If they are not honoured, the wronged party has an action for breach of contract. If however a statement is made during negotiations leading up to the contract, though not forming part of that contract and is not a collateral contract, then it is at best a representation. If the statement turns out to be untrue the wronged party has no action for breach of contract as it does not form part of a contractual bond. However, a remedy may be available if it satisfies the legal requirements of a misrepresentation.

(i) What is a Misrepresentation? It can be defined as '*a false statement of fact made by one party to another, which induces the other to enter a contract*'. Before going on to analyse this definition further, it should be noted that while the statement maker is usually a party to the contract, this is not essential; but in such a case the misled party's only remedy will lie in the law of tort for damages and the contract remains unaffected.

(a) False. A false statement can be fraudulent, negligent or innocent. The degree of falsity will be relevant in determining the remedies available to the misled party.

(b) Statement. It may be oral or written, and even conduct may qualify. In **Livesley v. Rathborne (1982)**, the plaintiff succeeded in misrepresentation. The defendant who was asked to confirm that the plaintiff would get at least two days work a week, smiled and nodded in response. His action was held to have constituted a misrepresentation by conduct.

As a general rule mere silence does not constitute misrepresentation. The following are exceptions to the rule:

1. Contracts of utmost good faith. These are special contracts (*uberrimae fidei*) which require one party to disclose all material facts on the ground that he alone knows facts which would influence the other party's decision of whether or not to enter into the contract. Contracts which fall within this category are insurance contracts and family arrangements.

2. Half-truths. This is a form of deception in which what is disclosed is true to a certain extent but will amount to a misrepresentation because the statement maker has knowledge of other facts, which if disclosed would have a detrimental effect in construing what was actually said. In **R v. Kylsant (1931),** a company gave a misleading impression to would-be investors that it was trading profitably during the depression years. It stated in a prospectus that it had paid a regular dividend during those years, but failed to disclose that it was only able to do so by drawing on its accumulated profits.

3. Change in circumstances. There is a duty to correct a statement which, at the time when made, was true but subsequently becomes untrue at the time the contract is entered into. In **With v. O'Flanagan (1936),** a statement about the fee income of a medical practice for sale was true when made but became untrue by the time the contract was signed because the income had dropped considerably as a result of the seller's illness. Failure to correct the statement was held to be a misrepresentation.

4. Fiduciary relationship (or constructive fraud). One party may be under a fiduciary duty to disclose information for the benefit of the other. A fiduciary duty will arise in certain relationships such as principal and agent, solicitor and client, and trustee and beneficiary.

(c) Fact. A misrepresentation must relate to an existing fact or past event. It therefore excludes statements of law; mere vague 'sales talk' (such as that a particular car for sale is 'the most popular car in Britain' or 'superb value for money'); and an expression of opinion or of future intention unless the opinion is not genuinely held (as in **Smith v. Land and House Property Corp (1884)** where the seller of a hotel described the tenant as 'most desirable' when he knew that the tenant was always late with his rent), or the statement maker does not intend to carry out his express intention (as in **Edington v. Fitzmaurice (1885)** where directors invited the public by prospectus to lend money to finance future expenditure on premises when their real intention was to use the money to pay off existing debts).

(d) Induces. The false statement must result in the misled party entering the contract. So no action will lie if he relied on his own skill and judgement (as in **Attwood v. Small (1838)** where the buyer relied on his own reports which wrongly confirmed the seller's statement about the ore-bearing capacity of a mine for sale). Also no action will lie if the misled party does not know of the misrepresentation **(Horsfall v. Thomas (1862)),** or does not believe it to be true.

(ii) Remedies for a Misrepresentation. The general effect of a misrepresentation is to render the contract voidable, the effect of which entitles the misled party to set aside the contract. Until this is done, the contract remains valid.

Accordingly, the misled party can choose to:

(a) Affirm the contract. He may enforce the contract as it stands, deciding that despite the misrepresentation, it is still overall beneficial to him. Affirmation may be evidenced by some act or conduct as well as by an express intention. Failure to exercise a right to cancel after a reasonable period of time may be evidence of affirmation. With fraudulent misrepresentation, time starts to run against the misled party when the untrue statement is discovered; but with a non-fraudulent misrepresentation time starts to run from the date the contract is made. In **Leaf v. International Galleries (1950),** Leaf failed in his claim to avoid a contract for an innocent misrepresentation that a painting sold to him was by Constable. Five years had lapsed since he bought the painting and the court held that he had by then affirmed the contract even though he brought an action as soon as he had discovered that the painting was not by Constable.

(b) Rescind the contract. He may cancel the contract if it has not yet been performed by either party (***informal rescission***), and can use the misrepresentation made to him as a defence to any action brought on the contract by the other party. If the misled party has already performed his part of the contract and the other party refuses to return matters to the pre-contractual position (such as by returning the purchase price and accepting the goods returned) then court action is necessary to obtain cancellation of the contract (***formal rescission***).

The misled party has no right to rescission if he has affirmed the contract; or if the parties cannot be restored substantially to their pre-contractual position or if the courts exercise their discretion under Section 2 (2) of the Misrepresentation Act 1967 to award damages instead of rescission.

In the typical case of fraud involving cheques, the victim is misled into accepting the cheque in consequence of a misrepresentation and so parts with his goods. If the victim has not been paid for the goods he cannot rescind the contract and recover his goods unless he has set aside the contract prior to the purchase of his goods by an innocent third party from the misrepresentor. Such avoidance of the contract normally requires giving notice to the misrepresentor. In practice, this may not be easy for as soon as the misrepresentor has obtained the goods he becomes impossible to find. However, **Car and Universal Finance Co. Ltd v. Caldwell (1965)** raises the possibility of effective avoidance, such as by notifying the police and the AA as soon as the misled party has become aware of the misrepresentation. As long as this is done before an innocent third party purchases the goods, the misled party can insist on restoration.

In addition to the above remedies, the misled party can claim damages.

(c) **Damages.** He has a right to recover damages from the statement maker where he has suffered loss if the misrepresentation was fraudulent or negligent. With a fraudulent misrepresentation the action is brought in the tort of fraud. With a negligent misrepresentation the action is brought either in the tort of negligence or under the Misrepresentation Act 1967.

Damages for misrepresentation are assessed according to tort rules, not contract rules. Tort rules aim to put the wronged party in the position he would have been in had the tort not been committed (in the case of misrepresentation, this means in the position before the contract was made), by making good any 'out of pocket' expenses caused by the misrepresentation. Contract rules aim to put the wronged party in the position he would have been in had the contract been performed properly (i.e. had the representation turned out to be true). Consequential foreseeable losses (e.g. loss of profit) are recoverable in contract. In tort, the wronged party can only recover loss of profit which he would have made from *another* business on the basis that if the misrepresentation had not been made, he would probably have bought another business and made (though not as extensive) some profit from that business **(East v. Maurer** (1991)**).**

1. Tort of fraud. In **Derry v.Peek (1889),** the House of Lords said that this requires the wronged party to prove that the statement maker knew when he made the statement that it was untrue, or do not believe it to be true or was reckless as to whether it was true or false. This is a very heavy burden to

discharge and in the case itself none of these yardsticks of proof was met.
Although the amount of damages recoverable in tort, like contract, is limited by the remoteness of damages rule, the rule has no application in the tort of fraud **(Doyle v. Olby (1969)).** Thus the misled party is entitled to recover all consequential losses (e.g. expenses incurred in running a business) directly flowing from the fraudulent inducement.

2. Tort of negligence. It was not until 1964, in **Hedley Byrne and Co. Ltd. v. Heller and Partners Ltd,** that pure economic loss resulting from a negligent statement became recoverable. In **Hedley Byrne,** it was said *obiter* that a duty of care can extend to negligent statements which cause financial loss as long as a special relationship exists between the statement maker and the misled party (see Chapter 14).

3. Misrepresentation Act 1967. It applies only to non-fraudulent misrepresentations (i.e. negligent and innocent misrepresentations). Section 2 (1) gives the misled party a right to recover damages for a negligent misrepresentation unless the statement maker can prove that he had reasonable grounds to believe and did believe the representation to be true. This route to damages has the advantage over the previously discussed common law routes in that the burden of proof is shifted from the misled party to the statement maker. However, it is narrower in other respects. The statement maker must also be the person with whom the misled party subsequently contracted. Also , only a principal is liable under the subsection for a representation by his agent. The agent himself cannot be made liable **(Resolute Maritime Inc. v. Nippon Kaiji Kyokoi** (1983)**).** Damages under section 2 (1) are assessed in the same way as in the tort of fraud **(Royscot Trust Ltd. v. Rogerson** (1991)**).** However, unlike the tort of fraud, the courts have power under the Law Reform

(Contributory Negligence) Act 1945 to reduce the amount of damages to be awarded for a negligent misrepresentation on grounds of the misled party's carelessness **(Gran Gelato Ltd. v. Richcliff (Group) Ltd. (1992).**

Section 2 (2) gives the courts a discretion to award damages in place of rescission. This subsection applies to both negligent and innocent misrepresentations. So the misled party may obtain damages under both subsections for a negligent misrepresentation although the courts are required to take account of the damages awarded under subsection 2 when awarding damages under subsection 1. According to dicta by Hoffman LJ and Evans LJ in **William Sindall plc v. Cambridgeshire County Council (1994)**, the measure of damages under subsection 2 is the amount by which the actual value at the time of contracting is less than the price paid by the misled party, with consequential losses being ignored altogether. While the misled party may be awarded damages under subsection 2 for an innocent misrepresentation, such damages are awarded at the courts'discretion. According to dicta by Jacobs J in **Thomas Witter Ltd. v. TBP Industries Ltd. (1996),** the courts can award damages under subsection 2 even though the misled party's right to rescind the contract is lost by the time judgement is given.

(iii) **Exemption Clauses and Misrepresentation.** Section 3 of the Misrepresentation Act (as amended by Section 8 of the Unfair Contract Terms Act) nullifies any clause in a contract which attempts to exclude or restrict liability for a misrepresentation unless it satisfies the test of reasonableness.

(iv) **Misrepresentation and Breach.** Where a misrepresentation is subsequently incorporated in a contract, the misled party may rescind for misrepresentation in addition to any remedy he may have for breach of contract **(S. 1 Misrepresentation Act).**

11 Mistake

This affects the state of mind of the parties and renders the contract void at common law so that no rights or liabilities can arise under it. Primarily because making a contract void can have an adverse effect on third party rights (e.g. a third party can only acquire title to goods if the contract he makes with the transferor of the goods is valid), the doctrine of mistake is confined to very narrow limits and will not be available as a relief for bad bargains or bad business decisions. It is no ground for relief that a manufacturer has erred in assessing his sales costs when pricing his product. This is a 'mistake' he has to bear or should have provided for in the contract by a **price escalation clause** (i.e. a clause which gives protection against unforeseen costs such as inflation and fluctuations in the exchange rates). For a party to have any chance at all to obtain relief at common law for a mistake he has made, the alleged mistake must be one of fact (not law) and must be fundamental.

Operative mistakes which may make a contract void at common law can be classified as follows:

(i) Mistake as to the existence of the subject-matter. Here, the parties reach an agreement but make the same mistake (a **common mistake**) that there is something to contract over. This may occur where the subject-matter of the contract has never existed (as in **Galloway v. Galloway (1914)**, where the parties entered into a separation agreement believing that they were validly married when unknown to them the man's first wife was still alive at the time they went through the marriage ceremony), or has ceased to exist (as in **Couturier v. Hastie (1852)**, where the seller purported to sell a cargo of corn to the buyer when unknown to both parties, it had fermented), or because unknown to both parties the contractual subject -matter already belongs to the buyer so that there is nothing for the buyer to buy (as in **Cooper v. Phibbs (1867)**, where fishing rights for rent already belonged to the hirer). If the subject-matter has never existed and the seller had no valid reason to believe that it did exist, then the Australian case , **McRae v. Commonwealth Disposal Commision (1950)** suggests that he can be sued for warranting the presence of a non-existing subject-matter. If the subject-matter of the contract exists but the parties are mistaken as to its quality, the mistake will not be sufficiently fundamental to invalidate the contract (**Leaf v. International Galleries (1950)**).

(ii) Mistake as to the identity of the subject-matter. Here, there is no agreement because each party is talking about different subject-matters (a **mutual mistake**). In **Raffles v. Wichelhaus (1864)**, a claim for mistake succeeded. The confusion related to ships carrying a cargo of cotton destined for the UK, one in October and the other in December. The seller intended to deliver the cotton on board the December vessel, but the buyer had in mind the October vessel. The court held that there was no agreement between the parties.

(iii) Mistake as to the identity of the other party. Here, one party, **A**, makes a mistake (a **unilateral mistake**) about the identity of the other party, **B**, usually where **B** makes some pretence of his own identity in order to bring about a contract with **A** or to obtain credit from him. In most cases **B** is a rogue who pretends to be wealthy and essentially the issue is whether the mistake is sufficiently fundamental to negate consent so as to make the contract void. As between the parties, the question of the contract being void is of little importance; **B**'s pretence will constitute fraud and so the contract is voidable anyway for misrepresentation. However, mistake is crucial when **B** obtains goods in consequence of the pretence and sells them to an innocent third party. If the contract is void for mistake, the third party gets no title; if only voidable for misrepresentation he gets a good title (unless the mistaken party had taken steps to rescind the contract with the misrepresentator before the sale to that third party).

For this type of mistake to succeed it is necessary for the mistaken party to satisfy three conditions:

(a) *The mistake was a crucial factor in the mistaken party's decision to contract* (i.e. the mistaken party must convince the courts that he intended to contract with some other person). Where the parties contracted face to face there is a strong presumption that they intended to contract with each other and that the mistake was only as to the attributes of the other party rather than to his identity. In **Lewis v. Averay (1972),** the Court of Appeal pointed out the difficulty of displacing this inference in face-to-face contracts. In **Lewis** , the conflict between the original owner of a Mini Cooper and an innocent third party was solved in the latter's favour. Lewis was offered a cheque by a rogue in payment when negotiating the sale of his car. He was reluctant to accept it but agreed after the rogue intimated that he was the well-known television actor, Richard Green, and backed this up by producing a Pinewood Film Studio pass with his assumed name upon it and a photograph clearly that of the rogue. The rogue quickly resold the car to Averay and on tracing his car Lewis brought an action to recover it, alleging that the original contract with the rogue was void for mistake. However, the Court of Appeal following **Phillips v. Brooks Ltd (1910)**, another face- to- face contract for the purchase of jewellery by a rogue who falsely represented himself as Sir George Bullough and giving the latter's address, held that the mistake was only as to the name and creditworthiness of the other party and not as to his identity. In **Ingram v. Little (1961)**, a face-to-face contract where a rogue induced two sisters to accept a cheque for their car by pretending to be 'P.G.M. Hutchinson of Stanstead House, Stanstead Road, Caterham', the sisters were able to convince the Court of Appeal that they intended to contract not with the rogue, but with the real P.G.H. Hutchinson. In consequence, they were allowed to recover their car from an innocent third party on grounds of mistake

. Where the parties did not contract with each other face to face, then mistake as to identity is easier to prove. In **Cundy v. Lindsay (1878)**, a rogue pretending to be Blenkiron , a well-known dealer, ordered linen through correspondence from Lindsay & Co. The rogue resold the linen to Cundy and absconded with the proceeds of sale. Lindsay & Co were able to recover the linen (or its value) from Cundy. The House of Lords was satisfied that they intended to contract only with Blenkiron.

(b) *The mistake involved two separate entities who actually exist, one being mistaken for the other.* In **King's Norton Metal Co Ltd v. Edridge, Merritt and Co Ltd (1897)** the plaintiffs received an order for wire from 'Hallan and Co', a firm which did not exist , merely being a creature of a rogue called Willis but which was described in order form as having depots in Belfast Lille and Ghent. Believing the firm to be real , the plaintiffs sent the wire on credit to the address shown on the order form. Willis obtained possession , sold the wire to the defendants and made off with the price. The unpaid sellers sought to recover the wire from the defendants, alleging that the contract with 'Hallan and Co' was void for mistake. However the Court of Appeal held against them on the basis that as 'Hallan and Co' did not exist, the plaintiffs must have intended to contract with Willis by letter.

(c) *The mistake was known to the other party.* Invariably, he does know as he has induced the mistake by fraud.

(iv) Mistake in signing a document. In certain circumstances the courts will allow a person who mistakenly signs a document to plead that the signature was not his act (*non est factum*) and will declare the document a nullity. As this plea can be a ready source of danger to innocent third parties who rely on signed documents, the law has introduced a number of restrictions on its scope.

The scope of the plea is limited in three respects:

(a) **Who can rely on it?** This , according to the leading case of **Saunders v. Anglia Building Society (1970)** is any person who has no real understanding of the document 'whether ...from defective education, illness or innate incapacity' or who has been induced by fraud. Thus it will not normally apply to a person who merely fails to read what is within his capacity to read and understand.

(b) **Nature of the mistake.** The document actually signed must be 'fundamentally different' from the document the signer thought he was signing. The House of Lords in **Saunders v. Anglia Building Society** formulated this test in place of the traditional test that the document must be different in nature and not just in contents. In the case itself, the plaintiff was originally a Mrs. Gallie, aged seventy-eight who died between the Court of Appeal decision and that of the House of Lords. Saunders who replaced her was the executrix of her estate. Mrs Gallie had signed a document which she thought was an assignment of her leasehold house as a gift to her nephew, Walter, so that he could raise a loan for his business. In fact, the document amounted to a transfer of the house to Walter's business partner, Lee, who induced the fraud. Lee raised a loan on the house from the Anglia Building Society and absconded.

On discovering the fraud, Mrs Gallie brought an action against the building society for a declaration that the assignment was void (*non est factum*). The court held that her mistake was not so fundamental as to avoid the assignment. She had intended to assign her house and the mistake was only as to the way in which she assigned it.

Ironically, Mrs Gallie's claim seems still to have fallen foul of the old 'contents only' test in that both the gift she believed she was making and the assignment she actually made were disposals of her property. However, the newly formulated test would seem to operate for the future since it is less rigid than the traditional test. So the plea may be available now for a person with limited capabilities who mistaken signs a document acknowledging a debt for £10,000 instead of £100 since the signed document will be fundamentally different from what the signer thinks he is signing.

(c) **Carelessness.** To rely on the plea, the signer must not have been careless in signing the document. In view of the statement in **Saunders** (see (a) above) the test will appear to be subjective (i.e. on the signer's actual capabilities). This is in line with **Foster v. Mackinnon (1869)**, where Mackinnon was held not to be careless because of old age, and weak eye sight when he signed a bill of exchange which was wrongly represented to him as a guarantee.

(v) Mistake in Equity. Equity has developed its own set of rules for a mistake and will treat a contract as voidable for mistake even though the mistake is not fundamental in the common law sense. However, a trivial mistake will not do . To obtain relief in equity, where common law does not recognise the mistake as being sufficient serious to invalidate the contract, the party claiming relief must show that he was no way at fault and that he acted promptly. Time runs from the date of the contract and not from the date of discovery of the mistake **(Leaf v. International Galleries).**

Equity intervenes in three ways to provide relief. It may grant rescission of the contract on such terms as it thinks fit **(Solle v. Butcher (1950));** it may reject any application for specific performance against the mistaken party, so leaving the plaintiff to his common law remedy of damages (**Wood v. Scarth** (**1855**)); and it may order rectification of a document where, by mistake , a written document does not accurately record the 'common intention' of the parties (as in**Craddock Bros Ltd v. Hunt (1923)** where a seller of land verbally agreed to sell a property and by mistake the written contract also included an adjoining yard which the parties had verbally agreed would be excluded from the sale).

III Duress and Undue Influence

In certain situations, the courts will intervene and give relief against contracts obtained by illegitimate and improper pressure. On the narrow front, where violence is inflicted or threatened to induce the contract **(duress)**, or more widely, in certain types of relationships where one party is in a position to exercise **undue influence** on the other party as a result of which a contract has ensued. As far as these two well-established forms of intervention are concerned the legal effect seems to render the contract voidable rather than void.

(i) Duress. A common law doctrine entitling the coerced party to avoid the contract. For the courts to intervene , unlawful violence (actual or threatened) to a party to 'persuade' him to contract was required. However, recent cases such as **The Sibeon and the Sibotre (1976)** and **Universe Tankships Inc. v. ITWF (1982)** suggest that the courts may now consider such factors as threat to destroy property or to cause serious economic consequences to a person's business .

(ii) **Undue Influence.** This line of approach developed by equity is much broader than duress. It permits victims of more subtle forms of pressure than duress to avoid a contract. Contracts which have been set aside for undue influence fall under two broad categories. There are those which have been affected by *actual undue influence* and those which have been affected by *presumed undue influence.*

With *actual undue influence*, the victim must prove that he has been subject to 'some unfair and improper conduct, some coercion from outside, some overreaching , some personal advantage obtained by' the party exercising the pressure (per Lindley LJ in **Allcard v. Skinner (1887)).** The contract need not be to the 'manifest disadvantage' of the victim before it could be set aside for actual undue influence. In **Williams v. Bayley (1866),** a son forged his father's signature on several promissory notes and the bank to whom they had been given threatened criminal proceedings against the son unless the father agreed to mortgage his mine to the bank as security for the son's debts. The father, unable to resist statements from the bank , such as 'this is a serious matter' and 'a case for transportation for life' was able to set aside the agreement to execute the mortgage because of the undue influence.

In some instances the courts will presume undue influence unless the contrary is proved. *Presumed undue influence* can arise in to ways. Firstly, where a recognised special relationship exists between the contracting parties. Examples of such relationships are doctor and patient, trustee and beneficiary, religious adviser and disciple (**Allcard v. Skinner**), guardian and ward, parent and child (as **Lancashire Loans Ltd. v. Black (1934)** shows this can still survive the child's marriage or the attaining of his majority if he is still not free of parental control), but not husband and wife **(Midland Bank plc v. Shepard (1988)).** Secondly, where there is no recognised special relationship between the contracting parties, presumed undue influence may be established if the victim proves that a relationship of influence has developed as a matter of fact, such as where the victim has place trust and confidence in the party exercising the influence or where he is dominated by that party. In **Re Craig (1971)**, a presumption of undue influence as of fact was said to exist between an eighty-four year old man and his secretary-companion on whom he was totally dependent, with the result that she had to return £30,000 with of gifts given to her during the six years preceding his death. For the courts to set aside a contract on grounds of presumed undue influence as of fact the contract must have been to the 'manifest disadvantage' of the influenced party **(National Westminster Bank plc v. Morgan (1985)).** Presumed undue influence can be rebutted if the victim was advised by an independent legal adviser.

Where the influence was exhorted by a third party, rather than by the other contracting party, (e.g. as in **BCCI v. Aboody (1990)** where a wife entered into a surety transaction with a bank in favour of her husband as a result of undue influence by the husband) the courts will set aside the contract only if the other contracting party had actual or constructive notice of the influence. Constructive notice will be imputed on the other contracting party if (a) the contract was on its face not to the financial advantage of the victim of the influence and (b)the relationship between the third party and the victim of the influence was such (e.g. based on marriage, cohabitation or a close family relationship) as to carry the risk of domination by that third party. In **CIBC Mortgages Ltd. v. Pitt (1994)**, a loan company brought an action for possession of the matrimonial home after a husband and wife defaulted with repayment of a joint loan. The wife attempted to have the security set aside on grounds of the husband's actual undue influence; but this argument failed as the loan company had no constructive notice of the influence since, on the face of the transaction, the loan was potentially for the benefit of both borrowers. The decision would have been different if the wife was only acting as surety for the husband's debts since, on the face of the transaction, it would not have been for the financial benefit of the wife **(Barclays Bank v. O'Brien (1994)).** The party with notice of the influence should take steps to counteract the influence (e.g. by advising the victim to seek legal advice) unless it is reasonable for him to expect that the victim had been advised by a solicitor **(Massey v. Midland Bank (1995)).**

As in misrepresentation, to right to avoid a contract (or gift) is lost in certain and similar cases (e.g. third party rights, affirmation after the influence ceases). In **Allcard v. Skinner (1887),** the plaintiff on joining a sisterhood transferred her property to it in accordance with its rules of poverty. Subsequently, she left the sisterhood and six years later attempted to recover her property on grounds of undue influence. Her action failed; the court concluded that she had lost her right to recovery due to her undue delay in pursuing her claim, which also amounte to evidence of affirmation of the gift.

(IV) Capacity

This is concerned with a person's ability to make a contract. At its crudest, and perhaps most graphic, to have full contractual capacity, a person must be human, an adult, sane, sober and not addicted to drugs. Corporations, minors and persons with mental disability are not fully liable on their own contracts.

(i) Corporations. A corporation is some legal person and it can only contract through human agents. A chartered corporation generally has power to do whatever a human adult can do; a statutory corporation is restricted to what is consistent with the particular statute which brought it into existence; and a registered corporation has contractual capacity to enter into transactions permitted by its memorandum of association.

(ii) Minors. The law reflects a piecemeal approach ; the general aim being to protect a minor or infant (i.e. a person under the age of eighteen) from his own inexperience. Originally, all contracts with a minor were voidable at his option; but this has been varied by common law acceptance that certain contracts shall have some effect (**binding contracts**) and others shall have no effect (**unenforceable contracts**). As a final general comment, a minor's parents are not liable as parents for his contracts unless they agree with the other contracting party to indemnify against loss suffered at their child's hands or if they guarantee the transaction.

Contracts which are binding on the minor are contracts for necessary goods and services and employment contracts . Whether or not goods and services are necessaries will depend on their suitability and the minor's needs. To be suitable , the goods and services must meet the minor's lifestyle as measured by status and income. Thus, where the usage of society require the use of certain things (such as food, clothing, furniture, textbooks and a wristwatch), they may be necessaries even though they may be luxurious in quality, if that is what a person in the minor's position ordinarily uses (**Clyde Clyde Co Ltd v. Hargraves (1898)).** Expensive items of gift are not usually necessaries unless they are engagement rings and wedding rings given by the minor to his fiancee **(Elkington v. Amery (1936)).** The minor must be in need of the goods and services at the time he receives them because he (or his spouse or infant child) lacks a sufficient supply (**Nash v. Inman (1908)).** A minor only has to pay a reasonable price for the necessary goods and services. Employment contracts cover apprenticeship contracts and all other contracts by which the minor earns a living or which would entitle him to do so (**Doyle v. White City Stadium (1935)).**

Voidable contracts concern contractual liability connected with property holding of a permanent form. Contracts such as leases, shares in a company, partnership contracts and marriage settlements are binding on a minor unless he avoids them during his minority or within a reasonable time after reaching eighteen. If a minor pays money under a voidable contract, he cannot recover the sum so paid unless he fails to receive any benefit whatsoever from the contract **(Steinberg v. Scala (Leeds) Ltd (1923)).** A minor who becomes a partner cannot be made liable for partnership debts arising while he is still a minor, but if he repudiates the partnership agreement , he cannot claim his share of the assets until all the firm's debts are paid.

Unenforceable contracts include contracts for the repayment of loans, contracts for non-necessary goods and services, and contracts made by the minor as self employed for the purpose of trade. The unenforceable nature of such contracts only adversely affects an adult who contracts with the minor. The minor himself can enforce these contracts though the courts will not grant him an order for specific performance (see Remedies for Breach of Contract). Unenforceable contracts can be ratified by the minor on reaching the age of eighteen, thus making him liable on them. In addition, the Minors' Contracts Act 1987 gives the courts power , where it is just and equitable to do so, to require the minor to return any property which he obtained under an unenforceable contract. Also, where the minor borrows money to purchase necessaries, the adult can recover all or any part of the loan as is spent on necessaries, under the equitable doctrine of subrogation **(Lewis v. Alleyne (1888)).**

A minor cannot be made indirectly liable on an unenforceable contract by suing him in tort. However if the tort is independent of the contract in the sense that the tortuous act was not contemplated by the contract or was expressly excluded by it, then he can be sued successfully **(Burnard v. Haggis (1863)).**

(iii) Persons under mental disability. If a person is insane or under the influence of drinks or drugs he can avoid the contract (unless it was for necessaries) if he can show that he was incapable of understanding the nature of the transaction **and** the other party knew of his disability.

V Contractual Formalities

Formalities, the precise observances of form, is not necessary in the formation of a contract. In the few cases where it is required, it is only because of the importance (now or in the past)of the type of contract involved. Some contracts such as promises not for consideration, a conveyance of land and a lease for over three years, must be made under seal. Here, the whole contract is written on a document which clearly indicates that it is intended to be a deed, it is then signed and witnessed and then delivered as a deed **(s.1 Law of Property (Miscellaneous Provisions) Act 1989).** Some contracts such as a contract of marine insurance (Marine Insurance Act 1906), a consumer credit agreement (Consumer Credit Act 1974) and a contract for the sale or disposition of an interest in land (Law of Property Act (Miscellaneous Provisions) Act 1989), are required to be in writing and signed before they can be valid. Some contracts such as a contract of guarantee (Statute of Frauds 1677) and an employment contract (Employment Rights Act 1996)require some written evidence.

VI Illegality

Some contracts are not actionable in court because they are declared illegal by statute or the common law. The illegality may affect the purpose of the contract or only the way in which the contract is carried out.

(i) Contracts affected by statute. Certain statutes expressly or by implication prohibit particular forms of activity.The effect of contravention may be to render the contract void or simply to impose a penalty without affecting the contract's validity. In the commercial field, a whole range of legislation exists to ensure competitiveness and to prevent unfair trading practices and it is these which will be considered here.

(a) The Restrictive Trade Practices Act 1976. A consolidating statute requiring agreements made between UK suppliers of goods and services to be registered with the Director General of Fair Trading if such agreements tend to restrict the prices to be charged for the goods and services, or the conditions of supply or the persons with whom or areas of places in which dealings are allowed. Certain agreements such as those which are to apply outside the UK; most sole agency agreements; and the supply of commercial services already subject to statutory control are exempted from the registration provisions of the Act.

Registrable agreements must normally be registered within three months of their making otherwise they are unenforceable between the parties. On registration, the Director General of Fair Trading may recommend to the Secretary of State that the agreement should be allowed to stand or he may refer it to the Restrictive Practices Court to determine its validity.

An agreement before the court is presumed to be contrary to public policy and therefore void unless it can escape through one of the 'gateways' provided by the Act **(s.10).** Among the most important gateways are that the restriction is reasonably necessary to protect the public; its removal will deny to the public other specific or substantial benefit; it maintains employment in concentrated areas; it maintains the export trade; and it countermands similar practices abroad. An agreement which passes through the gateways will then be upheld by the court if its benefit to the parties is not outweighed by its detriment to the public.

(b) Resale Prices Act 1976. It prohibits the imposition of minimum resale prices for goods by retailers and makes unlawful agreements between suppliers to enforce minimum resale prices by either trade fines or the withholding of supplies from dealers.

A minimum resale provision in a contract between the supplier and his dealer does not affect the validity of the agreement but the provision will be void. The Restrictive Practices Court has power to exempt contracts for the sale of certain goods from the provisions of the Act and will do so if it is convinced that without price fixing either the quality or variety of the goods would be substantially reduced or that the number of shops would decline or that the servicing of the goods would deteriorate, or that there would be a danger that the consumer's health would suffer, or that the price fixing is in the public interest Recommended sale prices (as opposed to the imposition of minimum sale prices) are not unlawful under the Act.

(c) **Trade Descriptions Act 1968.** Without affecting the validity of the contract, this Act imposes criminal liability on a business seller who sells or exposes for sale goods or services bearing a false trade description. Local authority trading standards officers, and not individuals, have to institute criminal proceedings against offenders. An individual seeking a civil remedy on account of a false trade description will have to rely on the common law remedies for misrepresentation, or on S.13 of the Sale of Goods Act 1979 which deals with sales by description.

Section 1(1) contains two offences where , in the course of a business, goods bear a false trade description; and in both cases liability is strict. Under subsection 1 (a) it is an offence to apply a false trade description to goods. The supplier must apply the trade description either before the sale is envisaged or at the time the contract is made. Under subsection 1(b) it is an offence to supply or offer to supply goods to which a false trade description is applied. 'Offer to supply' includes an invitation to treat such as where the supplier exposes goods in his possession for sale. Subsection 1 (b) is relevant where a retailer himself did not apply the false trade description. However, in such a case he may rely on the defence of innocent publication i.e. he did not know and could not with reasonable diligence have known that the goods did not correspond to the description or that the description had been applied to the goods.

'Trade description' means any assertion ' whether expressly or by implication, about the goods in relation to its characteristics (e.g. size, method of manufacture, fitness for purpose or strength) or its history (e.g. place or date of manufacture, previous owners, testing by a person and results). The false trade description may be applied orally or by markings. Moreover, it is not necessary for the buyer to be misled or for a sale to be concluded before the offences can be committed. While it is usually the business supplier who commits an offence under the Act, it may also be committed by a business buyer. In **Fletcher v. Budgen (1974),** a car dealer who wanted to buy a customer's car falsely informed the customer that the car could not be repaired and that it was only fit for scrap. The customer sold the car to the dealer for £2 and the dealer subsequently repaired it and advertised it for £136. It was held that the dealer had committed the subsection 1 (a) offence.

An offence is only committed if the false trade description was made 'in the course of a trade or business'. A transaction is in the course of a trade or business if it is either an integral part of the business or else if there is a sufficient degree of regularity or similar transaction **(Havering London Borough v. Stevenson (1970).** In **Davies v. Sumner (1984),** a self-employed courier who used his car for working purposes and claimed tax allowance for its use sold the car with a false odometer reading. It was held that he did not commit a offence under the Act because the sale of the car was not an integral part of his business.

Section 14 makes it an offence for any person in the course of a trade or business to make false statements deliberately or recklessly in relation to services, accommodation or facilities (e.g. as to their nature and the time at which, manner in which or persons by whom they are to be provided , also the location or amenities of any accommodation provided). 'Falsity' is judged at the time the statement is made, so that if a brochure issued by a travel agency indicates that a hotel is fully built when in fact the picture is only an artist's impression **(Yugotours Ltd. v. Wadsley (1988))** an offence is committed. However if a statement is true when made but subsequently becomes untrue, no offence is committed. A false statement in a travel brochure is made at each time the brochure is read by some one.

Misleading price indications as to goods , services , accommodation etc. are dealt with by S.20 of the Consumer Protection Act which makes it an offence for giving misleading information as to the price for such goods, services etc. A statement is misleading if it suggests that the price is less than it actually is, or that no additional charge is payable when this is not the case, or that a comparison made is a genuine one. Section 20 applies only in favour of consumers; this is in contrast to the offences under the Trade Descriptions Act where the offences can be committed regardless of the status of the buyer.It is a defence to a prosecution under S.20 if the defendant acted with due diligence to avoid committing the offence.

Section 24 of the Trade Descriptions Act provides to defences for its subsection 1 and section 14 offences, namely **innocent publication** (discussed earlier) and **general defences**. The general defences include mistake, accident or some other cause beyond the defendant's control, reliance on information provided to the defendant, and wilful default by a third party. In relation to the general defences, the defendant must also prove that he took all reasonable precautions and exercised due diligence to avoid committing the offence , such as by using a disclaimer notice. In **Simmons v. Potter (1975)** , the defendant car dealer sold a car which had a false odometer reading . The odometer had been tampered with by the previous owner but the defendant was not aware of it. Nevertheless, the defendant was convicted under subsection 1 (b) because he did not take all reasonable precautions to prevent commission of the offence, such as by placing a disclaimer notice near the odometer. A disclaimer notice is of no assistance to a trader who has deliberately made a false statement.

(d) Fair Trading Act 1973. This Act created the post of Director General of Fair Trading to protect the interest of consumers. The DG is responsible for monitoring business activities in the UK and for investigating the circumstances leading up to any monopoly or merger situation. A monopoly situation exists if at least one quarter of the goods or services of a particular kind are supplied either by a single person (or companies in the same group) or to a single person. With the approval of the in Secretary of State , the DG may refer a monopoly or merger situation to the Monopolies and Merger

Commission and if the business under investigation gives undertakings to the Commission, the DG monitors the observance of such undertakings.

(e) Competition Act 1980. This Act requires the DG to investigate anti-competitive practices. An 'anti-competitive practice' is a course of conduct which is likely to restrict, distort or prevent competition in connection with goods and services. If the DG finds that an anti-competitive practice exists, he can institute a process resulting in a statutory order to ban the practice. The validity of a contract made in the course of an ante-competitive practice prohibited by a statutory order is not affected but criminal sanction is imposed on the offender.

(f) Article 85 and 86. Article 85 of the Treaty of Rome prohibits any form of agreement or concerted practice between undertakings which significantly affects trade between member states and which could have an adverse effect on competition in the European Union. An agreement which infringes Art. 85 is void and unenforceable unless it is possible to severe the offending terms from the rest of the agreement. In addition, the European Commission can impose substantial fines on the parties to the agreement. Moreover, third parties who suffer loss as a result of the offending restrictions can sue all the parties to the agreement for damages in the national courts. The Commission has power to grant exemptions to agreements which infringe Art. 85. It can grant individual exemptions where the benefits of the agreement to consumers clearly outweigh any anti-competitive results. Block exemptions (i.e. automatic exemptions) are granted to certain types of commercial agreements (e.g. exclusive distribution, exclusive purchasing, and franchising) providing they fall within the terms of the exemption legislation.

Art. 86 prohibits abuses by monopolies within the European Union and does not, in contrast to English domestic law , actually prohibit monopolies.

(ii) Contracts affected by common law. Some contracts are declared illegal at common law either because they conflict with accepted standards of morality (e.g. contracts to commit a crime or a tort, or to promote sexual immorality, or to impede the course of justice), or because they are contrary to public policy (e.g. contracts in restraint of trade, or to oust the jurisdiction of the courts).

Contracts in restraint of trade. These are contracts which attempt to restrict a person's economic activities. They are *prima facie* void unless they are proved to be reasonable. They can be divided into three groups : restraints in employment contracts, restraints on the sale of a business and exclusive dealings agreements (**souls agreements).**

(a) Employment contracts. An employer can lawfully insert a provision in an employee's contract requiring him to render his services exclusively to the employer while the employment continues. However, any restraint imposed on the employee's freedom to set up in similar business or to work for a competing employer after his employment terminates will come under the close scrutiny of the courts.

The courts will uphold the restraint if they are satisfied that it is necessary for the protection of the employer's trade secrets (**Foster and Son v. Suggett** (**1918**)) or trade connections and it will not be giving the employer excessive protection.

Many restrains have been declared invalid as being unreasonable between the parties for the following reasons:

1. Area if restraint. The employee is prohibited from working in a wider area than the area of the employer's business (**Mason v. Provident Clothing and Supply Co Ltd** (**1913**)).

2. Duration of restraint. The employee is restrained for an excessively long time. Although a life-long restraint on a solicitor's clerk was held to be valid **(Fitch v. Dewes** (**1921**)), in general as the time of the restraint lengthens the onus of proving reasonableness grows too. Modern practice is to restrain the employee for a short period (1 - 2 years) within an area related to the employer's business or to prohibit him only from doing business with customers known to him. These so-called *solicitation clauses* are illustrated in cases such as **Home Counties Dairies v. Skilton (1970)**, where a milkman was restrained for a year after leaving his employer's business from selling milk to his employer's customers.

3. Activities covered. The employee is restrained from engaging in modes of employment where he lacks the skill to present any serious threat to his employer (**Attwood v. Lamont (1920)**).

(b) Restraints on the sale of a business. A person who buys a business not only buys its assets but also it s goodwill (i.e. the information and contacts built up by the seller before he sold the business). The buyer is entitled to protect the goodwill and normally does so by including a clause in the contract of sale preventing the seller from setting up his business again within the area covered by the existing business. Such a restraint is valid unless it is excessive **(Nordenfelt v. Nordenfelt Gun and Ammunition Co Ltd (1894))**.

(c) Solus agreements. These are agreements by which a manufacturer or supplier contracts to supply one distributor in return for the latter's promise to sell only the manufacturer's or supplier's range of goods. In **Esso Petroleum Co v. Harper's Garage (1967)**, the House of Lords said that such agreements will be valid only if their duration is not excessive. In the case itself, an agreement tying a garage to take Esso products for 4 . 5 years was valid, but another tying a second garage for 21 years was excessive. So the first agreement was upheld but the second one was declared void.

(iii) Effect of illegality. A contract which is wholly illegal on formation is void so that no rights or liabilities can arise under it. Moreover, money or property transferred under such contract cannot be recovered under a court action unless the parties were not *in pari delicto* (i.e. equally to be blamed , such as where one party entered into the contract under duress or fraud) in which case the innocent party can obtain recovery, or one party has repudiated voluntarily the illegal contract before performance could begin **(Bigos v. Bousted (1951)).**

If the contract is partly illegal at common law on grounds of public policy, the courts may sever the illegal part and enforce the legal part. Severance is possible only if the courts are in a position to delete by pencil the illegal part without having to reword the contract. In **Goldsoll v. Goldman (1915),** the defendant who traded in imitation jewellery in the UK sold his business to the plaintiff and agreed not to trade in imitation or real jewellery for two years in any part of the UK or in certain overseas countries. The court severed reference to real jewellery and foreign countries which were too wide since it was possible to do so without having to reword the contract and the effect of severance did not alter the basic character of the contract.

If a lawful contract is being used for an unlawful purpose and both parties were aware that it was going to be used for such purpose, then the contract is treated as if it was illegal from the time it was made. In **Pearce v. Brooks (1866),** the court refused to allow the owner of a horse-drawn coach to recover the hire charge from a prostitute because he knew that she was hiring the coach to ply her trade. However, if one party was unaware of the illegal purpose, then he alone can enforce the contract **(Archbolds Ltd v. S. Spanglett (1961)).**

Chapter 6

Discharge of a Contract

Introduction

To discharge a contract means to bring the contract to an end. This is usually achieved by the parties each performing their part of the contract, by agreement, frustration or by breach.

I Performance

As a method of termination this may not give rise to many problems if the contractual promises are clear. The law requires performance to be precise before contractual obligations can be discharged. Thus, the contract price is not payable unless performance is exact and to the letter of the contract. In **Cutter v. Powell (1795),** a seaman contracted to work on a ship for a complete voyage from Jamaica to England for 30 guineas. The widow of the seaman failed to recover any of his wages after he died a few days before the ship arrived in England, as performance of the contract was entire.

The rule that the contract price is not payable to a party unless he has fully performed his part of the contract will not apply if the contract does not demand complete performance before payment is due (e.g. in employment contracts salaries are fixed on an annual basis, yet are paid monthly). The common law also concedes exceptions where some payment may be recovered in exchange for incomplete performance. These exceptions are discussed below.

(a) Divisible contracts. Where performance of the contract is by instalments, payment can be recovered for work already done, although an action may lie for failure to complete performance.
In **Richie v. Atkinson (1808),** the court held that a shipowner who had agreed to carry cargo at a stipulated rate per ton could recover freight *pro rata* when he only carried part of the cargo. However, the shipowner was held liable, in a later action, for failing to carry the whole cargo. Whether or not a contract is divisible will be ascertained from the terms of the contract.

(b) Fault of the other party. Where one party has partly performed his part of the contract and is prevented from completing performance by the other party who is due to pay, the performing party is entitled to be paid for the work he has done on a *quantum meruit* basis. In **Planche v. Colburn (1831),** the plaintiff could not complete a book which was to be serialised in the defendants' magazine because the defendants had ceased publication of the journal. The court felt that he should be paid on a *quantum meruit* basis for work already done.

(c) Acceptance of partial performance. Where partial performance by one party is accepted by the other party, the other must pay for the work done on a *quantum meruit* basis. Acceptance must be voluntary. If the other party had no choice but to accept (as in **Sumpter v. Hedges (1898)** where the defendant had engaged the plaintiff to build two houses and stables, and had to complete the work himself after the plaintiff had abandoned the job) no money is payable.

(d) Substantial performance. Where the contract is substantially performed subject to minor omissions or defects, the performing party is entitled to the contract price less the cost of remedying the defects. What amounts to substantial performance is a question of fact. In **Hoenig v. Isaac (1952),** the plaintiff contracted to decorate the defendant's flat and to fit a wardrobe and bookcase for £750. When the work was completed it cost the defendant £55 to put right the defects. The court held that the contract was substantially performed. However, in **Bolton v. Mahadeva (1972),** where the cost of putting right defects in a central heating system which the plaintiff had agreed to install in the defendant's home amounted to between one third and a quarter of the contract price, the court held that the contract was not substantially performed.

Two other matters relating to performance require comment:

(i) Tender of performance. A tender to perform is as good as actual performance. So if the party to whom performance is tendered refuses to accept, the tenderer will be free from liability and entitled to the price of the goods or services tendered. In the case of tender of money which is refused by the other party, this will not discharge the tenderer from liability, but if he pays the money into court he will have a good defence to an action brought against him and the debt bears no interest.

(ii) Time of performance. If there is a fixed contractual date for performance and it is not met, the guilty party may perform at a later date unless prompt performance is an essential condition of the contract, in which case the innocent party may treat the contract as discharged by breach.

'Time will be of the essence' if the parties expressly make it a condition of the contract; or where it was not originally of the essence, but the innocent party makes it of the essence after the time of performance has passed, by giving the guilty party notice to complete performance within a reasonable time (**Charles Rickards Ltd v. Oppenheim (1950)**); or where the circumstances of the case are such that the contract ought to be performed at the agreed time (e.g. as with perishable goods or shares in a volatile market).

II Agreement

In the same way as a contract is created by agreement, so too can it be terminated by agreement. But because we are dealing here with contractual rights, any agreement to discharge the contract must be made under seal or else consideration must be provided. Where the contract is still executory (i.e. neither party has yet commenced performance) the consideration is met by each party agreeing to give up his right to enforce the other's promise (**bilateral discharge**). Where, however, one party has already performed his side of the contract an agreement to release the other party from his contractual obligation (**unilateral discharge**) requires new consideration from the other (e.g. a cancellation fee). This process is called 'accord and satisfaction'. The agreement to end the contract is known as the accord; the new consideration provided by the other party to support the agreement to release him from performance is the satisfaction.

III Frustration

After the contract is made but before performance is completed circumstances beyond the control and contemplation of the parties may intervene making the performance impossible or meaningless. In such a case the law will excuse the parties from further performance and the contract is terminated.

There are a series of events which the law will consider as sufficiently grave to terminate the contract automatically:

(a) Destruction of the subject matter. If the subject matter necessary to the performance of the contract is destroyed or seriously damaged, so that performance according to the contractual terms becomes impossible (as in **Taylor v. Caldwell (1863)** where a music hall which was hired for concerts was accidentally destroyed by fire before any performance had taken place), the contract is frustrated.

(b) Death or other personal incapacity. If a person who has to perform a contract of service dies or becomes physically incapable of performing it (as in **Robinson v. Davison (1871)** where a pianist became too ill to perform at a concert), the contract is frustrated.

(c) Subsequent illegality. If a contract is lawful when made but becomes unlawful before performance is completed as a result of government action or legislation (as in **Metropolitan Water Board v. Dick Kerr & Co (1918)** where the government delayed the performance of a contract to build a reservoir within 6 years because of the war) the contract is frustrated.

(d) Non-occurrence of an event. If a venture upon which a contract is based does not take place the contract is frustrated. In **Krell v. Henry (1903)**, a room was let in Pall Mall for the sole purpose of viewing the coronation procession of King Edward VII from the window of the room. When the king's illness caused the procession to be postponed, the court held the contract to be frustrated. However, in **Herne Bay Steamboat Co. v. Hutton (1903),** where the defendant hired a boat to take passengers to view the royal review of a fleet and to cruise around the anchored fleet, the court held that the contract was not frustrated even though the review was cancelled, because it was still possible to cruise around the fleet which remained in place. Thus the review did not form the basis of the contract.

Limitations on the doctrine of frustration
The doctrine does not apply in the following cases:

(a) Self-induced frustration. If one party is responsible for the event which makes performance of the contract impossible, the contract will not be discharged by frustration but the party at fault will be liable for breach of contract. In **Maritime National Fish v. Ocean Trawlers (1935),** the appellants chartered a trawler from the respondents. The use of the trawler required a licence from the Canadian government. The appellants applied for 5 licences (4 for their own vessels and 1 for the chartered trawler). They were only granted 3 licences but were to apply them to any three of the vessels. They chose three of their own vessels and argued that the contract for the chartered trawler had been frustrated as the trawler could not be used lawfully. The plea failed; in exercising their choice, that act had caused the frustration. The plea would have succeeded if the Canadian government had named the vessels to which the licences were to apply and the chartered trawler was not among the ones named.

(b) Express provision made for the event. The parties may have included an express provision in their contract as to what will happen if an unexpected event occurs. Sometimes known as an *hardship clause*, it has the effect of either cancelling the contract or simply suspending it for a while to enable normality to be restored.

(c) Absolute undertaking to perform. If one party has undertaken to perform his side of the contract, whatever happens, he will be liable for breach of contract if he is unable to perform.

(d) Onerous contracts. If a contract becomes more difficult to perform through inflation or labour shortages, this will not be enough to frustrate the contract. In **Davis Contractors Ltd. v. Fareham UDC (1956),** the plaintiffs who had contracted to build 78 houses within 8 months at a price of £92,425 could not finish the work until after twenty two months and at a cost of £115,000 owing to labour shortages. The contract was held not to have been frustrated.

(e) Leases. This rests on the notion that a lease is more than a contract in that it is an interest in land and as land itself is indestructible, so too the interest cannot be destroyed.

The parties' rights after frustration.

In most cases the parties' rights are determined by the Law Reform (Frustrated Contracts) Act 1943 which provides that;

(1) All moneys paid before discharge are recoverable **(S.1(2)).**

(2) All moneys due to be paid at the time of discharge cease to be payable **(S.1(2)).**

(3) Expenses incurred by one party before discharge are recoverable but only up to the limit of any moneys paid or payable to the other party before the frustrating event **(S.1(2)).**

(4) Where one party has received a benefit (other than a money payment) before discharge, the courts have a discretion to see that he pays for the benefit. In **BP (Libya) Ltd v. Hunt (1982),** BP was able to recover to recover 35 million dollars from Hunt after it participated in an oil concession granted to Hunt by the Libyan government and supplied him with oil before the government was overthrown.

Certain contracts, such as insurance and sale of goods, are excluded from the provisions of the Act.

(IV) Breach

The wronged party always has a right to damages as compensation for breach of contract. But in addition, he can treat the breach as a ground for terminating the contract if it is significant (as with conditions and certain innominate terms).

A breach may occur where one party has renounced all his obligations in advance or disables him from performing (called an ***anticipatory breach***). With an anticipatory breach the wronged party has a choice. He can treat the contract as discharged forthwith in which case he is certain to obtain a remedy, although it is restricted to damages. So in **Hochester v. De La Tour (1853),** the plaintiff successfully sued for damages when the defendants terminated in advance a contract of employment hiring the plaintiff as courier for three months. Alternatively, the plaintiff can wait until the actual breach in which case he may be able to obtain a remedy other than damages (e.g. specific performance), but he runs the risk of unforeseen events occurring during the waiting period (the time between the anticipatory breach and the time performance of the contract is due), which may frustrate the contract (as in **Avery v. Bowden (1855)** where the defendant who had committed an anticipatory breach by informing the shipowner that he would no longer be able to obtain a cargo for the ship when the time for loading arrived, was able to avoid liability by pleading frustration when the Crimean War broke out during the waiting period). Thus, if a frustrating event occurs in the waiting period, the wronged party also runs the risk of losing his right of action if he does not accept repudiation of the contract.

Chapter 7

Remedies for Breach of Contract

Introduction

It was discussed in the previous chapter that the remedy of 'self-help' is available to the wronged party for breach of contract. The wronged party can terminate the contract without the courts' assistance where a condition is broken or where the breach is sufficiently serious. If some other remedy is preferred an action will have to be brought in the courts. This chapter examines the main remedies which the courts can grant for breach of contract and the persons who are entitled to them.

(i) Damages. This is the standard common law remedy for breach of contract and the amount recoverable will either be assessed by the courts or may be agreed by the parties in their contract.

(a) Assessed damages. This type of damages is also known as *unliquidated damages*; and its purpose is to compensate the plaintiff for the financial loss he has suffered as a result of the defendant's breach of contract. Such loss could be some benefit which the plaintiff has been deprived of because of the defective performance or non-performance (expectation loss) or expenses incurred by the plaintiff in relying on the contract (reliance loss) . Even pre-contractual expenses could be recovered as long as it is not too remote. In **Anglia Television Ltd. v. Reed (1972),** the defendant contracted to take the leading role of a TV play but pulled out of it at the last moment, making it impossible for the plaintiffs to find a suitable replacement actor in time. The court allowed the plaintiffs to recover from the defendant pre-contractual expenditure of £2,750 which they incurred in the preparation of the play because the defendant would have known that money had been spent by the plaintiffs on the play before he contracted to take the leading role and that that money would be lost if he broke the contract.

The choice is with the plaintiff whether to claim damages for loss of benefit or for expenses incurred. He will usually claim for expenses where he is unable to calculate the value of the benefit he expected from the contract. However, the courts will not allow him to recover all his expenses if the defendant proves that the plaintiff had made a bad bargain and to allow him to recover his entire expenses would leave him in a better position than he would have been in had the contract been performed fully (**C and P Haulage v. Middleton** (1983)**).** In addition to financial loss, non-financial losses such as physical inconvenience and pain and suffering upon physical injury caused by the breach may also be recovered.However, damages for mental distress and disappointment are not recoverable **(Addis v. Gramophone Co. (1909))** unless the purpose of the contract is to provide pleasure and entertainment **(Jackson v. Horizon Holidays Ltd. (1973**)**).**

To make an award of damages, it is necessary to quantify the losses in money terms. With loss of benefit, the basis of assessment will be either the 'difference in value' or the 'cost of repair'. An award will not be based on the cost of repair if the defective performance did not materially affect the purpose or value of the benefit and the cost of putting the defective performance right is out of all proportion to the benefit to be obtained from the contract **(Ruxley Electronics and Construction Ltd. v. Forsyth** (1995)**).**

In contracts for the sale of goods the basis of assessment is usually 'the difference in value' with reference made either to market value or actual value. For example, if the seller fails to deliver goods for which there is a market, the buyer's loss will be the difference between the market price for identical goods at the time the goods ought to have been delivered and the contract price. If the goods cannot be replaced by buying in the market, the buyer's loss will be the cost of the goods and of their carriage and a reasonable profit where they were bought for resale. If the buyer refuses to accept delivery and pay for the goods, the seller's loss will be the amount (if any) by which the contract price exceeds the market price. If the goods cannot be disposed of in open market (because there is no market for the goods) the seller's loss will be the contract price.

Speculative damages may be awarded in contract. If the plaintiff loses the chance of obtaining a benefit, damages may be awarded for loss of chance as long as it is possible to calculate the value of the chance lost. In **Chaplin v. Hicks (1911),** the plaintiff was awarded damages for loss of chance to compete in the finals of a beauty contest. In assessing an award of damages in such cases the courts will take account of the value of the benefit under the contract and the probability of the plaintiff actually obtaining the benefit.

The amount of damages recoverable is limited by the remoteness of damages rule and by the duty of the plaintiff to mitigate his losses. The leading case on the remoteness of damages rule is **Hadley v. Baxendale (1854),** where Alderson B identified the losses which are legally recoverable as (a) those losses which arose naturally as a result of the breach of contract (i.e. which were an inevitable consequence of the breach) and (b) those losses (exceptional or special losses) which were in the contemplation of the parties at the time they made the contract. In **Hadley,** the plaintiffs suffered loss of profit as a result of their mill being kept idle after the defendant carriers failed to deliver a repaired mill shaft in time. The court held that the loss was not an inevitable consequence of the breach since the defendants could not foresee that their delay would keep the mill idle (as the plaintiffs may have had a spare mill shaft). As the loss was not an inevitable consequence of the breach the defendants should have been told of the special circumstances which caused the loss for the loss to have been in the contemplation of the parties.

The second limb of **Hadley v. Baxendale** (i.e. special losses) was considered by the Court of Appeal in **Victoria Laundry Ltd. v. Newman Industries Ltd. (1949),** and then again by the House of Lords in **The Heron II (1969),** where the courts said that for the defendant to be liable for special loss, there had to be a high degree of probability (a 'real danger' or 'serious possibility') of the loss occurring , and not just the remote possibility (a low degree of probability) as is applied in tort. In **Victoria Laundry,** the defendants knew that the plaintiff needed an additional boiler for a new laundry business they were setting up and delivered it five months late. The defendants were held liable for loss of ordinary day to day profits which would have resulted from its use had the boiler been delivered in time, but not for the loss of certain exceptionally profitable contracts which the plaintiff would have obtained from the government.

The amount of damages awarded by the courts is also reduced to reflect a party's duty to take reasonable steps to mitigate his losses (e.g. by selling or buying the goods elsewhere).

(b) Agreed damages. This type of damages is also known as *liquidated damages* and it is usually inserted in the contract by the parties in order to avoid the complicated rules governing unliquidated damages. In sale of goods contracts and building contracts, for example, the parties frequently provide for a fixed sum to be payable for each day of delay. Such provision will be enforced by the courts as liquidated damages if it is a genuine attempt to pre-estimate the likely loss. If it is unreasonable and simply put in the contract to compel performance it is a penalty and the courts will ignore it and assess the damages.

The question whether a provision is liquidated damages or a penalty will depend on how the courts view it. The fact that it is described in the contract as 'liquidated damages' (as in **Kemble v. Farren (1829)** or a 'penalty' (as in **Cellulose Acetate Silk Co v. Widnes Foundry Ltd (1933)**) is relevant but not conclusive. In **Dunlop Pneumatic Tyre Co Ltd v. New Garage & Motor Co Ltd (1915)** , Lord Dunedin suggested the following test:

(1) If the sum stipulated for is extravagant and unconscionable in amount in comparison with the greatest loss that could conceivably be proved to have followed from the breach, it is a penalty.

(2) If the breach consists only in not paying a sum of money and the sum stipulated is a sum greater that the sum which ought to have been paid, it is a penalty.

(3) If a single lump sum is made payable on the occurrence of one or more or all of several events, some of which may be serious and others not, there is a presumption that this is a penalty.

Once the courts regard a provision as a 'genuine pre-estimate of actual loss' it is enforceable even though the damages obtained through its application include damages for loss which is irrecoverable as being too remote.

(ii) Quantum Meruit. This is compensation to prevent the unjust enrichment by one party at the expense of the other party. It rests not on the original contract but on an implied promise through acceptance by the other party of the benefit of the work done. This remedy may be claimed where one party cannot complete performance because of the other party's fault

(**Planche v. Colburn**) or where partial performance is accepted voluntarily. The courts have power to grant *quantum meruit* even if the contract is void (**Craven-Ellis v. Canons Ltd (1936)).**

(iii) Specific Performance. This is an equitable remedy requiring a party to carry out his contractual obligations. It may be granted instead or in addition to damages but will not be granted where the courts are satisfied that damages alone would compensate the wronged party. Nor will it be granted when the performance of the contract requires the constant supervision of the courts (as with building contracts which are of a continuing nature and performance is usually in stages), or involves personal skill (as with employment contracts where the courts are incapable to compelling the complete execution of such contracts properly). The courts will not grant this remedy to a party unless it would have been awarded against him (i.e. specific performance must be mutual). Thus specific performance will not be granted where one of the parties is an infant.

Contracts which may be specifically enforced are land contracts (sale or lease), contracts for the purchase of shares or debentures in a company and contracts for the sale of unique articles such as great works of art and heirlooms.

(iv) Injunction. This is an equitable remedy restraining the doing, continuance or repetition of a wrongful act. In contract law, an injunction is usually granted to enforce a negative stipulation and is a useful remedy where specific performance will not be granted (as with employment contracts). As Lord St. Leonards in **Lumley v. Wagner (1852)** said ' It is true I have no means of compelling her (the defendant) to sing, but she has no cause of complaint if I compel her to abstain from the commission of an act which she has bound herself not to do and thus possible cause her to fulfil her engagement'. An injunction will only be granted if the stipulation is reasonable and its effect does not indirectly compel the defendant to specifically perform the contract. In **Warner Bros. v. Nelson (1937)**, the defendant agreed (a) to act for the plaintiffs for a fixed period (b) not to act for any third party, and (c) not to engage in any other occupation without the plaintiffs' consent. It was held that an injunction would only be granted for (b).

Who can sue? While contract law provides remedies for breach of contract the right to a remedy, the liability for the duty , only exists where the plaintiff and the defendant are parties to the same contract. A third party cannot sue under the contract even if it was expressly made for his benefit. This is known as the **doctrine of Privity of Contract** and it has its origin in**Tweddle v. Atkinson (1861)** where a plaintiff sued his father-in-law's estate for £200 which the father-in-law had promised the persons who the plaintiff's father that he would give the plaintiff on the latter's marriage.

This rule which has the effect of restricting contractual rights and obligations to the persons who are parties to the contract is subject to exceptions. These include :

(1) **Assignment of rights.** Contractual rights (other that a right which is so personal to the original contracting parties that assignment to a third party will alter it fundamentally) can be transferred and so allowing the transferee to enforce them.

(2) **Trusts.** A beneficiary under a trust can sue the trustee even though he was not a party to the contract setting up the trust.

(3) **Agency.** An undisclosed principal can enforce a contract made on his behalf with a third party (see Chapter 10).

(4) **Road Traffic Act 1988.** A third party can sue not only the driver of the vehicle for personal injuries but also his insurance company.

(5) **Bills of Exchange Act 1882.** The holder of a negotiable instrument can sue not only the person who gave it to him but also all persons who signed the instrument (see Chapter 11).

(6) **Restrictive Covenants.** An obligation restricting the use of land can bind not only the buyer himself but also any later owner who had notice of the restriction (**Tulk v. Moxhay (1848)**).

Chapter 8

Sale of Goods

Introduction

It was seen in Chapter 4 that the parties to a contract need not work out in meticulous detail the terms of the contract before the contract can become complete, as some terms are predetermined by law partly for the protection of the weaker party. One instance of statutory intervention is the Sale of Goods Act 1979 which regulates the terms on which goods are sold. Some of these terms will be implied automatically in the contract of sale (e.g. conditions and warranties which are for the protection of the buyer). Others will apply only if a matter is not covered by the parties expressly, or through a course of dealings by them, or through trade usage (e.g. matters regarding price, title and the time and place for delivery).

The Act applies only to a contract for the sale of goods, which is a contract to pass title to goods from one person (the seller) to another person (the buyer) for a money consideration called price. The phrase 'title to goods' means 'property in goods'. 'Goods' means tangible moveable property other than money. It includes animals, ships, minerals detached from land at the time of the sale, and crops (e.g. potatoes and wheat) grown by man even though they have not yet been harvested at the time of the sale (but not things grown naturally on the land such as timber or grass unless they are severed before the sale or the contract expressly requires them to be severed after the sale). Although the price must be a money consideration, it includes a part-exchange of goods together with money. Unless the contract provides otherwise, the price is deemed to include VAT **(Value Added TAX 1983 S.10 (2)).** A definite sum of money must be fixed in the contract or in a manner agreed by the parties in the usual course of their business. The contract may permit the price to be fixed by a third party but if he cannot make a valuation, the contract is avoided **(s.8)** except if the buyer has used the goods he must pay a reasonable price **(s.9)**; or if the failure to make a valuation was due to the fault of either the buyer or seller, then that party will be liable in damages. Where there is no reference to price in the contract the buyer must pay a reasonable price.

The Act covers two types of transactions, namely, a 'sale' and an 'agreement to sell'. A contract is a sale where title is to be transferred at once, and is an agreement to sell where title is to be transferred at some future time or upon some condition being satisfied. An agreement to sell becomes a sale when title to the goods passes to the buyer. The distinction between a 'sale' and an 'agreement to sell' is an important one. The risk of accidental loss or damage to goods will generally be on the buyer in the case of a sale, and on the seller in the case of an agreement to sell. Normally the buyer will be able to claim the goods on the seller's bankruptcy in the case of a sale, but not in the case of an agreement to sell. Also the passing of title to the buyer enables the seller to sue him for the price.

I Implied Terms

Terms implied under the Sale of Goods Act for the benefit of the buyer are contained in sections 12 to 15. They are implied so that the buyer need not ensure that they are written down in the contract. Moreover, in a consumer sale (see Chapter 4) the seller cannot exclude them by use of an exemption clause. In essence, they provide two categories of protection, namely, against failing to get ownership and against getting unsuitable or defective goods.

(i) **Failing to get ownership.** Section 12(1) implies a condition that the seller 'has a right to sell the goods'. This obligation is normally satisfied if the seller has title to the goods at the time ownership is to pass to the buyer. However, the seller will still be in breach of this condition, notwithstanding that he has title to the goods, if he transfers the goods in such a way that the sale could have been stopped by an injunction (as in **Niblett v. Confectioners Materials Co (1921)**, where the seller could have been prevented by law from selling because he infringed a trade mark of another company. The court held that he had no right to sell, even though he had title to the goods).

If the seller breaches section 12(1), there will be a total failure of consideration on his part and the buyer can recover the whole price notwithstanding that he had the use of the goods for some time. In **Roland v. Divall (1923)**, the court allowed the buyer to recover the full contract price he had paid the seller for a car even though he used the car for four months before the police took it away on grounds that it was stolen property, a fact which was unknown to either party at the time of the sale. However, the buyer loses his right to a refund of the price if the seller remedies the defect in title before the buyer rejects the contract **(c.f. Butterworth v. Kingsway Motors Ltd (1954)).** In addition to the purchase price, the buyer may recover from the seller any expenses, such as the cost of necessary repairs, incurred on the goods **(Mason v. Burningham (1949)).**

Section 12(2) implies warranties that the goods will be free from any encumbrance in favour of a third party (e.g. a hire purchase agreement) and that the buyer will enjoy quiet possession. These warranties are not normally relied on since the condition in section 12(1) provides the same protection; but they may be important for time limits for claims under the Limitation Act 1980 as time starts to run against the buyer at the date of the sale under section 12(1), but only when he is dispossessed under section 12(2).

The condition and warranties implied under section 12 apply to both private sales and sales in the course of a business and they cannot be excluded by use of an exemption clause **(s.6 Unfair Contract Terms Act).** However, a seller who is doubtful of his title may sell goods on the basis that 'I am transferring only such title as I may have,' and to this extent the implied condition and warranties can be modified.

(ii) Unsuitable or defective goods. Four conditions are implied here in favour of the buyer.

(a) Goods to correspond with contract description. Section 13 states that where goods are sold by description, there is an implied condition that the goods will correspond with the description. There is a sale by description whenever words are used which identify 'an essential part of the description of the goods' (per Lord Wilberforce in **Readon Smith Fire Line Ltd v. Yngvan Hansen-Tanger (1976)).** In **Beale v Taylor (1967)**, a buyer bought a specific car which he saw prior to the sale but was relying on an advertisement describing the car as a 'Herald convertible white 1961'. The court awarded the buyer damages for breach of description when the front of the car was later found to be part of an earlier model. There is no sale by description if the buyer buys specific goods such as a suite of furniture and signs the invoice 'bought as seen' **(Cavendish-Woodhouse Ltd v Manley (1984))**, or if the circumstances are such that it is not in the reasonable contemplation of the parties that the buyer is relying on the description. In **Harlingdon & Leinster Ltd v. Christopher Hull Fine Art Ltd (1990)**, art dealers stated that they had for sale two paintings by Gabriele Munter of the German impressionist school. The art dealers had no training, experience or knowledge of German impressionist paintings and the buyer knew this. Nevertheless the buyer bought the paintings after inspecting them. The buyer later found that the paintings were not by Munter and sued for breach of section 13. The Court of Appeal held that there was no sale by description because the buyer did not rely on the art dealers' statement as to the artist but rather on his own skill and judgement.

'Description' covers a variety of matters such as ingredients, age, date of shipment, manner of packing and quality. Moreover, each item which describes the goods is a condition and must be exact. Thus even a slight divergence of the goods from the contract description will amount to a breach of section 13. In **Arcos v. E & A Ronaasen (1933)**, the contract was for the sale of half-inch wooden staves but most of the staves turned out to be between one-half and nine-sixteenths of an inch thick. The court decided that the buyer was entitled to reject the whole consignment. Section 15A of the Sale of Goods Act now provides that where the buyer is a business and a breach of a term in sections 13, 14 or 15 is so slight (but greater than for the *de minimis* rule to apply) that it would be unreasonable for the buyer to reject the goods, the buyer will have to keep the goods and claim damages. The seller can always protect himself from liability under section 13 by qualifying descriptive items (such as with words 'more or less' or 'thereabouts') and by relying on the *de minimis* rule (i.e. the rule which allows the courts not to award any compensation where the breach is so minute as to be insignificant).

Section 13 applies regardless of the status of the seller. However, unlike section 12, the seller may exclude this implied condition in a non-consumer sale if the exemption clause satisfies the test of reasonableness (see Chapter 4 on 'Exemption Clauses').

(b) Goods to be of satisfactory quality. Section 14 (2) provides that where goods are sold in the course of a business there is an implied condition that the goods supplied under the contract will be of satisfactory quality. 'Satisfactory quality' means that the goods must meet the standard that a reasonable person would consider as good , having regard to any description applied to them, the price (if relevant) and all other circumstances **(s.14 (2A).** Thus if goods are described as 'second-hand' or 'shop-soiled' the buyer must reasonably expect them to be of a lower quality and cannot complain of their quality even though they would not be satisfactory if sold new in that condition. Similarly, if the goods are offered for sale at a very low price the buyer must reasonably expect them to be inferior goods unless the seller offers some other explanation for their cheapness or if it is reasonable to draw some other inference from the circumstances (e.g. they are part of a clearance sale).

The standard that can be expected from the goods includes the fitness of the goods for all their common purposes, their appearance and finish (particularly relevant with highly visible goods such as expensive cars and kitchen units), freedom from minor defects, their safety and durability. The importance of each factor will vary depending on the type of goods being purchased.

The requirement of satisfactory quality is only relevant if the goods are sold in the course of a business. It is not applicable to a sale by a private seller where the common law rule '*caveat emptor*' (let the buyer beware) is retained by section 14 (1). 'Course of a buainess' is liberally construed under section 14. Thus a merchant fisherman who makes a one-off sale of his fishing boat will be selling the boat in the course of his business **(Steveson v. Rogers (1998)**). An agent acting in the course of a business for an undisclosed private seller (e.g. an auctioneer) is liable if the goods are not of satisfactory quality **(s.14(5).** The private seller (whether disclosed or undisclosed) is himself liable **(Boyter v. Thomson (1995)**) unless the buyer knew or reasonable steps were taken to let him know that he was a private seller.

Like section 13, the seller can exclude section 14 in a non - consumer sale. Regardless of the status of the buyer, the buyer loses his right under subsection 2 if the seller specifically draws the defects to the buyer's attention before the sale or the buyer examines the goods before purchasing them and the examination ought to reveal the defects, or in the case of a sale by sample the defects would be apparent on a reasonable inspection of the sample.

(c) Goods to be fit for their purpose. Section 14(3) implies a condition that where goods are sold in the course of a business and the buyer informs the seller (either expressly or impliedly) of the particular purpose for which he intends to use the goods, the goods will be reasonably fit for that purpose unless the circumstances show that the buyer does not or that it is unreasonable for him to rely on the seller's skill and judgement. There is no real distinction between this condition and 'satisfactory quality' because if the goods are not fit for the particular of the buyer, they will not be fit for all their common purposes as required by section 14 (2) so that the seller will be in breach of both subsections. Nevertheless, because section 14 (3) is not expressly excluded where the buyer knew of the defects or ought to have known of them before purchasing the goods, he may still sue the seller for breach of section 14(3) despite his knowledge of the condition of the goods as long as he relied on the seller's skill and judgement that the goods were reasonably fit for his purpose.

(d) Sample. Section 15 implies two conditions in a contract of sale by sample, namely, that the bulk will correspond with the sample, and that the bulk will be free from any defect making their quality unsatisfactory which would not be apparent on a reasonable examination of the sample

II Passing of Property and Risk

As was indicated earlier, it is crucial to know when property in goods (i.e. title) passes from the seller to the buyer because risk passes with the title (*res perit domino*). If goods are of satisfactory quality when sold but are accidentally damaged or destroyed later, then the loss is borne by the party with title **(s.20).**

The rules for the passing of property in goods are found in sections 16 to 19. They depend on whether the goods are specific goods or unascertained goods..

(i) Specific Goods. These are goods identified and agreed upon at the time of the sale **(s.61).** Where there is a contract for the sale of specific goods property in the goods will pass to the buyer when the parties intend it to pass **(s.17).** Unless there is a contrary intention the rules in section 18 will apply as to the passing of property.

Rule 1. Where the contract is an unconditional contract for the sale of specific goods in a deliverable state, property passes when the contract is made and it is immaterial whether payment or delivery is postponed. Goods are in a deliverable state when they are in such a condition that the buyer would be bound under the contract to take delivery of them **(61).**

Rule 2. Where specific goods are not in a deliverable state, property passes when they are put in a deliverable state and the buyer is notified. In **Underwood Ltd v. Burgh Castle Brick and Cement Syndicate (1922)**, the buyer bought a 30 ton engine which at the time of the sale was embedded in a concrete floor. While the engine was being detached from the floor and loaded on a railway truck, it broke down but the seller still sued for the price. The Court of Appeal dismissed the claim since the machine was not in a deliverable state when it was accidentally broken.

Rule 3. Where specific goods are in a deliverable state but the seller has to do some act to ascertain their price (e.g. weigh or measure them), property passes when the act is done and the buyer is notified.

Rule 4. Where specific goods are delivered to the buyer on approval or on a sale or return basis, property passes to the buyer when he signifies his approval or acceptance, or does any act adopting the transaction (e.g. by pawning jewellery which is sent to him on approval as in **Kirkham v. Attenborough (1897)**), or retaining the goods beyond a reasonable time without intimating rejection. A contract may be a sale or return contract whether or not the recipient of the goods intends to buy them himself or to sell them to a third party. In **Poole v. Smith's Car Sales (Balham) Ltd (1961)**, a car owner gave dealers his car to sell for not less than £325. On November 7, he demanded the return of his car within three days or payment of £325; but the dealers did not return the car until the end of November. The Court of Appeal held that the parties intended the transaction to be a sale or return basis and since more that an reasonable time had lapsed, the property in the car had passed to the dealers and they were liable for the price.

(ii) Unascertained Goods. Goods are unascertained if they have no separate identity at the time the contract is made. They include generic goods (e.g. the purchase of a Ford Escort), goods forming part of a larger consignment (e.g. the purchase of ten gallons of petrol from a tank containing 200 gallons), and future goods (i.e. goods to be manufactured or acquired by the seller after the contract is made). No property in unascertained goods can pass to the buyer until the goods become ascertained i.e. are identified and agreed on after the making of the contract (**Re Wait (1927)**) after which the parties' intention becomes relevant. Unless the parties show a contrary intention, section 18 rule 5 provides that where there is a contract for the sale of unascertained or future goods by description in a deliverable state, property will pass when the goods are unconditionally appropriated to the contract with the express or implied assent of the parties (e.g. when ten gallons of petrol are put in the tank of the buyer's car). The act of setting aside the goods by the seller is not enough to constitute 'unconditional appropriation'; there must also be the intention that those goods and no others will be the buyer's (**Carlos Federspiel & Co v. Twigg & Co Ltd 1957).** Goods may also become ascertained by exhaustion . This occurs where the buyer purchases an unascertained part of an identified bulk and a series of sales diminishes the bulk to the point where only the amount sold to the buyer is left (**Karlshamns Oljefabriker v. East Port Navigation Corp, The Elasi (1982)).** Delivery of the correct goods to a carrier for transmission to the buyer is also an act of appropriation **(rule 5(2))** unless the seller has reserved the right of disposal.

(iii) Reservation of Right of Disposal. This is dealt with in section 19. It may be by express reservation; or there is a deemed reservation when the seller sends a bill of exchange for the price of the goods to the buyer for his acceptance together with the bill of lading , and the buyer retains the bill of lading but dishonours the bill of exchange.

The effect of reservation by the seller is that notwithstanding the delivery of the goods to the buyer or to the carrier for transmission to the buyer, the property in the goods does not pass to him until the conditions imposed by the seller are fulfilled. However, it does not prevent an innocent third party for value from obtaining a good title to the goods if the buyer wrongfully resells the goods to him **(s.25)**, although the unpaid seller may be able, in appropriate cases, to recover the proceeds of resale through a tracing order (**Aluminium Industrie BV v. Romalpa Ltd (1976)).**

(iv) Risk. The general rule is that risk passes with title **(s.20).** This rule is subject to the following exceptions:

(a) If delivery has been delayed through the fault of either party, that party bears the risk as regards any loss that might not have occurred but for such fault.

(b) If, after the property in the goods has passed to the buyer, the seller agrees to look after the goods until the buyer wants them, the seller becomes a bailee and will be liable if the goods perish as a result of his negligence.

(c) If the parties agree that risk is to pass at a time before or after the property in the goods has passed to the buyer, then risk will pass at such time. This agreement may be implied by custom (as in **Bevington v. Dale (1902),** where the buyer had to pay the price for furs which were stolen during the approval period, because of the recognised custom in the fur trade that goods out on approval should be at the buyer's risk).

(d) If the seller agrees to deliver the goods at his risk to a place other than the place where the goods were sold, the buyer must nevertheless take any risk of deterioration in the goods necessarily incidental to the course of transit **(s.33).** However, the seller will be liable for any deterioration not caused by transit even though the property in the goods has already passed to the buyer and the goods are of satisfactory quality at the time of the sale **(Marsh & Murrell Ltd v. J I Emmanuel Ltd (1961)).**

(e) In c.i.f. contracts, risk passes to the buyer once the goods are over the ship's rails although property in the goods does not pass until shipping documents (i.e. the bill of lading, insurance and invoice) are handed over to the buyer.

(v) Perishing Goods. A seller who contracts to sell goods which have perished (i.e. destroyed physically or commercially) before the risk has passed to the buyer may find that he loses not only the goods but also is liable to the buyer for failure to deliver. This is particularly so in the case of one type of unascertained goods, namely generic goods. However with other types of unascertained goods, such as goods to be manufactured or grown by the seller and the sale of an unascertained part of an identified bulk, if the goods have perished after the contract is made but before the risk has passed to the buyer, the contract is discharged by frustration . In addition, the Sale of Goods Act gives limited protection to the seller where he contracts to sell specific goods. Section 6 provides that if the goods are accidentally destroyed without the seller's knowledge *before* the contract is made, the contract is void for mistake. Section 7 provides that if the goods are accidentally destroyed *after* the contract is made but before the risk passes to the buyer the contract is destroyed by frustration and neither party can sue the other. The effect of such frustration is governed by common law rules , as the Law Reform (Frustrated Contract) Act 1943 does not apply to sale of goods contracts. Accordingly, all moneys paid by the buyer to the seller are refundable if the buyer did not receive any benefit from the contract and there is no set off for expenses incurred by the seller before the frustration occurred.

III Delivery of Goods

Delivery is the voluntary transfer of possession from one person to the other. It is the duty of the seller to deliver the goods and of the buyer to accept and pay for them in accordance with the terms of the contract **(s.27).** Unless otherwise agreed, the following provisions are implied in the contract :

(a) Delivery and payment are concurrent conditions.

(b) The place of delivery is *prima facie* the seller's place of business; but if the goods are specific goods and the parties know that the goods are at another place, then that place will be the place of delivery.

(c) Where the goods are in the possession of a third party at the time of the sale, then delivery takes place when the third party acknowledges to the buyer that he is holding the goods on his behalf.

(d) The seller is under a duty to deliver the exact quantity of goods required. If he delivers less than he has contracted to sell, the buyer may reject the contract altogether or accept the goods at the contract rate. The same applies where the seller delivers more than the buyer has contracted for, although if the buyer decided to keep the excess, he must pay for them at the contract rate. A business buyer is not allowed to reject the goods contracted for, where the breach is not serious; he must keep the goods and claim damages for breach of contract. Where goods not contracted for have also been delivered and the buyer agrees to keep them he must pay for them at the market rate **(s.30).**

(e) If the seller delivers the goods by instalments, the buyer need not accept them unless he has agreed to do so. In such a case, the goods are to be paid for separately and if there is a failure to make or take delivery of one or more instalments, the breach may constitute either a repudiation of the whole contract or a severable breach giving rise to damages only. The test is the quantity of goods involved in relation to the contract as a whole and the likelihood of the repetition of the breach **(s.31).**

(f) If the goods are to be sent to the buyer, then in a domestic sale, delivery to a carrier for transmission to the buyer is *prima facie* delivery to the buyer. Different rules apply to international contracts.

IV Remedies of an Unpaid Seller

(a) Against the buyer. The seller has an action for the price where the buyer wrongfully refuses to pay for the goods. Unless otherwise agreed, an action for the price can only be brought when the property in the goods has passed to the buyer **(s. 49).** Additionally, where the buyer wrongfully refuses to accept delivery of the goods and the seller incurs expenses (e.g. storage charges) he may bring an action for damages for non-acceptance **(s. 50).** Sometimes, this may be the only remedy available to the seller. In **Colley v. Overseas Exporters (1992)**, the buyers failed to nominate a ship for the goods under a f.o.b. contract with the result that the seller could not put the goods on board in order to transfer property in the goods to the buyer. The seller successfully claimed damages for non-acceptance although he was unable to sue for the price.

(b) Against the goods. The seller has four remedies against goods sold by him, three of them (lien, stoppage in transit and resale) are statutory rights under the Sale of Goods Act and the fourth arising out of case law, namely **Aluminium Industrie BV v. Romalpa Ltd (1976)**. The statutory rights are available whether or not the property in the goods has passed to the buyer; the right under case law applies only if the property in the goods is still with the seller.

(1) **Lien.** This is a right to withhold delivery of the goods until the price is paid. However, payment of the price must be due to the seller. This right is lost if the seller loses possession of the goods lawfully (e.g. he gives the goods to the carrier for transmission to the buyer), and if he waives the lien (e.g. he agrees to a sub-sale by the buyer).

(2) **Stoppage in transit.** This is a right to resume possession of the goods if they are with the carrier. It is exercisable only if the buyer is *insolvent* and the goods are still

in transit. A person is deemed to be insolvent if he has ceased to pay his debts in the ordinary course of business or is unable to pay his debts when they fall due, whether he has committed an act of bankruptcy or not. Transit ends when the buyer or his agent acquires possession of the goods or when the carrier informs the buyer that he is holding the goods on his behalf. The seller can stop the goods notwithstanding that carriage was arranged by the buyer, and his right is not affected if the buyer has resold the goods while they are still in transit unless he did so with the seller's consent.

(3) **Resale.** This is a right to dispose of the goods to third parties and to pass a good title to them. The seller can resell the goods if they are perishable, or if he reserves this right in the contract with the buyer, or if he serves notice on the buyer of his intention to resell the goods and the buyer does not pay or tender the price within a reasonable time.

(4) **Romalpa Clause.** In its simplest form, this clause reserves title to the goods in the seller until the contract goods are paid for, or all sums due from the buyer (an all moneys clause) are paid. The effect is to enable the seller to recover the goods on the buyer's insolvency and this prevents them from being used by the buyer's secured creditors. The clause may be elaborately drafted to create a fiduciary relationship between the buyer and the seller with the result that the seller acquires extensive rights, such as rights against the proceeds of resale. In **Aluminium Industrie BV v. Romalpa Ltd,** AIV sold aluminium foil to Romalpa and reserved ownership in the foil until all moneys owed by Romalpa to AIV were paid. The contract also required the foil to be stored separately and provided that if Romalpa resold the foil it should hold the proceeds of sale as agent of AIV. On the insolvency of Romalpa, the Court of Appeal held that the foil still held by

Romalpa and the proceeds from foil sold could be recovered by AIV under a tracing order.

To acquire rights against the proceeds of sale, the contract must expressly state that if the buyer resells the goods he resells them as agent of the seller. In practice, the seller may be reluctant to go this far since it would make him liable to sub-purchasers for defects etc. of the goods sold. A Romalpa clause is ineffectual as a reservation of title clause if it is too elaborate. Thus a clause which states that if the seller's goods are mixed with other goods by the buyer to make a new component the seller will have the legal ownership of the new component, will not extend the seller's title to the new component but may give him a valid charge on the new component if the charge is registered under the Companies Act 1985 (**Borden (UK) Ltd v. Scottish Timber Products (1979)).** However, the seller may be able to retain ownership of his own goods if they are readily detachable from the new component. In **Hendy Lennox Ltd v. Graham Puttick Ltd (1984)**, a supplier sold an engine to the defendants for use in a diesel generator. The engine sold was subject to a reservation of title clause. When the defendants went into receivership the court held that the supplier still had ownership of the engine even though it was incorporated in the generator set, since the engine was still identifiable by its serial number and could be disconnected easily from the set. To be effective, a Romalpa clause must reserve the legal title to goods sold. If the seller only reserves the 'equitable and beneficial ownership' in the goods, he will only have a charge on them (**Re Bond Worth (1979)).**

V Remedies of the buyer

Where the seller is in breach of contract, the buyer will have the following remedies :

(a) Repudiation of the contract. For breach of any of the implied conditions (i.e. ss 12 - 15), the buyer may reject the goods and claim damages. A business buyer is restricted to damages where the breach is a minor breach. The buyer's right to reject the goods is also lost if he elects to treat the breach as a breach of warranty (i.e. he keeps the goods and claims damages from the seller); or if the contract is not severable and he accepts the goods. The buyer is deemed to have accepted the goods if he retains the goods for an unreasonable length of time without telling the seller that he has rejected the goods, or if the goods are delivered to him and he has had a reasonable opportunity of examining the goods and then does some act which is consistent with the ownership of the goods.

(b) Damages. Damages may be recovered for non-delivery and breach of a warranty. The measure of damages and the question of remoteness are the same as in contract generally.

(c) Specific Performance. This remedy is available only if the goods are unique or of special value to the buyer.

(d) Set-off against price. The buyer may use a breach of warranty to reduce or extinguish the price he has to pay the seller.

VI Sale by Non-owners

The transfer of property (i.e. title) is the central feature of a contract for the sale of goods. Therefore, the seller must be either the owner of the goods or must have sold them under the authority or with the consent of the owner. If not, the buyer can obtain no better title than the seller had. This principle is often expressed in the latin maxim *nemo dat quod non habet* (no one can give what he doe not have).

Where the buyer obtains no title to the goods, he must return them to the true owner or face a court action in the tort of conversion. However, he can sue the seller for damages for breach of section 12. This may not always be an appropriate remedy especially if the seller is bankrupt or has absconded. Accordingly, the law has introduced a number of exceptions to the strict *nemo dat* rule for the protection of innocent buyers and these are discussed below.

(1) **Sale by agent.** Whether or not an agent who has exceeded his authority can pass a good title to his principal's goods to an innocent buyer will depend on the status of the agent. If he is an ordinary agent , no title passes and the principal can recover the goods from the buyer. If he is a mercantile agent (i.e. a professional selling agent such as an auctioneer or a car dealer) he can pass a good title and the principal's only remedy is against the agent personally **(s. 2 Factors Act 1889).** The agent must be in possession of the goods in his capacity as mercantile agent (i.e. to sell the goods) and with the owner's consent. In the case of second hand motor vehicles, the registration book of the vehicle forms part of the vehicle so that if the owner of the vehicle leaves the vehicle with car dealers for display but retains the registration book no buyer can claim title to the vehicle under the Factors Act **(Stadium Finance Ltd v. Robbins (1962)).**

(2) **Estoppel.** The owner of goods who, by word or conduct, represents to the buyer that the seller has a right to sell is precluded from denying the seller's right to sell **(s.21).**

(3) **Sale under a voidable title.** Where the seller of goods has a voidable title to them and his title has not been avoided at the time of the sale, the buyer will obtain a good title to the goods provided he buys in good faith and without notice of the seller's defective title **(s.23).** A voidable title can be acquired

under a voidable contract (such as in **Lewis v. Averay** discussed in Chapter 5).

(4) **Resale by seller in possession.** Where a seller having sold goods remains in possession of them or of document of title to them, any subsequent sale of those goods by him to an innocent buyer will give the new buyer a good title as soon as he takes physical possession of the goods or document of title **(s.24).** If there is no transfer of possession to the new buyer title will not pass to him **(Ladbroke Leasing Ltd v. Reekie Plant (1983)**) and his only remedy against the seller will be an action in damages for non-delivery. Section 24 applies notwithstanding that the seller is in possession of the goods without the consent of the first buyer.

(5) **Resale by buyer in possession.** Where a buyer in possession of goods or document of title to them under a contract of sale with the seller's consent, resells them to an innocent person, that person will obtain a good title even though the buyer has no title because, for example, the seller had reserved the title to the goods **(s.25).** Title only passes to the new buyer when the goods are actually delivered to him. It should be noted that this exception does not apply to transactions where the 'buyer' in possession only has an option to purchase, as in a hire purchase agreement **(Helby v. Matthews (1895)),** and where the buyer is in possession of the goods under a conditional sale agreement within the Consumer Credit Act 1974.

(6) **Motor vehicle on hire purchase.** The hirer or buyer of a motor vehicle under a hire purchase agreement or a conditional sale agreement who sells the vehicle to a private purchaser taking in good faith and without notice of the agreement can pass a good title to the vehicle **(Hire Purchase Act 1964 Part III).** 'Private purchaser' includes a private individual as well as

a company. It excludes a trade or finance purchaser i.e. anyone who has a business which buys motor vehicles for resale (e.g. a car dealer) or which provides finance by buying motor vehicles and letting them out on hire purchase or conditional sale terms (e.g. a hire purchase company). Although the Act does not protect a trade or finance purchaser, the first private purchaser who takes the vehicle in good faith from the trade or finance purchaser will obtain a good title.

Chapter 9

Consumer Credit

Introduction

It was observed in the previous chapter, that delivery of the goods and payment of the price were concurrent implied terms. Thus, if the buyer could not pay the price all at once he was not entitled to the possession and use of the goods in view of the seller's lien on them. This problem is usually overcome by the use of credit facilities. The buyer may be able to raise a loan quite independently (e.g. from a bank), acquire the goods and later repay the loan. Or, the buyer and seller may enter into an agreement which makes provision for the price (plus interest) to be paid on an instalment basis. Such an agreement may take any one of three forms. It may be a *credit sale* whereby title passes to the buyer immediately on the goods coming into his possession; or a *conditional sale* whereby title passes only when all the instalments are paid (this allows the seller to sue for possession of the goods before title passes); or a *hire purchase agreement* whereby the goods are only hired out to the buyer but with an option , though not a commitment, for him to purchase the goods (this option is usually exercised on payment of the last instalment).

Credit transactions often lead to the imposition of onerous terms on the debtor and because of this, statutory control in the form of the Consumer Credit Act 1974 exists where credit is given to a consumer. For the purpose of the Act, a consumer is any individual other than a company who is given credit not exceeding a statutory limit (at present £25,000). The statutory limit is reached after excluding all sums payable by way of deposit, interest and credit charges. The Act applies only to regulated agreements and linked transactions. Regulated agreements are defined as consumer credit agreements (e.g.,credit sales, conditional sales, hire purchase agreements and credit card transactions), and consumer hire agreements exceeding three months. Linked transactions are transactions entered into between the debtor (or his relative) and another person in compliance with a term of the credit agreement (e.g. an insurance contract which the creditor requires the debtor to enter before the creditor will finance the principal credit agreement). Linked transactions stand or fall with principal credit agreements. Thus, if the debtor cancels or withdraws from a principal credit agreement, the linked transaction also comes to an end. Agreements covered by the Act are enforceable only if they satisfy a prescribed form and content and if the person carrying on the business of consumer credit is licensed by the Director General of Fair Trading.

Credit includes both cash loans and other forms of financial accommodation. Thus, most types of credit transactions are within the provisions of the Act. The Act identifies a running account credit where the consumer is able to obtain from tine to time cash, goods or services up to a maximum fixed limit (e.g. bank overdrafts and shop budget accounts); or a fixed sum credit where the loan is for a definite sum whether provided in one amount or by instalments (e.g. credit and conditional sale, and hire purchase agreements). The credit may be given for a particular purpose only (as with hire purchase transactions and Access cards used to pay for goods and services) in which case it is called restricted-use credit; or the credit may be used for any purpose the consumer chooses (as with Access cards used to obtain cash or personal bank loans) called unrestricted -use credit.

Where the credit is provided by the supplier of the goods or by some other person who has an arrangement with him to finance the transaction , the agreement is called a debtor -

creditor-supplier agreement. It may be a two party debtor-creditor-supplied agreement (e.g. the dealer sells the goods to a finance company and then arranges the credit agreement on behalf of the finance company with the customer) or a three party debtor-creditor- agreement (e.g. the dealer sells the goods to the debtor and arranges a loan from a finance company to finance the purchase; also where goods are purchased with a credit card such as Access or Barclaycard). Section 75 provides that in a three party debtor-creditor -supplier agreement, any claim by the debtor against the supplier (dealer) for misrepresentation or breach of contract will also attach to the creditor (finance company), so that the creditor will become jointly and severally liable with the supplier/ dealer. Section 75 does not apply where the cash price of the goods is less than £100 or more than £30,000. Moreover, if the supplier can avoid liability by relying on an exemption clause (e.g. the debtor is a business buyer or the goods are not of the type used for consumer use and the exemption clause satisfies the reasonableness test under UCTA) the clause equally protects the creditor.

Certain consumer credit agreements are outside the scope of the Consumer Credit Act because they are exempt agreements (e.g. loans by building societies for the purchase of land; fixed sum debtor-creditor- supplier agreements, other than hire purchase and conditional sale agreements, with four or fewer instalments; and low cost debtor-creditor-supplier agreements where the annual percentage rate does not exceed 13% or 1% over Base Rate). Other credit agreements are partly exempted from some of the formalities and cancellation provisions of the Act either because they are small agreements (*viz.* credit sales where the credit does not exceed £50) or because the agreements were not made in the course of a business.

The Consumer Credit Act requires two types of business dealing with regulated agreements to be licensed, namely, consumer credit and consumer hire businesses and ancillary businesses. The former include a business in which goods are sold on credit or hire purchase. Thus not only must the finance company obtain a licence but also the supplier of the goods. The latter include the business of credit brokerage (as in the case of mortgage brokers), debt counselling (as in the case of solicitors who give advice to debtors about the liquidation of their debts due under regulated agreements, debt collecting and a credit reference agency (i.e. a business which collects information about the financial position of a person and passes it on to potential creditors).

Licences are of two types - standard and group. A standard licence is issued to a named person (or partnership) authorising him to carry on business under the name specified in the licence as long as the person is a fit person to engage in activities covered by the licence and the name under which he applies to be licensed is not undesirable. A group licence is issued to those categories of creditors or credit business where personal examination of the individual is not necessary in the public interest (e.g. the Law Society). Unlicensed trading is not only a criminal offence but will render agreements unenforceable by the creditor unless the Director General of Fair Trading orders otherwise.

I Formalities of Regulated Agreements

(i) Pre-contractual disclosure. The consumer should be given certain information in a prescribed manner (e.g. the annual percentage rate of charge, the required deposit, the amount of credit provided and a comparison of the cash price and the credit price).

(ii) Form and content. The agreement itself must be in writing and must describe the parties, inform the consumer of his right to pay off his debt at an earlier date and (if relevant) his right to cancel the agreement. It must then be signed by both the consumer and the creditor (or the creditor's agent) after which it becomes executed (i.e. the contract is concluded).

(iii) Copies. The consumer is always entitled to copies of the agreement which he signs. Depending on the circumstances, he must be given one, sometimes two copies. He is always entitled to a copy immediately after he signs the agreement. If the creditor (or his agent) does not sign the agreement at the same time as the consumer but at a later date, so that the agreement is still unexecuted, the consumer is entitled to a second copy to be sent to him within seven days after the creditor signs. In the case of cancellable agreements, this second copy must be sent to the consumer *by post*; and it must notify him that he has a right to cancel the agreement within five days after receiving the second copy and the person to whom notice of cancellation should be sent. The consumer can always withdraw from the agreement whilst it is still unexecuted but notice of this must be served on the creditor or his agent.

(iv) Non-compliance with formalities. The agreement is treated as 'improperly executed' and is unenforceable unless the courts direct otherwise. However, in three cases the courts have no discretion on the matter and *must* refuse to enforce the agreement: (a) where the agreement was not signed by the consumer, (b) where the consumer was not given a copy of the fully signed agreement up to the time of commencement of proceedings, and (c) where the second copy of a cancellable agreement does not contain the required notice. In these three cases, the consumer can retain possession of the goods and cannot be sued for any instalment or other expenses.

(v) Cancellable agreements. These are agreements made off the trading premises of the creditor or any dealer with whom the consumer originally negotiated (e.g. if made at the consumer's home) and where oral representations were made to the consumer during antecedent negotiations.

Notice of cancellation must be in writing and if sent by post, it takes effect as soon as it is properly posted, whether or not it is actually received. The effect of cancellation is to treat the agreement and any linked transaction, as if it had not been made. Thus the consumer is entitled to a refund of all moneys paid by him under the agreement but he must also surrender the goods (if they were already sent to him) although he does not have to return them personally. If the goods were perishable goods or were consumed before cancellation, the consumer incurs no liability to the creditor. However, if the consumer is not in a position to hand back the goods simply because they were incorporated in land or any thing not comprised in the cancellable agreement, he remains liable to pay the full price of the goods, though not the credit part of the transaction. The consumer is under a duty to take reasonable care of the goods for up to twenty one days after cancellation, thereafter this duty ends.

II Extortionate Credit Bargains

The parties are at liberty to decide on what terms they are prepared to contract. However, if it appears to the courts that a credit-bargain entered into by an individual (other than a company) with the creditor is extortionate, they may re-open the credit agreement so as to do justice to the parties **(s.137).**

A credit -bargain is extortionate if the debtor has to make payments which are grossly exorbitant (as in **Barcabe Ltd v. Edwards (1982)** where the court reduced a flate rate interest of 100% on a loan to 40%) or which grossly contravenes the ordinary principles of fair dealing. In considering the fairness of the agreement, the courts must take account of prevailing interest rates; the age, business capacity and health of the debtor, together with any pressure which he might have been under when entering the agreement; and the degree of risk accepted by the creditor, his relationship to the debtor and whether an inflated cash price was quoted so as to make the rate of interest look attractive.

III Enforcement and Termination

(i) By the creditor. He has common law rights where the consumer breaches the agreement (e.g. by defaulting with his payments). He may sue for arrears of instalments; and if the breach is sufficiently serious, he may terminate the agreement, claim damages and recover the goods. Even in the absence of breach, where the creditor expressly gives himself power, he may terminate the agrement at will (e.g. on the death of the consumer, or on any third party levying execution against him).

The exercise of the creditor's common law rights are statutorily controlled where the Consumer Credit Act applies. Section 129 gives the courts power to make a 'time order' allowing the consumer additional time to pay; section 87 provides that the creditor cannot terminate the agreement or retake possession of the goods where the consumer breaches the agreement, without first serving a *notice of default* in the prescribed form on the consumer giving him at least seven day in which to remedy the breach; and section 98 suspends his right to terminate the agreement at will until a seven days notice in the prescribed form is served. Moreover, if the transaction is a conditional sale or a hire purchase agreement and the goods are **protected goods,** the creditor is further required to obtain a court order before he can recover possession of his goods from the consumer **(s.90).** 'Protected goods' are goods where one-third of the total price has been paid by the consumer who does not himself terminate the agreement and who does not surrender possession of the goods voluntarily, nor transfers them for value to a third party. If the creditor contravenes section 90, the agreement is automatically terminated; the consumer is discharged from future liabilities, and is entitled to a refund of all moneys paid by him under the agreement. The agreement is terminated by operation of law so the consumer cannot claim a return of the goods (**Carr v. Broderick & Co Ltd (1942)**), and the creditor cannot revive it by returning the goods to the consumer (**Capital Finance Co Ltd v. Bray (1964)).**

(ii) By the consumer. He has a common law right to terminate the agreement for breach of any condition by the creditor and to claim damages for breach of any warranty. In addition, section 94 gives him a right to pay off the debt early and to obtain any rebate which may be due to early repayment; and in the case of a conditional sale or hire purchase agreement section 99 permits him to terminate the agreement at any time before the last instalment becomes payable.

A consumer who wishes to exercise his right under section 99 must do so in writing and it takes effect when the creditor or his agent (usually the dealer) receives the notice of termination.

The consumer must then return the goods and pay all instalments due before termination. His liability normally ends there; he does not have to complete his payments under the agreement even though the goods may have depreciated badly whilst they were in his possession. To guard against loss due to depreciation, creditors usually include a *minimum payment clause* in credit agreements. Section 100 provides that where such a clause exists, the amount to be paid by the consumer should not exceed the amount (if any) to bring his total payments up to one half of the total price. This amount may be reduced if the courts are satisfied that the creditor has suffered less than that sum. On the other hand, should it be established that the consumer had failed to take reasonable care of the goods whilst they were in his possession, the courts may require him to pay a greater sum to compensate the creditor for his loss.

IV Effect of Sale by the Consumer

As the consumer obtains no title to goods under a conditional sale or hire purchase agreement until he completes all his payments, he cannot pass a good title to an innocent third party while the goods are still the subject of the credit agreement. This is the essence of the *nemo dat* rule discussed in the previous chapter; but the standard exception (sale of motor vehicles to private purchasers) equally applies. In addition, unless the credit agreement provides otherwise, the consumer does have the contractual right to acquire ownership so he can assign the benefit of the contract to another person and the assignee can obtain a good title on completing the outstanding instalments. The burden of the contract remains with the consumer so that he will still have to ensure that the instalments are paid and that the assignee takes care of the goods.

V Death of the Consumer.

If the consumer dies during the currency of the agreement, the finance company cannot terminate the agreement even if it expressly reserves this right **(s.86).** The consumer's personal representatives have a right to keep up the instalments and the finance company has a claim against the consumer's estate for the credit.

VI Defective Goods

Schedule 4 of the Consumer Credit Act imposes essentially the same strict liability on the supplier in relation to the basic implied terms that are imposed by the Sale of Goods Act on the seller in a sale. So, for example, the goods must still be of satisfactory quality and fit for their purpose. Equally section 6 of the Unfair Contract Terms Act prevents contracting out by the creditor by means of an exemption clause in a consumer transaction.

Chapter 10

Agency

Introduction

The purpose of agency in contract law is for someone (the agent) to enter into contractual relations on behalf of another (the principal) with a third party. In modern commerce, agency is used frequently to effect commercial transactions (e.g. through the employment of brokers, factors and auctioneers). Sometimes a person described commercially as an agent (e.g. a sole agent for some article or commodity) is not legally an agent since he buys and resells on his own account and is directly liable on the contract as a principal.

An agent may be either a servant or an independent contractor. A servant is a person employed under a contract of service. An example of such an agent is a cashier in a supermarket. An independent contractor is a person employed under a contract for service. He is his own master and the method he uses to carry out his function is not under the control of his principal. An example of such an agent is a commercial agent. If a commercial agent has *continuing* authority to negotiate the sale or purchase of goods on behalf of his principal or to negotiate and conclude the sale or purchase of goods on behalf of and in the name of his principal, then his relationship with the principal will be governed by the Commercial Agents (Council Directive) Regulations 1993. The Regulations enhance the position of such agents. They require the agents to be given a written statement of the terms of their agency; provide them with commission for their work; and for minimum periods of notice (one month in the first year, two months in the second year, and three months in the third and subsequent years) to be given before a party can terminate a non-fixed term agency. Unless the agency agreement states otherwise, commercial agents are given the right to receive compensation or indemnity from principals who terminate non- fixed term agencies where there is not breach of contract by such agents. The Regulations also set out in some detail the otherwise implied duties of the parties, such as the duty of the agent to act in good faith and of the principal to keep the agent informed of all relevant matters.

It is not necessary for an agent to have contractual capacity; but the principal must have legal capacity to enter into the contract for which he employs the agent. The contract must also be of a type which, under the general law, can be made on behalf of another. A contract of marriage cannot be made by an agent for his principal because English law does not permit marriage by proxy.

1 Types of Agents

Agents may be divided into various categories according to their **authority** (e.g. general and special agents); their **functions** (e.g. factors and auctioneers); and their **liability** (e.g. personal and del credere agents). Some agents may even fall into more than one category (e.g. an auctioneer may have general or special authority, while his liability is personal).

General Agent - one with authority to represent his principal in all business of a certain type (e.g. a partner is a general agent of the firm and of his other partners for the firm's business).

Special Agent - one with authority to act on a particular occasion or for a particular purpose (e.g. to sign a cheque on his principal's account or to buy a particular article for him).

Universal Agent - one appointed to handle all the affairs of his principal and with unlimited authority to act for that principal in any capacity. Such an agent is rare nowadays and has to be appointed by deed.

Mercantile Agent - one having in the customary course of his business as such an agent, the authority either to sell goods or to consign goods for the purpose of sale, or to buy goods or to raise money on the security of goods.

Factor - one employed to sell goods or merchandise consigned or delivered to him by or for his principal for commission. He has possession of his principal's goods, sells them in his own name and can receive payments for the goods sold, give valid receipts and grant credit.

Broker - one employed to make bargains and contracts in matters of trade, commerce and navigation between parties for compensation commonly called brokerage. He does not have possession of the goods and cannot sell them in his own name unless authorised to do so.

Del Credere Agent - one, who for extra commission, undertakes responsibility for the due performance of contract by persons introduced by him. For example, a person who buys and sells goods for his principal on a commission basis (i.e. a factor) may enter into a del credere agreement to guard his principal against losses from sales on credit. A del credere agent only undertakes that the buyer will pay and therefore is not liable if the contract fails for some other reason.

11 Creation of Agency

Agency may be created in any one of three ways - by express agreement, by implication or by ratification.

(i) Express agreement. As a basis rule, an express agency does not require any special form. It can be created orally although it may be prudent to reduce the terms of the agreement into writing. If however, the agent is required to contract under seal, then he too must be appointed by deed. This usually occurs under the Power of Attorney Act 1971 when the agent has to execute a deed such as a conveyance. A universal agent also has to be appointed by deed as he may be required to execute documents under seal.

In certain cases, written form is required by statute. For example, a lease for over three years cannot be made by an agent unless he has been appointed in writing **(section 2 of the Law of Property (Miscellaneous Provisions) Act 1989)**. Similarly, an agent cannot sign a prospectus on behalf of a director unless he is authorised in writing to do so **(Financial Services Act 1986).** Also, a commercial agent has a right to be given written particulars of his agency, on request **(Commercial Agents (Council Directive) Regulations 1993)**.

(ii) Implication. In certain circumstances, a contract of agency may be implied from the conduct or position of the parties rather than from any express grant of authority. Such agencies include agency by estoppel and agency of necessity.

(a) *Agency by estoppel.* If one person by words or conduct holds out another as having authority to make contracts on his behalf, he will be estopped from denying that such an agency exists. Thus, a wife living with her husband and managing his household is presumed to be his agent for the purpose of purchasing necessities for the household on credit.

(*b*) *Agency of necessity.* It arises where circumstances amount to an emergency and one person acts to protect another person's property. The law will confer authority on the person taking the action because of the necessity, and the person on whose behalf the action is taken may be obliged to indemnify the agent for any expense incurred even though he did not authorise the act or ratify it.

Agency of necessity can arise only if certain requirements are satisfied:

(1) The person taking the action to protect the property must have been unable to communicate with its owner and to obtain his instructions in time. Whether this condition is satisfied will depend on the nature of the emergency. In **Springer v. Great Western Railway (1921)**, carriers who had received a late delivery of a consignment of tomatoes on behalf of the plaintiff sold them locally because they feared that an existing rail strike would have caused further delay. The court held that they were not agents of necessity because they made no attempt to communicate with the plaintiff for instructions. Accordingly, they had no authority to sell and were liable to damages. On the other hand, in **Great Northern Rail Co v. Swaffield (1874)**, the plaintiffs had to stable a horse which they had agreed to carry because there was no one at the destination to receive it. The court held that they could recover their expenses because they had acted in an emergency.

(2) The action taken must be reasonably necessary and done in good faith to preserve the property (**Sachs v. Miklos (1948)**).

(3) There must be already some existing contractual relationship between the parties. Doubts were expressed in **Jebara v. Ottoman Bank (1927)** as to whether a stranger could plead an agency of necessity, since this would have the effect of depriving a person of his property or imposing obligations on him without his consent.

Agency of necessity may lead to three different consequences. It may give the agent authority to create a contract between the principal and a third party (**The Winston (1982)**); it may entitle the agent to dispose of the principal's property (**Springer v. Great West Railway**); and it may allow the agent to claim expenses incurred in protecting the interest of the principal (**Great Northern Rail Co v. Swaffield**).

(iii) Ratification. If a person without authority to contract on behalf of another does so, the latter may later confirm and adopt the contract. In this way an agency may arise though no such agency existed at the time the contract was made. This procedure may also be used to validate unauthorised acts by a properly appointed agent.

For ratification to be effective, the following conditions must be satisfied:

(a) The agent must have contracted as agent and either named or clearly identified the principal. In **Keighley, Maxted & Co v. Durant (1901)**, an agent who was authorised by his principal to buy wheat at a certain price for both the principal and himself, bought the wheat at a higher price in his own name. The undisclosed principal purported to ratify the purchase but later refused to accept delivery. It was held that ratification was ineffective and the principal was not liable.

(b) The principal must have had contractual capacity at the time of the contract. In **Boston Deep Sea Fishing & Ice Co Ltd v. Farnham (1957)**, a principal who was an alien enemy when the contract was made, attempted to ratify after he ceased to be an enemy. It was held that his ratification was ineffective.

(c) The principal must have been in existence at the time the contract was made. In **Kelner v. Baxter (1866)**, a company attempted to ratify a pre-incorporation contract made by its promoter on its behalf. It was held that this was not possible as the company was not yet in existence when the contract was made.

(d) The principal must have full knowledge of all material facts or intend to ratify the contract whatever the facts may be, at the date of ratification **(Marsh v. Joseph (1897)).**

(e) The principal must have ratified the contract in time. Ratification has to take place within a reasonable time and in any case before the time fixed for the performance of the contract has passed. In **Metropolitan Asylum Board v. Kingham & Son (1890)**, an agent, without authority, accepted an offer by a third party to supply eggs from September 30. The principal purported to ratify the agent's acceptance on October 6. It was held that it was too late to ratify and so the principal could not claim damages for non-delivery.

Effect of Ratification. It relates back to the original act of the agent, making it lawful. Accordingly, the third party is in a precarious position in the interim. He cannot sue the principal unless and until the latter ratifies, nor can he withdraw from the contract if the principal chooses to ratify **(Bolton & Partners Ltd v. Lambert (1889)).**

111 Duties and Rights of Agents

The duties and rights of an agent against his principal (to which the principal has corresponding rights and duties) can be summarised as follows:

(i) Duties of an agent

(a) To exercise due care and skill. The degree of care and skill depends on the agency and skill which the agent professes to have. A paid agent is bound to use such skill as he claims to possess, or such as may be expected of him or may be implied from his position. In **Keppel v. Wheeler (1927)**, an estate agent was employed to sell a block of flats. He received an offer of £6,150 which the owner accepted 'subject to contract.' Before the sale was effected, the estate agent received a second offer of £6,750 from another prospective buyer but said the house was already sold. It was held that as the contract involving the offer of £6,150 was not yet concluded, the house should have been sold to the second prospective buyer. Accordingly, the estate agent was liable to the owner for £600 (the difference between the two offers) but was entitled to the commission on the first offer and on the damages he had to pay because he *bona fide* believed that his duty ceased when the first offer was accepted 'subject to contract'.

An unpaid agent is under no duty to carry out his task, but if he chooses to do so, he must use the same amount of care and skill which he would give to his own affairs.

(b) To account. The agent must account to his principal for all moneys received during his agency and must keep 'agency money' separate from his own. Any money received under a void or illegal contract must be transferred to his principal **(De Mattos v. Benjamin (1894))**.

(c) To act in good faith. An agent is in a fiduciary position towards his principal and so he must not allow his interest to conflict with his duty, nor should he disclose confidential information acquired during his agency **(Lamb v. Evans (1893))**, nor should he make secret profits or take bribes **(Armstrong v. Jackson (1917))**.

The principal has a number of remedies where the agent makes a secret profit or takes bribes. He may dismiss the agent summarily (**Boston Deep Sea Fishing & Ice Co v. Ansell** (**1888**)); he may recover the secret profit or bribe from the agent or third party in an action for money had and received (**Andrews v. Ramsay & Co** (**1903**)), and in the case of bribes, as an alternative to money had and received, he may claim damages against the agent and the third party in actions for conspiracy to defraud or for deceit. In **Salford Corp v. Lever** (**1891**), the defendant paid the corporation's agent a bribe so that his tender would be accepted by the corporation. It was held that the corporation was entitled to damages from the defendant for deceit.

(d) To obey the lawful instructions of his principal. The agent's instructions will normally be set out in the agency agreement. These instructions will indicate the *express authority* of the agent. The courts will generally place a strict construction on this authority but may imply incidental powers necessary to carry out the tasks. Such incidental powers constitute the agent's *implied authority*. A power to receive pre-contractual deposits from a prospective purchaser will not be implied, however, in an estate agent's contract (**Sorrell v. Finch** (**1976**)). The express and implied authority of an agent constitute his ***actual*** or ***real authority.***

If the agent exceeds his actual authority and the principal suffers a loss, he will be liable in damages and has no claim to any agreed remuneration (**Turpin v. Bilton** (**1843**)), unless the instructions were ambiguous and the agent acted in accordance with a reasonable construction of them (**Ireland v. Livingston** (**1872**)). An agent who exceeds his actual authority is liable to his principal notwithstanding that he possesses ***ostensible*** or ***apparent authority***.

Ostensible or ***apparent authority*** is authority which third parties are entitled to infer from the words or conduct of the principal whether or not there is any actual authority. In **Rama Corp v. Proved Tin and General Investments Ltd (1952)**, Slade J said ' Ostensible or apparent authority ......is merely a form of estoppel, indeed , it has been termed agency by estoppel and you cannot call in aid an estoppel unless you have three ingredients : (i) a representation (ii) a reliance on the representation and (iii) an alteration of your position resulting from such a reliance '. The representation must be made by the principal and it could be given expressly or implied by conduct or through previous dealings. Moreover, any private limitation on ostensible authority will not be binding on third parties unless it is known to them **(Overbrooke Estates Ltd v. Glencombe Properties Ltd).**

Sometimes an agent is said to have 'usual authority' when referring to his incidental powers implied by the courts and also to those powers conferred on him as a result of some holding out by the principal. ***Usual authority*** can also be used in another sense, to describe those exceptional cases where the principal is bound even though the agent had no express or implied power or ostensible authority to act as he did. Such a case was **Watteau v. Fenwick (1893)**. In that case, a manager of a public house who was forbidden to purchase certain articles including cigars, bought cigars in his name for his principal's business. The third party from whom the cigars were purchased did not know or believe the manager to be an agent. Nevertheless, the court held the owner of the public house liable for the price because the manager was acting within the authority usually conferred upon an agent of his particular character. Wills J said that a private limitation had not effect on such authority unless it was known to the third party.

The extent of the agent's usual authority in the **Watteau v. Fenwick** sense will depend on the type of agent and the customs of the particular trade with which he is involved. Thus if the agent is appointed for an isolated transaction, the doctrine of usual authority will not apply. Similarly, if the agent enters into a particular transaction which is not normal in the trade, the doctrine cannot apply. In **Daun v. Simmins (1879)**, the manager of a tied public house was held to have no usual authority to order alcohol from any person he liked. The agent must also have entered into the unauthorised transaction for the principal's business before the courts will confer such authority on him.

(e) To act personally. An agent's function normally requires skill and competence to perform (**John McCann & Co v. Pow (1975)**). So he should not delegate his authority (*delegatus non potest delegare*). If this duty is contravened, the principal may refuse to accept the work of the sub-agent and the agent will be liable for any loss suffered by the principal.

Tasks may be delegated only if the principal consents, or if it is customary to delegate, or if the work is of such a nature that it does not require any special discretion on the part of the sub-agent, or in the case of necessity. However, even where delegation is lawful there is still no contractual relationship between the principal and the delegate so that neither can sue the other. Rights will have to be enforced through the agent.

(ii) Rights of the agent

(a) To receive remuneration. Remuneration or commission is payable to the agent only if it is expressly or impliedly agreed with the principal. In the absence of any provision for remuneration and subject to any contrary intention in the agency contract, a professional agent is entitled to a quantum meruit for work done (**Bryant v. Flight (1839)**). If remuneration is payable on the occurrence of a certain event, such as the sale of the principal's house, the agent is entitled to the remuneration only if the event is caused by his effort **(Tribe v. Taylor (1876)).**

(b) To be indemnified against losses. This right exists only insofar as the agent incurred the liability in the proper execution of his agency.

(c) Lien on the principal's goods. To satisfy claims by the agent against his principal, the agent has a right to hold on to any of his principal's property which has come into his possession until the claims are satisfied. Every agent has a ***particular*** lien for claims arising out of the agency, and may have a ***general*** lien by custom or by special contract for all claims whether arising out of the agency or not.

1V Relations with Third Parties

The liability of the parties depends on their intention but if no contrary intention appears, the following general rules apply:

(i) If the agent has authority and names his principal. Generally, the principal alone can be sued on the contract.

(ii) If the agent has authority and discloses the existence but not the name of the principal. Again, the general rule is that the principal alone can sue and be sued on the contract.

(iii) Special cases. Whether the principal has been named or not, there are three exceptional cases where the agent will be personally liable to the third party.

(a) If he makes the contract under seal on behalf of his principal and signs it in his own name, the agent will be personally liable and entitled under it and his principal will have no rights or liabilities, unless the agent was appointed by a power of attorney **(s. 7 Power of Attorney Act 1971).**

(b) If the agent signs a negotiable instrument as drawer or endorser in his own name without adding words showing clearly that he is signing as agent for another, he will incur personal liability on the instrument **(s. 23 Bills of Exchange Act 1882).** It is not enough for the agent to describe himself as being an agent (e.g. AB,director).

(c) Trade custom may also make the agent personally liable on the transaction with the third party. However, it was held in **Teheran-Europe Co Ltd v. S.T. Belton (Tractors) Ltd (1968),** that there is no trade custom that an English agent who contracts on behalf of a foreign principal should be personally liable.

(iv) If the agent has authority but does not disclose the existence of his principal. This is known as the ***doctrine of undisclosed principal***. The agent himself may sue and be sued on the contract **(Sims v. Bond (1833)**). The undisclosed principal can also sue the third party unless the terms of the contract are incompatible with agency (as in **Humble Hunter (1848)**, where the agent described himself in a contract of charter as 'owner' of the ship); or where the agent's identity is material to the contract. In **Said v. Butt (1920)**, the plaintiff wanted to go to the first night of a play but knew that the theatre would not sell him a ticket. He sent a friend to buy a ticket for him and was refused admission. It was held that the contract was of a personal nature and so the undisclosed principal could not take its benefits.

As a corollary to the undisclosed principal's right to intervene and enforce the contract against the third party, the latter may on discovering his existence elect to sue him instead of the agent. An election once made is irrevocable; but there can be no election before the principal is discovered.

If judgement obtained against the agent is unsatisfied, the third party can sue the principal for the balance of the debt (**Civil Liability (Contribution) Act 1978 s.3**). This is only possible though if the third party does not know of the principal before judgement is entered against the agent, otherwise his knowledge together with his act of pursuing the claim against the agent, will amount to an election.

(v) Settlement with the agent.

(a) Where the principal pays the agent money due to the third party and the agent fails to pass on the money, the principal remains liable to the third party even if the principal was undisclosed **(Heald v. Kenworthy (1855)**), unless the third party had represented to the principal that he would settle with the agent (e.g. where the payment to the agent was made at the third party's request as in **Smythe v. Anderson (1849)**); or where the third party looked to the agent for payment and so induced the principal to settle with the agent, as in **Wyatt v. Hertford (1802).**

(b) Where the third party pays the agent who fails to pass on the money to his principal, the third party is not discharged unless the agent had actual or ostensible authority to receive the money. It was held in **Butwick v. Grant (1924)** that an agent authorised to sell is not authorised to receive payment. This rule is rebuttable by any unusual or well-known practice in a particular type of agency.

(c) If an agent for the sale of goods owes a personal debt to the third party, the latter can only set off that debt against the price of the goods if he thought that the agent was the principal, that the agent owned the goods and that the debt accrued before the third party discovered otherwise **(Montagu v. Forwood (1893)).**

(vi) Where the purported agent is in fact the principal. Here, the agent is personally liable **(Jenkins v. Hutchinson (1849))** and can himself enforce the contract provided that the supposed principal was not named and the terms of the contract show that the identity of the party is not material **(Schmaltz v. Avery (1851)).**

(vii) Where the agent has no authority to act. If disclosed, the principal may be bound by ratification. If undisclosed, the principal is not bound unless the agent had ostensible authority to enter into the transaction. In the event of the principal not being liable, then if the agency is disclosed, the agent will be liable in damages to the third party for breach of his implied *warranty of authority* where the agent acted innocently (e.g. he wrongly believed that he had authority to lease the principal's farm as in **Collen v. Wright (1857)**, or he was unaware that his authority to commence legal proceedings against the third party had been terminated by his principal's insanity as in **Yonge v. Toynbee (1910)**). If the agent knew that he had no authority he will be liable also in the tort of deceit (as in **Polhill v. Walter (1832)**, where the agent accepted a bill of exchange on behalf of his principal realising that he lacked the authority to do so but wrongly believed that his principal would ratify).

An agent who disclosed his agency without naming his principal can enforce the contract against the third party if his principal cannot be made liable on it **(Schmaltz v. Avery)**.

V Termination of Agency

An agency may be terminated by act of the parties or by operation of law.

(i) By act of the parites. This may occur:

(a) by **mutual agreement,**

(b) by **renunciation,** if the agent terminates the agency. But if it is a contractual agency analogous to a contract of employment reasonable notice must be given to the principal,

(c) by **revocation**, if the principal withdraws the agency.

Under (c) the principal has a right to revoke the agency at any time before the agency has been completely performed, by giving notice. But if this amounts to a breach of contract with the agent, he may be liable to the agent in damages for loss of the agent's commission or other remuneration and the agent may also be able to restrain by injunction the breach of a negative stipulation in the agency contract (such as an undertaking by the principal not to appoint another agent to conduct the business in question **(Decro-Wall International SA v. Practitioners in Marketing Ltd (1971)).** Third parties must be advised if the revocation is to be effective or there should be a reasonable inference that the authority has been cancelled. Otherwise, the principal will be liable to any third party who acted in good faith on the strength of the previous authority.

In certain cases, an agency cannot be revoked and if revoked the revocation will have no effect. If the agent is given authority to act on behalf of his principal as security for some debt or obligation owed by the principal to the agent, the authority cannot be revoked without the agent's consent. Thus an **agency coupled with an interest** is irrevocable as long as the creation of the agency was intended for the protection of the interest **(Frith v. Frith (1906))**; but not if the agency existed before the interest was created **(Smart v. Sanders (1848)).** A power of attorney which is expressed to be irrevocable and is given to secure a proprietary interest of, or the performance of an obligation owed to, the donee cannot be revoked without the donee's consent **(Power of Attorney Act 1971 s. 4).**

(ii) By operation of law. This may occur:

(a) on any event making the continuance of the agency unlawful (e.g. if the principal or agent becomes an alien enemy as a result of war).

(b) on the death of the principal or agent, whether the survivor knows of the death or not. However, death of the principal and other events which terminate an agency by operation of law cannot terminate an irrevocable power of attorney given to secure a proprietary interest **(Power of Attorney Act).**

(c) on the supervening insanity of the principal or agent. But the principal's insanity does not affect the ostensible authority of the agent unless the third party had actual notice of it. Thus in **Drew v. Nunn (1879)**, where a husband held out his wife as having authority to pledge his credit and she continued to pledge his credit after he became insane, he was held liable on recovery, for the price of the goods supplied during his insanity.

Chapter 11

Negotiable Instruments

Introduction

A negotiable instrument is a written document which represents money. Its chief characteristics are (a) it must be freely transferable like cash; (b) no notice to drawers (i.e. debtors) is required; (c) the person who holds it for the time being must be able to sue in his own name; (d) the person who takes it for value and in good faith acquires a good title even though he acquires it from a person without title; and (e) it must have been made negotiable by statute or commercial custom.

Instruments which are regarded as negotiable include bills of exchange, promissory notes, cheques, exchequer bills, treasury bills and share warrants. By far the most important are bills of exchange, cheques and promissory notes and they are governed by the Bills of Exchange Act 1882. Postal orders, money orders and share certificates are not negotiable because they cannot pass a better title than that of the transferor.

I Bills of Exchange

Section 3 (1) of the Bills of Exchange Act 1882 defines a bill of exchange as 'an unconditional order in writing , addressed by one person to another, signed by the person giving it, requiring the person to whom it is addressed to pay on demand, or at a fixed or determinable future time, a sum certain in money to, or to the order of, a specified person, or to bearer.'

The following are, or may be, parties to a bill of exchange:

Drawer	-	the person giving the bill.
Drawee	-	the person required to pay.
Payee	-	the person to be paid.
Acceptor	-	the drawee once he accepts liability to pay.
Indorser	-	the payee or an indorsee who negotiates by indorsement to a third party.
Holder	-	the payee or an indorsee in physical possession of a bill either by an indorsement completed by delivery or, in the case of a bearer bill, by mere delivery.

The following points relating to the definition of a bill of exchange should also be noted:

(1) Unconditional order. The bill must be a clear order to your drawee to pay. A mere request (e.g. 'You will oblige your humble servant' if you pay, as in **Little v. Slackford (1828)**) is not enough.

Also the order must be unconditional as between the drawer and drawee. So if the order is conditional upon some event (e.g. 'Pay £69 7s ... provided that receipt form at foot hereof is duly signed' as in **Bavins & Sims v. London & South East Bank (1900)**) it is not a valid bill. An order to pay out of a particular fund is conditional but if the order is only coupled with an indication of the fund out of which the drawee is to reimburse himself (e.g. 'Pay Michelle £10,000 and debit my No. 1 account) it will be unconditional **(S.3(3)).**

(2) Writing. It can be printed and even in pencil but the latter is discouraged by banks.

(3) Addressed by one person to another. The drawer and the drawee must be different persons although the drawer and the payee may be the same person. Where the drawer and the drawee are the same person or where the drawee is a fictitious person, the bill is treated as a promissory note. The holder of a promissory note has fewer duties than a holder of a bill of exchange (see later).

The drawee of the bill must be clearly identifiable. So whilst the bill may be addressed to two or more persons (e.g. 'To A and B') it will not be valid if addressed to two drawees in the alternative (e.g. 'To A or B'). If the drawee is a banker, the bill will take the form of a cheque.

(4) Signed by the person giving it. Only when the drawer signs the bill will he incur liability on it.

(5) Payable on demand. The bill is payable on demand where it so provides, or where it is payable at sight, or on presentation, or where not time for payment is expressed.

(6) Fixed or determinable future time. This means that it is payable either (a) at a fixed period after date or sight. 'Sight' means when the drawee signifies his acceptance or, (b) on or at a fixed period after occurrence of a specified event which is certain to happen, though the time of happening may be uncertain (e.g. '30 days after sight'). If the bill is payable on a contingency, it is not valid even though the event does in fact occur (**Williamson v. Rider (1963)**).

(7) A sum certain in money. A sum is certain if required to be paid (a) with interest, (b) by instalments, or (c) according to a specified rate of exchange. Where there is a discrepancy between the sum stated in words and the sum stated in figures, the former will prevail **(S.9(2)).**

(8) To or to the order of a specified person. A bill is an order bill if it is payable to a specified person **(S.8).** Payment to 'wages' or 'cash' is not valid because this is not a specified person. But payment to the Borough Treasurer will be all right. Banks often treat impersonal cheques (i.e. cheques marked 'Pay cash') as payment to bearer and it has been held in **North & South Insurance Corp v. National Provincial Bank (1936)** that they are entitled to do so.

A bill is not an order bill if it contains words prohibiting transfer or indicating an intention that it should not be transferable. Such an instrument is only valid between the parties themselves. So if a bill is drawn 'To Michelle only' and is indorsed by Michelle to Beth, Beth cannot sue in her own name. A crossing 'not negotiable' on a bill of exchange (other than a cheque) has been held to have the same effect (**Hiberian Bank Ltd v. Gysin & Hanson(1939)**).

(9) To bearer. A bill is a bearer bill if it is originally drawn 'Pay bearer', or if the bill was originally drawn payable to a specified person and a subsequent indorser indorses it in blank or if is to a payee who does not exist (as in **Clutton v. Attenborough (1897)**, where a clerk fraudulently asked his employer to sign cheques in favour of a non-existing person on pretence that the latter had done work for the employer and then forged the indorsement and negotiated the cheques to an innocent third party) or if to the name of a real person known to the drawer but whom the drawer did not intend to receive payment (as in **Bank of England v. Vagliano Bros (1891)** where a fraudulent clerk forged some of his employer's customers' names as drawers of bills and got his employer to accept them on pretence that they were to be paid to the employer's other customers when the clerk had no intention that they should receive payment. The court held that the clerk was in fact the drawer and the bills were bearer bills).

The importance of a fictitious payee being treated as payable to bearer is that any forgery of the indorsement of such a payee will not affect the title of subsequent holders as the bill (because it is treated as a bearer bill) does not require indorsement.

II Negotiation of Bills

Negotiation means the transfer of a bill from one person to another so that the latter can obtain a perfect title to it if he takes the bill in good faith and for value, even though the transferor has a defective title. A bearer bill is negotiated by mere delivery; an order bill requires indorsement and delivery.

Indorsement may be done by signing the back of the bill. An indorsement may be in *blank* (i.e. where no indorsee is specified); or *special* (i.e. it specifies the person to whom or to whose order the bill is payable); or *restrictive* (i.e. it prohibits further negotiations, for example, 'Pay Michelle only').

When a bill is negotiated, the holder will be either a holder for value or a holder in due course. A ***holder for value*** is one who provides consideration for the bill or who is part of a chain of indorsees one at least of whom has given consideration for the bill. A ***holder in due course*** is one who has received the bill, complete and regular on the face of it where (a) he became a holder of it before it was overdue and without notice of any previous dishonour and (b) he took it in good faith and for value and at the time of negotiation had no notice of any defect in title of the negotiator. A bill is incomplete or irregular if the name of the drawer or payee is missing; and as 'face' includes the back of the bill, if the indorsement is inaccurate, or if an alteration is not initialled.

The same person may be both a holder for value and a holder in due course, but it is possible to be the former without being the latter; and the former status will often be sufficient for the holder unless there is some defect in the bill. A payee of a bill can never be a holder in due course (**R E Jones Ltd v. Warring & Gillow Ltd (1926)**).

The law on the rights of a holder seems to be this:

(1) If a person is a holder of a bill which has been dishonoured and he gave consideration for it, he can proceed against any of the other parties who signed the bill. He is presumed to have given consideration and therefore is a holder for value unless one of the parties challenges this.

If the holder received the bill as a gift, he can still sue all prior parties except the one from whom he received the bill as long as some prior party had given value. He is allowed to rely on that value (i.e. past consideration).

(2) To be a holder for value will not be enough if there is some defect in the title of the bill because, consistent with the nemo dat rule, no one can give a better title than he himself has. The doctrine of holder in due course is an exception to the nemo dat rule. If, before reaching the present holder's hands, title to the bill in earlier negotiations is defective (e.g. a signature was obtained by fraud or misrepresentation, or the consideration was illegal) he must be able to show that he is a holder in due course (e.g. he must prove that he himself gave consideration for the bill and that he received it in good faith and was unaware of the defective title). An innocent holder who has not himself given consideration cannot be a holder in due course even if some prior party had given consideration because the conditions for holding in due course cannot be split among successive holders.

A holder in due course cannot take a bill free of the following defects:

(a) a defect for which any indorser (or drawer) has excluded liability by adding the words '*sans recourse*' after his signature.

(b) a defect in a party's signature resulting from forgery or without authority unless that party is estopped from denying his signature. A '*per procurationem*' (per prop. or p.p.) signature on an instrument shows that the actual signatory has only limited authority and operates as notice of this to third parties to whom it is negotiated or delivered.

(c) where as a result of a misrepresentation, a party signed the instrument believing it to be something fundamentally different and he did so without negligence, his defence of *non est factum* will defeat a claim by a holder in due course.

(d) where a party lacked capacity at the time of signing the instrument (e.g. he was a minor at the time) or he signed the instrument in a representative capacity (e.g. he signed as agent of a named principal) he cannot be sued by a holder in due course for defects in title.

III Acceptance of Bills

The drawee is under no liability unless he 'accepts' the bill (i.e. signs the bill agreeing to pay the sum of money); and no other person than the drawee can be liable as acceptor of the bill. Presentment for acceptance is therefore desirable. In three cases it is also necessary and if the holder fails to present the bill for acceptance, the drawer and indorsers will be discharged from liability. These three cases are:

(1) Where the bill is expressed to be payable 'after sight'.

(2) Where the bill expressly stipulates that it shall be presented for acceptance.

(3) Where the bill is drawn elsewhere than at the place of business or residence of the drawee.

The holder may be excused in cases (2) and (3) if he is not to blame where the time factor makes it impossible to present the bill for acceptance before maturity (e.g. where as a result of postal delays, the bill only reaches the holder on the day it matures).

Where the drawee gives a qualified acceptance, the holder need not take it and can treat the bill as dishonoured (i.e. rejected). But if he decided to take it, he must give notice to the drawer and all indorsers if he is to preserve his rights against them. Acceptance is qualified if it is *partial* (i.e. to pay part of the amount only); or *conditional* (i.e. when it makes payment by the acceptor dependent upon the fulfilment of a condition stated in the acceptance); or *local* (i.e. to pay only at a particular place); or qualified as to *time* (i.e. to pay at a different date from that specified in the bill); or qualified *as to parties* (i.e. where it is accepted only by some of the drawees).

IV Presentment for Payment

The holder of the bill is only entitled to receive the money payable on the bill when the time for payment arrives. He or his agent will take the bill to the acceptor to receive payment. The bill must be presented within a reasonable hour on a business day; if it is payable at a bank it must be presented during banking hours and if payable at a private residence it must be presented before bedtime. Delay in making presentment for payment will discharge the drawer and indorsers (but not the acceptor) from liability unless the delay is caused by circumstances beyond the control of the holder and not caused by his default, misconduct or negligence.

Presentment for payment is unnecessary and the holder can treat the bill as dishonoured where the drawee cannot be found or where he is a fictitious or non-existent person or is dead.

V Dishonour of Bills

If the drawee fails to accept the bill or to make payment on its maturity, he is said to dishonour it. All parties who are prior in time to the present holder are liable on the bill as long as they have been given notice that the bill has been dishonoured. Notice must be given within a reasonable time. A 'reasonable time' is the day after dishonour if the parties live in the same postal district, or if they live in different postal districts then the notice need only be sent on the day after the dishonour of the bill.

Notice of dishonour may be waived or dispensed with where it is impossible to give notice (e.g. the drawer has moved from his last known address and has left no forwarding address). Where a foreign bill is dishonoured, it must be noted and protested, in order to retain the liability of the parties to the bill. The bill is handed to a notary public who formally presents it for acceptance or payment in order to obtain legal proof of dishonour. If acceptance or payment is still not forthcoming the notary will note this fact and make a formal declaration of what he has done (i.e. a protest). A foreign bill is one which is either drawn or payable outside the British Isle or drawn within the British Isle on a person not resident therein.

VI Order of Liability on a Dishonoured Bill

Before acceptance, the drawer is primarily liable. After acceptance, the acceptor is primarily liable and the drawer and indorsees are secondarily liable as sureties.

Measure of Damages. The measure of damages where a bill is dishonoured will include the face value of the bill, interest thereon and expenses of dishonour. Damages may be limited if a party adds to his signature on the bill the phrase '*sans frais*' (without dishonour expenses).

VII Discharge of Bills

Discharge of a bill (as opposed to discharge of some of the parties by failing to give them notice of dishonour, or to present the bill for payment on the due date or by taking a qualified acceptance etc.) may occur in the following ways:

(1) By payment. Payment of the amount by the acceptor on or after the maturity of the bill will discharge the bill provided the payment is made to the holder or his authorised agent in good faith and without notice of any defect in the holder's title **(s.59).** Payment to the drawer or to an indorser does not discharge the bill unless it is an accommodation bill and the payment is made by the accommodated party. An accommodated party is one who gets another person (usually some well-known person whose credit is good) to sign a bill as drawer, indorser or acceptor and the latter does not receive any value for lending his name on the bill.

(2) By renunciation. This must be in writing by the holder.

(3) By cancellation. This is only valid if done intentionally and written on the bill itself.

(4) By negotiation. The acceptor receives the bill as holder on or after its maturity.

VIII Forgery on Bills

There are two types of forgery: forged signatures and material alterations to the bill without the assent of all parties liable on the instrument. Where the drawer's signature is forged, the bill is invalid from the outset; and where the indorser's signature is forged the bill becomes inoperative after the forgery and no subsequent holder can obtain a good title to the bill. Nevertheless, a signatory (who may be previous to the forgery or subsequent to it) can be estopped from denying liability to a holder in due course. Thus, if the signature of the drawer is forged, the acceptor of the bill remains liable on it to a holder in due course; and if the signature of the acceptor is forged a holder in due course can sue the drawer on the bill. Similarly, an indorser of a bill, by indorsing it, is estopped from denying to a holder in due course the genuineness and regularity in all respects of the drawer's signature and all previous indorsements. Estoppel does not permit a good title to pass after a forged signature is placed on the bill. It simply allows certain rights as between the parties. As a bearer bill does not require indorsement, forgery of an indorsement on such a bill will not affect the bill in such a way. An order bill is treated as a bearer bill where the payee is a fictitious or non-existent person.

Material alterations include change of date, time payable, amount payable and place of payment. Where made, such an alteration will discharge all parties who did not assent to it., though it would bind subsequent indorsers. If the alteration was not apparent, a holder in due course may sue on the bill as it was before the alteration **(s.64).** In **Scholfield v. Earl of Londesborough (1896),** a third party presented a bill for £500 for acceptance with a stamp of a much higher value than was necessary for this amount with space left vacant. The Earl accepted the bill and returned it to the third party who altered the amount payable to £3,500 and transferred it to the plaintiff, a holder in due course. The court held that the plaintiff could enforce the instrument in its original form and recover £500 from the Earl.

Transferor by delivery. The holder of a bill payable to bearer who negotiates it without indorsement is called '*transferor by delivery.*' By section 58, he does not incur liability on the bill since he does not sign it. However, by negotiating it he warrants to his immediate transferee that (a) the bill is what it purports to be; (b) he has a right to transfer it; and (c) at the time of the transfer he knows of no fact which renders it valueless.

IX The Law Concerning Cheques

Section 73 defines a cheque as 'a bill of exchange drawn on a banker payable on demand.' The rules governing cheques are in most respects similar to those governing other bills payable on demand but:

(1) It is usually unnecessary for the payee to indorse a cheque unless he wishes to negotiate it.

(2) The provisions of the Bills of Exchange Act relating to crossings only apply to cheques.

(3) Cheques do not have to be presented for acceptance.

(4) Unlike a demand bill, the drawer of a cheque is not discharged if the holder fails to present it for payment within a reasonable time.

(5) In certain circumstances, a banker on whom a cheque is drawn is given statutory protection if he pays out an a forged indorsement; but there is no such protection for a drawee of demand bill who is not a banker.

(6) Cheques marked 'not negotiable' can still be transferred although they cease to be negotiable.

Relationship of banker and customer. This relationship arises out of contract and embraces a number of implied duties at common law. These duties may be summarised as follows:

Duties of a customer

(a) To indemnify his banker. This includes repaying sums overdrawn on his account.

(b) To take reasonable care with his cheques. A customer must be careful when drawing his cheques. If he is careless, he has no claim against the banker for any loss attributable to his carelessness (**London Joint Stock Bank Ltd v. Macmillan & Arthur (1918)**).

Duties of a bank

(a) To take reasonable care. A banker is expected to know his customer's signature. Similarly, if he knows or ought to know that a cheque is being drawn by the customer's agent for an unauthorised purpose, the banker should not pay out on the cheque. A banker who gives his customer an inaccurate bank statement of his account may be estopped from denying its accuracy if the customer acts on it in good faith and to his detriment. So, in **Skyring v. Greenwood (1925),** where a customer maintained a higher standard of living than he would otherwise have done as a result of an inaccurate bank statement as to his credit balance, the banker was prevented by the courts from enforcing repayment. A banker, however, may rectify the inaccuracy within a reasonable time and before the customer acts on the bank statement.

(b) To obey the customer's mandate. A banker must obey the instructions of his customer and should pay out of his account only if the customer or his agent has signed the cheque. This duty is broken if a banker pays a company cheque drawn by one director only when two directors have to sign it **(Liggett (Liverpool) Ltd v. Barclays Bank (1928));** and if a banker pays a cheque on which the customer's signature has been forged unless the customer is estopped by his conduct from setting up the forgery (as in **Greenwood v. Martins Bank Ltd (1933),** where a customer failed to inform his bank of previous forgeries of his cheques).

The customer's mandate is terminated by his death, notice of his insanity or bankruptcy, and by his countermand of payment (i.e. stopping the cheque). The countermand must be clear and unambiguous and must be communicated to the branch where he holds his account. Moreover, countermand is only effective when actual notice is received by the bank to stop payment.

(c) To honour cheques. This duty exists only to the extent that the customer has a credit balance or is given overdraft facilities. A banker is not required to pay part of a cheque. He must pay the cheque in full or not at all. So, if a cheque is for £20 and the customer's credit is £15, the banker may dishonour the cheque entirely.

A banker who wrongly dishonours a cheque may be liable to his customer for special loss where the customer is a trader and as a result of dishonour, his credit is affected.

(d) To observe secrecy. A banker is under a duty of secrecy in relation to the financial affairs of his customer and may only make a disclosure under a court order, where there is a public duty to disclose, where the banker's own interests require disclosure, and where the customer has consented to the disclosure.

(e) To collect cheques paid in. The banker acts here as a collecting banker and agent of the customer and may obtain statutory protection if the customer has a defective title to cheques paid into his account.

Crossing on Cheques. A cheque is said to be 'crossed' where two parallel lines are written or printed across its face **(s.76).** The effect of a crossing is that the paying banker is under a duty to pay to a bank and not to pay cash over the counter. Crossed cheques minimise the risk of cheques being cashed by persons having no title to them. There is not any statutory provision for the cancellation of a crossing on cheques, but bankers who provide their customers with crossed cheque books, will cash their cheques if the drawers mark 'Pay cash' over the crossing, sign them, and collect the cash in person.

In addition to the parallel lines, words may be written acros the cheque and these words determine the nature of the crossing, which may be:

(a) General - this consists of the lines and possibly the additions of the meaningless words 'and co'. A cheque bearing a general crossing must be paid only to a banker.

(b) Special - the name of the banker is stated between the crossing.

(c) 'Not negotiable' - the cheque loses its characteristic as a negotiable instrument (i.e. it is not free from equities). So, the holder can have no better title than the transferor.

(d) 'Account payee' - these words require the payee to bank the cheque. He cannot indorse it to others (Cheques Act 1992).

The holder of a cheque may alter the crossing to make it more severe (i.e. from 'general' to 'special'). A cheque which is crossed specially cannot be re-crossed generally and may only be re-crossed specially by the banker.

Protection for bankers. A banker who wrongfully pays or collects a cheque will be liable to the true owner for the face value of the cheque in the tort of conversion. Conversion is the wrongful interference of goods (including documents) by some act which denies the owner of his rights of ownership over the goods. It is a statutory tort under the Tort (Interference of Goods) Act 1977.

Certain statutory defences are available to a banker in such an event and these are discussed below.

(i) Paying Banker

(a) A banker who pays a bearer cheque in good faith and without notice of the holder's defective title will not be liable to the true owner and may even debit his account for the amount **(s.59).**

(b) A banker who pays an order cheque drawn on himself in good faith and in the ordinary course of business will not be liable to the true owner and may even debit his customer's account even though the cheque bears a forged *indorsement*

(s.60). 'Ordinary course of business' means during banking hours (as in **Bains v. National Provincial Bank (1927),** where a cheque was presented and paid at 3.5pm when closing time was 3pm), and in the manner adopted generally by bankers. Thus, to pay a crossed cheque over the counter would not be acting in the ordinary course of business.

Section 60 applies to both crossed and uncrossed cheques and notwithstanding that the banker was negligent as long as he was acting in good faith. Instances of lack of good faith are: where the banker knows that an indorsement has been forged, and where he knows that a cheque payable to order has been lost or stolen whilst still unindorsed by the payee but nevertheless pays the cheque when it is presented.

(c) A banker who pays a crossed cheque drawn on himself in good faith and without negligence and in accordance with the crossing is placed in the same position and thus receives the same protection as if he had paid the true owner of the cheque **(s.80).** This section also covers cheques bearing a forged indorsement, but unlike section 60, the drawer will also be discharged from liability to the payee if the cheque had come into the payee's possession before the indorsement was forged.

(d) A banker who pays a cheque into the account of the payee will incur no liability if the payee had no title to it and can debit the drawer's account even though the cheque bore no indorsement or an irregular indorsement. But the banker must have paid the cheque in good faith and in the ordinary course of business **(s.1 Cheques Act 1957).**

Uncrossed cheques paid over the counter are still required to be indorsed, so the paying banker will only obtain protection from section 1 if the cheque is irregularly indorsed. This does not apply to forged indorsements.

Collecting Banker
A collecting banker is the bank which collects the proceeds of a cheque from the paying banking on behalf of a customer who paid it in for the credit of his account. He is protected in two cases where the customer has no title to the cheque.

(a) A collecting banker who receives payment for a customer in good faith and without negligence to which the customer has no title will incur no liability to the true owner of the cheque **(s. 4 Cheques Act).** The collection of the cheque must be for a customer (i.e. for a person with an account at the bank even though the account was opened with the disputed cheque).

The following have been held to constitute negligence on the part of the collecting banker: failure to take up references when opening the customer's account **(Ladbroke & Co v. Todd (1914));** to receive payment of a cheque for a customer when the cheque is drawn in favour of the customer's employer without enquiring as to the customer's title to the cheque (**Lloyds Bank Ltd v. E.B. Savoy & Co (1933));** and to collect a cheque marked 'account payee' for some other account **(Bevan v. National Bank Ltd (1906)).**

(b) A collecting banker may obtain a cheque as holder in due course and will obtain a good title even if he was negligent. This may arise where the banker buys the cheque from the holder (i.e. cashes the cheque for someone who is not a customer) or takes it to reduce the customer's overdraft or where the cheque is drawn by the customer before it is cleared.

X The Law Concerning Promissory Notes.

Section 83 of the Bills of Exchange Act defines a promissory note as an 'unconditional promise in writing made by one person to another signed by the maker, engaging to pay, on demand or at a fixed or determinable future time, a sum certain in money, to, or to the order of, a specified person or to bearer.

To qualify as a promissory note, an instrument must be a promise to pay. So, I.O.U.s, being only acknowledgement of debts, are not promissory notes. Unlike bills of exchange, a promissory note involves only two persons, the maker and the payee. A Bank of England note is a good example of a promissory note. The holder of a promissory note has far fewer duties than the holder of a bill. Since there is no drawee, the holder does not have to present the note for acceptance. Also it does not generally have to be presented to the maker for payment in order to make him liable on it

Chapter 12

Business Organisations

Introduction

A person wishing to go into business has to decide whether to run it as a sole trade, partnership or a limited company. A sole trade is a one-man business. It can employ others but the responsibility for its success or failure rests with one person - the proprietor. The proprietor has greater freedom and takes all the profits but also bears all the losses and has limited resources. The business may trade under a name different from that of the proprietor but will not be a separate person from its proprietor so that all legal actions against the business will be brought against the proprietor.

A partnership is similar to a sole trade in that it also does not have separate legal personality from the partners. However resources are pooled and the partners share the losses. The law imposes a maximum of twenty partners for any partnership unless it is a professional partnership such as a firm of accountants or solicitors. A partner cannot transfer his/ her interest in the partnership to an outsider without the consent of the fellow partners.

A limited company has separate legal personality from its proprietors (the members or shareholders). It can have as many members as it wishes. It can own its own property and can enter into contracts in its own name, and in relation to such activities, the company itself is primarily liable, not its members or its directors. A principal reason for forming a limited company rather than a partnership is the privilege of limited liability enjoyed by the members in the event of the business failing. The extent of this protection depends on the type of limited company. If the company is limited by shares, as with commercial companies, members are liable to the company's creditors up to any amount unpaid on their shares. If the company is limited by guarantee, as with companies formed for a non-commercial purpose such as to promote education, religion or a charity, the members are liable up to the amount guaranteed by them in the company's constitution. Companies limited by shares and companies limited by guarantee are formed by registration under the Companies Act 1985.

This chapter considers the main features of the partnership and the limited company.

1 Partnerships

The principal statute governing partnerships is the Partnership Act 1890 which defines a partnership as 'the relation which subsists between persons carrying on a business in common with a view of profit.' A partnership is formed by contract. This contract may be express, oral, in writing or under seal or it can be inferred from the conduct of the parties. If written, the document is called *Articles of Partnership*, and if under seal, it is called *Deed of Partnership*. This document will deal with such matters as the name, place and nature of the business; the proportion in which capital is to be provided and whether interest is to be paid on capital before profits are divided; the partners who will manage the business; and what will happen in the event of the death or retirement of a partner. If the partnership is oral or inferred by conduct or a matter is not dealt with in the agreement, recourse must distinct from gross returns of the business, is *prima facie* evidence of the existence of a partnership except in the circumstances be had to the Partnership Act

Where it is unclear from the conduct of the parties or the manner in which the business is carried on as to whether a partnership exists, the Partnership Act lays down rules to help resolve the uncertainty. Section 2 states that co-ownership of property does not in itself create a partnership, even though the co-owners share the profits. However, the sharing of profits, as specified by the Act. These include the receipt of instalments of a debt out of profits, payment of wages by a share of profits and payment for the goodwill of the business out of its future profits.

(i) Types of Partners. Although the Act does not make any distinction between the different types of partners, partners are often classified according to the function they perform. Thus, there is the ***general*** or ***active*** partner who has a right to take part in the management of the business and is liable for the firm's debts. Then there is the ***dormant*** or ***sleeping*** partner who is not entitled to take part in the management of the business but remains liable for all debts ostensibly incurred for the firm by the other partners. There is also the ***limited*** partner whose liability is restricted by the amount of capital invested by him in the business. He too is not allowed to be involved in the management of the firm. A firm which has limited partners must have at least one general partner. Finally, there is the ***retiring*** partner who is not liable for debts incurred by the firm after he retires unless he continues to allow the firm to use his name after he leaves.

(ii) Authority of Partners. Every partner is deemed to be an agent of the firm for the purpose of its business, and any contract he makes in pursuance of this object will be binding on the firm and his co-partners **(s. 5).** The only exception to this is where the partner acting has no authority to act (because the firm has limited his powers to act for it) and the person with whom he is dealing is aware of this fact or does not know that he is a partner.

(iii) Liability of Partners to Outsiders. Every partner is jointly and severally liable for all debts and contractual obligations of the firm and for all torts committed in the ordinary course of the firm's business or with the authority of co-partners. 'Jointly and severally liable' means that the outsider can sue all the partners (jointly) or may sue each partner in separate actions. Therefore an action against some partners is no bar to a later action against the others.

(iv) Relationship of Partners to each other. Partners are under a duty to act in good faith towards each other. Thus, they must render accounts and disclose to each other all matters affecting the firm. If a partner makes a secret profit or uses the firm's name or business connections to obtain a benefit, that benefit is treated as partnership property unless the other partners otherwise agree.

Subject to any contrary intention, the Partnership Act also lays down rules governing the relationship of the partners. It provides that all partners are entitled to manage the business , profits and losses are to be shared equally; no interest is payable on original capital; no person can be introduced as a partner without the consent of all existing partners although such consent cannot be withheld unreasonably.

(v) Dissolution of Partnerships. A partnership can be dissolved with or without recourse to the courts. With recourse to the courts by a creditor on the ground that the firm is unable to pay its debts; and by a partner on the ground that a partner has become a mental patient, or is guilty of such conduct as is calculated prejudicial to affect the carrying on of the firm's business, or is guilty of wilful or persistent breach of the partnership agreement, or the business can only be carried on at

a loss, or that there are circumstances which would render it just and equitable to dissolve the partnership.
Without the involvement of the courts, a partnership will terminate where it is formed for a particular purpose or for a fixed time and that purpose has been fulfilled or the time has expired; where a partner dies or becomes bankrupt unless the partnership agreement provides otherwise; where a partner serves notice to dissolve the partnership and where an event makes it unlawful to continue business. If a partnership becomes illegal (e.g. it exceeds the statutory maximum number of partners, or one or more of the partners resides or trades in a foreign country and war is declared against that country) third parties ignorant of the illegality can still sue the firm as long as their transaction with the firm is not tainted with illegality. However, the partners themselves cannot sue each other, since in the eyes of the law the association does not exist.

11 Registered Companies

The principal statute governing registered companies is the Companies Act 1985. This Act is supplemented by the Financial Services Act 1986 which regulates the raising of corporate finance, the Insolvency Act 1986 which deals with corporate insolvency, and the Companies Act 1989. Unless otherwise indicated, all references to sections in the text will be to the Companies Act 1985.

A company's constitution is contained in two documents: a ***memorandum of association*** which regulates the relations between the company and outsiders and limits its activities to those set down in the object clause of this document; and ***articles of association*** which is a subordinate document regulating the company's internal affairs. A company also has two controlling elements: the ***General Meeting*** and the ***Board of Directors.*** The ***General Meeting*** comprises the company's members (or shareholders, if the company has a share capital) who act collectively by resolution. A resolution is a motion which is passed at the meeting. Company legislation identifies four types of resolutions: an *ordinary* resolution which is a resolution passed by a simple majority at the meeting; a *special* resolution which requires seventy five per cent majority but with a minimum of 21 days notice of the meeting at which the resolution is to be passed; an *extraordinary* resolution which also requires a seventy five per cent majority but the length of notice (14 or 21) depends on the type of meeting at which the resolution is to be passed; and an *elective* resolution (relevant only to private companies) which requires the consent of all the members and with a minimum of 21 days notice of the terms of the resolution and of the meeting. The ***Board of Directors*** is appointed by the members and is given the task and powers to run the company.

The Act recognises two types of limited companies - public and private. A public company is defined as a company limited by shares whose memorandum states that it is a public company and which is properly registered as a public company. Its main features are that its name ends in the abbreviation 'plc'; its capital is not less than the authorised minimum (at present £50,000); and its certificate of incorporation states that it is a public company. It cannot issue its shares for services and it must obtain a trading certificate before it can commence trading. To obtain a trading certificate, the company must satisfy certain conditions set out in section 117, which include the requirement that the company's issued share capital is not less than the statutory minimum (£50,000). The principal reason for running a business as a public company is that it alone can offer its shares to the public and gain access to the stock market **(Financial Services Act 1986).**

A private company may be limited or unlimited. If limited , it may be limited by shares or by guarantee. A company limited by guarantee is not suitable for trading since it is formed for a non-commercial purpose. A private company can be incorporated or run as a single-member company. The statutory provisions regulating a private company are not as stringent as those governing a public company, especially those relating to capital, payment for shares and dividends. A private company does not need any minimum capital as such and can commence trading as soon as it is incorporated. It can issue shares for services and need only make good its accumulated realised losses before it can declare a dividend. Moreover, if it is qualified by its size (this depends on the number of its employees, turnover figure, and balance sheet total), a private company can obtain useful accounting exemptions - a small-sized private company need not file a copy of its profit and loss account or directors' report at Companies Registry, and a medium-sized private company need not disclose its turnover figure. A practical advantage of running a business through a private company rather than a public company is that the company and thus the business remains under the control of its founders. This is achieved by a clause in the articles restricting the right of shareholders to transfer their shares in the company to outsiders **(Lyle Scott v. Scott's Trustees (1959)).**

In a move to deregulate private companies, sections 115 - 117 of the Companies Act 1989 allow the members of a private company to pass an elective resolution to opt out of certain requirements of the Companies Act 1985, namely, to re-appoint the auditor annually; to extend by resolution every five years directors' authority to issue shares if such authority is to continue; to lay financial statements and other reports before the annual general meeting; to hold annual general meetings; and to reduce the percentage required for shorter notice for an extra-ordinary general meeting from ninety five per cent of the total voting share capital to not less than ninety per cent. An elective resolution (like all special resolutions) must be filed at Companies Registry within 15 days after it is passed. Moreover, it can be revoked by ordinary resolution at any time. A private company can also use 'the written resolution' procedure to pass a resolution without having to convene any formal general meeting. This procedure requires all the members who are entitled to attend and vote at a general meeting to give their written consent in support of the resolution. The procedure cannot be used to pass an ordinary resolution to remove a director or the auditor from office.

The main advantages of running a business through a limited company rather than a partnership are that its proprietors enjoy the privilege of limited liability ; the company has perpetual existence in that it continues to exist even though it has no members left; it can raise loans by giving as security a provision called a 'floating charge' (see later); and the interests of its proprietors (measured in terms of shares) are freely transferable subject to any restrictions on transfer contained in the company's articles. The main disadvantages are that the company has to comply with all the formalities imposed by company legislation; it has to file financial and other information at Companies Registry and these are open to public scrutiny; it incurs expenses in having to have its accounts audited and in filing fees; and its ability to trade is restricted by the *ultra vires* rule which confines the company to those activities set out in its constitution

.

Registration of New Companies. The person who takes steps to form a company and to set it going is called 'the promoter'. A promoter is under a fiduciary duty towards the company he is forming; so he must not accept bribes or make secret profits and must make a full disclosure of his interest either to an independent board of directors or to the members. When a breach of this duty occurs the company can obtain damages for any loss it suffers **(Re Leeds & Hanley Theatre of Varieties Ltd (1902)).** The company may rescind the transaction where the promoter sells to it his own property (i.e. property acquired before he became a promoter) or if it is not possible to rescind the transaction, it may recover the profit where the promoter buys property ***after*** assuming this office and sells it to the company at a profit without disclosing the fact. In **Gluckstein v. Barnes (1900)**, a syndicate was established to promote a company to purchase the Olympia. The syndicate first purchased cheaply existing charges on the Olympia and later purchased the Olympia for £140,000. It then registered the company it was promoting and then sold the Olympia to the company for £180,000. The syndicate disclosed the profit of £40,000 it made on the resale but failed to disclosed a further profit of £20,000 it made when charges it had purchased were redeemed. This was discovered four years later when the company went into liquidation. In an action by the liquidator to recover the £20,000 the court held it was a secret profit made by the syndicate as promoter of the company and it was required to repay the profit to the company.

The promoter may enter into contracts on behalf of the company before it is registered (e.g. he may purchase office accommodation). Such contracts are called ***pre-incorporation contracts*** and the promoter is personally liable on them **(s.36).** However, he may avoid personal liability by including in the pre-incorporation contract a clause that he should not be liable (e.g. a clause allowing him to rescind the contract without liability if the company does not take up the contract, or a clause stating that his liability should cease when the company, after incorporation, takes up the contract). For a company to be bound by a pre-incorporation contract it must accept the contract by novation (i.e. make a new contract on the same terms as the pre-incorporation contract in which case the old contract is discharged and the new contract takes it place). Novation may also be inferred by the act of the parties, for example, where the company re-negotiates the terms of the pre-incorporation contract **(Howard v. Patent Ivory Manufacturing Co.** ((**1888**)). Ratification of the pre-incorporation contract by the company is not sufficient to make the company liable on the contract **(Kelner v. Baxter** (**1866**)).

The payment of promoter's expenses and remuneration is at the discretion of the company.

The promoter must prepare and file with the Registrar of Companies the following documents in order to obtain registration of the company: a memorandum of association; articles of association if necessary; a statement in the prescribed form (known as **Form 10**) signed by the subscribers of the memorandum containing the name and particulars of the first directors and secretary together with their written consent to act, and specifying the postal address of the company's registered office; a statement of the company's capital unless the company is to have no capital; and a statutory declaration (**Form 12**) by the solicitor engaged in the formation of the company or by any person named as director or secretary. If the Registrar is satisfied with these documents, he will give the company a registered number, issue a certificate of incorporation and publish this in the appropriate Gazette. The certificate of incorporation is *conclusive* evidence that the requirements for registration were complied with and in the case of a public company, is a statement of the fact. The accuracy of the certificate cannot be questioned **(s.13)**.

A company is incorporated on the date specified in the certificate of incorporation and it becomes a legal person separate from its members. It has a name and may have a common seal under which legal documents such as written contracts and share certificates can be signed on its behalf. This concept of corporate personality is something called ***'the doctrine of incorporation'***. The doctrine is amply illustrated by the well-known case, **Salomon v. Salomon & Co Ltd (1897).** In this case, a sole trader, Salomon, converted his boot business into a limited company and minimised the risk to the assets transferred to the company by taking the price for the assets partly in full paid shares and in a debenture secured on the company's assets (a debenture is a document evidencing a debt and it has to be repaid before shareholders' capital. This is important where the company does not have enough assets to repay everyone). Salomon held all of the company's 20,007 shares except for 6 shares which were held by his wife and five children; and he was appointed managing director. A year later the company went into liquidation and it was discovered that the company's assets were only sufficient to discharge Salomon's debenture and that there was nothing left for the unsecured creditors. The liquidator challenged the validity of the debenture on the grounds that (1) Salomon and the company were in reality one and the same person so that the company could not have owed him any money and (2) Salomon had wilfully overvalued his business when he sold it to the company. However, the House of Lords rejected both arguments and laid down the following principles: (a) once a company is incorporated legally, it has to be treated like any other independent person, with rights and liabilities appropriate to itself; (b) where a promoter sells property to a company he has set up no one can complain that the price is extravagant if there is a full and frank disclosure to members.

Company legislation lays down instances where the separate personality of the company from its members and directors will be ignored. If a public company trades for more that six months with only one member left then if that member is aware of this, he will be personally liable for all those debts of the company contracted after the six months have expired **(s.24).** An officer of a company who signs a cheque or order for goods on behalf of the company without mentioning its corporate name in full, will incur personal liability if the company dishonours the document **(s.349).** If a company has subsidiaries, the separate identity of each subsidiary company is ignored for accounting purposes, and the holding company has to lay the subsidiaries' accounts before its annual general meeting when its own accounts are being considered so that the group's financial position is properly reflected **(s.229).** The directors of a public company who commence trading or exercise any borrowing powers of the company before the company receives its trading certificate will be personally liable for the company's debts if the company is unable to pay those debts **(s.117).** If a company is in insolvent liquidation the liquidator can apply to the courts for an order that any person who was trading on behalf of the company to defraud the creditors should contribute towards the assets of the company **(s.213 IA).** For a person to be made liable for fraudulent trading there must be 'actual dishonesty' or 'recklessness' on his part and this can often be difficult to prove. A contribution order can also be made against any director who was involved in wrongful trading **(s.214 IA).** Wrongful trading arises where a director continues to trade on behalf of the company beyond a period when a reasonable person would have reached the conclusion that there was no possibility of the company surviving. This catches 'the honest but incompetent director'.

The courts too will 'lift the veil' of incorporation where justice demands it. They will do so in times of war, to determine the nationality of the company. In **Daimler Co Ltd v. Continental Tyre & Rubber Co. Ltd (1916)**, the court ignored the fact that the defendant company was incorporated in England and held the company to be a German company because its majority shareholders and directors were all resident in Germany which was at war with England. If the company is formed for a fraudulent or unlawful purpose, the courts will also ignore its corporate personality. In **Gilford Motors Co Ltd v. Horne (1933)**, a former director of the plaintiff company who had bound himself by a restraint of trade clause formed a company with his wife for the purpose of enabling him to commit a breach of his covenant. An injunction was granted against the company from carrying on the business even though it was not a party to the covenant, because it was 'a mere cloak or sham'. The courts may treat a parent company and its subsidiary as a single unit where one is acting as agent or trustee for the other. In **DHN Food Distributors Ltd v.**

London Borough of Tower Hamlets (1976), the Court of Appeal treated a holding company and its subsidiary as a single unit, even though there was no agency relationship between them, because they were involved in what amounted to a single business, rather than separate business. In that case, a holding company carried on business from premises owned by a subsidiary. The subsidiary did not itself carry on any business and the two companies had the same directors. It was held that the two companies were a single economic entity so that when the Council compulsorily purchased the premises it had to pay compensation for both the site and for disturbance of the business (the Council had argued that because the subsidiary carried on no business on the site the Council was not obliged to pay compensation for disturbance of a business). The 'economic entity' approach has not been followed in recent cases (see **Adams v. Cape Industries plc (1990)**).

(i) Memorandum of Association. This document contains the fundamental conditions upon which the company is allowed to be incorporated. It should contain the following clauses : (a) the name clause; (b) the public company clause, if relevant; (c) the registered office clause; (d) the objects clause; (e) the liability clause, if relevant; (f) the capital clause, if relevant.

(a) ***Name.*** The choice of name is limited by two factors, namely, the Registrars' sanction and a passing-off action. The Registrar will not register the company if the last word in the name does not end in 'limited' , 'public limited company', or 'unlimited' (or their abbreviations); or if the name is the same as one appearing in the index of names kept at the Registry; if the name is offensive or unlawful or gives the impression that the company is connected with central or local government; or if the name is designated by the Secretary of State as a protected name **(s.26).** Also if the name should be similar to that of an existing company so as to impinge on its goodwill and connections, that company may apply to the courts in a passing-off action for an injunction to restrain the new company from carrying on business under that name (**Manchester Brewery Co v. North Cheshire & Manchester Brewery Co (1899**)).

A company which carries on business under a name other than its corporate name must include its corporate name and its address whenever the business name appears on any business premises or business documents **(s. 4 Business Names Act 1985).** Where an officer of a company misstates the company's corporate name on any bill of exchange cheque or order for goods he will be personally liable on that instrument if the company dishonours it **(s.349).** In **British Airway Board v. Parish (1979),** a managing director signed a cheque on behalf of his company but omitted to include 'limited' after its name. He was held personally liable to the payee when the cheque was dishonoured by the company.

A company can freely change its name by passing a special resolution and by altering its constitution to reflect the change **(s.28).** The Department of Trade and Industry (DTI) can also compel the company to change its name but its power to do so is statutorily regulated. If the name is similar to that of an existing company, this power must be exercised within one year of incorporation; if misleading information was given to the Registrar for the purpose of registration, this power must be exercised within five years of incorporation; if the name is misleading then the DTI can exercise this power at any time. The courts too can force the company to change its name as a result of a successful passing- off action. A change of name takes effect when the Registrar issues an amended certificate of incorporation.

(b) Registered Office. The memorandum must state whether the registered office of the company is to be situated in

England and Wales, Wales or Scotland. This information determines the domicile and nationality of the company. If it is stated that the registered office will be situated in England and Wales, the company will be an English company and English law will govern the company (e.g. to decide whether it is validly incorporated). The postal address of the registered office is not included in the memorandum but is filed separately with the Registrar when an application is made to register the company.

The registered office is necessary for communications and legal notices to be sent to the company (e.g. a winding up petition can only be served on the company at its registered office). It is also the place where statutory books and documents can be inspected. The following books and registers *must* be kept at the registered office: the register of charges, the register of directors and secretary, and the minute book of the members' meeting. All other books (e.g. registers of members, of debenture holders, of directors' interest in shares and debentures, and the accounting records) may be kept elsewhere if not made up at the registered office; but the Registrar must be notified of this. The members are entitled to inspect all the above books except the directors' minute book and the accounting records.

The registered office clause cannot be altered. However, the postal address of the registered office can be changed from one address to another within the country of domicile. An ordinary resolution is necessary to effect the change and the Registrar must be notified within 14 days.

(c) Objects. The memorandum must set out the activities which the company intends to pursue and constitutes the limits on the company. If the company engages in an activity outside its objects it will be acting *ultra vires* (i.e. beyond its capacity) and any of its members can apply to the courts for an injunction to prevent the company from continuing that activity. However, no injunction can be granted to prevent the company from fulfilling a legal obligation to a third party even if it arises out of an *ultra vires* activity**(s.35(2)).** Moreover, since members can now ratify by special resolution anything which is outside the company's objects clause **(s.35(3)),** a member will be unable to bring injunctive proceedings against the company where members' approval of the unauthorised activity is obtained by the directors before the proceedings are instituted.

A third party other than a director or connected person (e.g. the director's spouse, infant child or step child, business partners, or another company in which the director has a 20% shareholding) can enforce an *ultra vires* contract against the company if he/she enters into it in good faith **(s.35 A)** or the contract is ratified by the members. 'Good faith' is presumed and it is not enough for the company to show that the third party knew that the contract or act was outside the company's constitution in order to defeat the presumption. If the third party is dealing with a charitable company he can enforce the *ultra vires* transaction against the company only if either he has given value ***and*** does not know that the transaction is outside the company's constitution or else is unaware at the time that he is dealing with a charitable company. Where the third party is a director or a connected person, the company can set aside the *ultra vires* contract unless its members ratify the contract by special resolution; or restitution is no longer possible; it would prejudice the rights of innocent third parties for value; or the company is indemnified against any loss or damage arising from the contract. A company can enforce an *ultra vires* against a third party only if its members ratify the contract. If the company suffers a loss as a result of an *ultra vires* contract the directors will be liable to the company for the loss (unless the members had ratified the contract by special resolution and then passed another special resolution releasing the directors from liability).

Companies have been able to evade the *ultra vires* rule by relying on various drafting devices aimed at giving even greater freedom of action. The most well-known drafting device is the subjective objects clause. This is a statement in the objects clause enabling the company to carry on any activity which, in the directors' opinion, is of benefit to the company's business **(Bell Houses Ltd v. City Wall Properties Ltd (1966)).** In addition, section 3A permits a draftsman to include a statement in the company's memorandum that the company's object is 'to carry on business as a general commercial company'. This enables the company to carry on any trade or business whatsoever and to have power to do all things as are incidental or conducive to the carrying on of that trade or business. However such a statement does not cover charitable and political donations, and other *ex-gratia* payments and so they would require a separate object.

A company can alter its objects by special resolution **(s.4).** The courts' confirmation is not required unless the holders of 15 per cent of the company's share capital or 15 per cent of the members (where the company does not have a share capital) who did not vote for the alteration, apply to the courts within 21 days to have the alteration cancelled **(s.5).** A copy of the amended memorandum and the special resolution must be filed at Companies Registry.

(d) Limited Liability. If the company is to be limited by shares or by guarantee, the memorandum must indicate this. The liability clause can be altered once only in the company's lifetime and this is done by re-registration. If the company is limited it may re-register as an unlimited company, but it must first obtain the written consent al all of its members **(s.49).** If the company is unlimited it may re-register as limited by special resolution **(s.51).**

(e) Share Capital. If the company is to have a share capital the memorandum must state the amount of capital with which the company proposes to be registered. This capital is known as the *authorised* or *nominal capital* and, in the case of a public company, cannot be less than £50,000. The authorised capital is divided into shares of fixed value; the fixed value of each share is called 'nominal' or 'par' value, and subject to section 24 of the Companies Act (a public company trading with only one member left) and section 213 of the Insolvency Act (fraudulent trading), it determines the maximum liability of each member for the company's unsatisfied debts. A company can only issue shares up to its authorised share capital.

The method of altering the share capital depends on whether or not the issued share capital will be reduced. The *issued share capital* is that part of the authorised capital which has been allotted to investors. If the alteration will not affect the issued capital and the articles authorise the alteration, then an ordinary resolution can be used **(s.121).** Section 121 applies where the company wishes to increase its authorised capital, cancel unissued shares, consolidate or sub-divide its shares and convert fully paid shares into stock. It was held in **Russell v. Northern Bank Development Corp (1992)** that a company cannot lawfully contract out of its statutory right to increase its authorised capital.

If the alteration in authorised capital will reduce the issued capital then, as long as the articles authorise it, a special resolution and confirmation by the courts is required **(s.135).** Section 135 specifies three instances where it will apply: to extinguish or reduce members' liability for unpaid capital; to return capital in excess of the company's needs; and to cancel paid up capital which has been lost or unrepresented by available assets.

In deciding whether to sanction a reduction of capital under section 135, the courts have to take into account the interests both of the creditors and of the members. Any creditor who does not consent to a reduction of capital, where such reduction prejudices creditors, will have to be paid off or given some security before the courts will dispense with his consent. If the company wishes to repay excess capital or to reduce the nominal value of the issued shares because of a loss of assets, the reduction must be carried out as in a winding up and the rules of repayment of capital complied with. Thus, if some shareholders are preferential as to repayment of capital they will have to be repaid first, whether or not they agree to it (**Prudential Assurance Co Ltd v. Chatterley-Whitfield Collieries Ltd (1949**)). However, they will bear the loss of capital last. A reduction of capital takes effect when it is registered at Companies Registry.

(ii) Articles of Association. This document specifies the manner in which the business of the company is to be conducted, and regulates the rights of members among themselves. A model set of articles, called Table A, is contained in Statutory Instrument 1985 No.805. If a company limited by shares does not register articles, Table A will apply automatically to that company **(s.8).** Even if it does register its own articles, the provisions of Table A will still apply to the extent that they are not excluded altogether by the registered articles. Companies limited by guarantee must register articles as Table A does not apply to them.

By section 14, the memorandum and articles constitute a ***statutory contract*** between the company and its members, and between the members themselves, but only in so far as the relevant provisions in the company's constitution are membership matters. Therefore if a member breaks the contract, the company can sue him in its own name. In **Hickman v. Kent (1915**), the articles provided that if a member had a dispute with the company the matter should go to arbitration. Hickman, a member, brought a court action against his company in connection with his expulsion therefrom. The court held that the company was entitled to have the action discontinued since the member had contractually agreed by the articles that all disputes would go to arbitration. Conversely, the member can sue the company for breach of any right given to him as member. In **Pender v. Lushington (1877),** the articles provided that each member should be entitled to one vote for every 10 shares, but that no member would be entitled to more than 100 votes. One member had more than 1000 shares and to avoid that limit he transferred some shares to a nominee, who was then registered as owner of the shares. Subsequently, the chairman at a general meeting improperly rejected the votes cast by the nominee on the grounds that the transfer was merely a device to avoid the provision in the articles. The court held that the articles bound the company to the shareholder, whose votes must therefore be counted.

The company is bound to the member only in respect of membership matters. So in **Eley v. Positive Life Assurance Co Ltd (1876),** where the articles provided that Eley would be employed as solicitor for life and the company later dismissed him, the court held that Eley could not rely on the statutory contract even though he was a member because the relevant provision in the articles referred to him in his capacity as solicitor rather than as a member (i.e. it was not a membership right).

Each member is bound to the other members. Therefore if the articles give a member some personal right, then the contract is directly enforceable by that member against other members without making the company a party to the action. In **Rayfield v. Hands (1960),** the articles provided that if a member wished to sell his shares he should inform the directors who will take the shares equally between them at a fair price. The court held that the directors, as members, were bound by the statutory contract to take up the shares of the member who wished to sell.

The statutory contract is unique in that it is subject to the right of the company to alter its constitution. Thus any action by a member against the company for a reduction in the enjoyment of his membership rights, caused by a valid alteration of the articles, will be defeated.

A company can alter its articles at any time by special resolution in a general meeting **(s.9).** However, no alteration can be made under section 9 if the effect of the alteration is to provide the articles with more power than the memorandum permits; or to increase a member's liability without his consent; or to change any provision inserted in the articles by the courts (e.g. under s. 459) without the courts' consent; or to vary class rights contained in the articles without the consent of the class concerned **(s.125).** In addition, the power to alter the articles under section 9 must be exercised in good faith and for the benefit of the company otherwise the alteration might be set aside by the courts on grounds that it is fraud on the minority. The test whether an alteration is 'in good faith' is a subjective one (i.e. whether the majority of members honestly believe that their action will benefit the general membership of the company). If their belief is honest, then the alteration will be valid even though it prejudices the minority of members. In **Brown v. British Abrasive Wheel Co (1919),** a company wanted more money. The majority of members agreed to provide more, but the minority did not want to contribute. The majority decided to alter the articles to purchase compulsorily the minority's shares. The court said that it was fraud on the minority. However in **Sidebottom v. Kershaw Leese (1920)**, where a similar *expropriation clause* was included in the articles to prevent members from competing with the company, it was upheld by the courts on the ground that it was inserted to protect the company's trade secrets from its competitors.

A person who has a separate contract with the company, some terms of which are contained in the articles, cannot obtain an injunction to prevent the articles being altered; but he is entitled to damages from the company for breach of contract. In **Southern Foundries Ltd v. Shirlaw (1940),** Shirlaw had a separate contract to manage the company for ten years. The articles provided that if the managing director ceased to be a director he would lose his appointment as director. The company altered its articles, permitting it to remove a director on notice. Shirlaw was subsequently removed , and as a result lost his appointment. Lord Porter held that, although the courts could not prevent the company from altering its articles when it could lawfully do so, Shirlaw was entitled to damages for breach of contract.

When the articles are altered, a copy of the resolution and the amended articles must be filed with the Registrar of Companies.

(iii) Financing Company Activities. The two most common methods of funding a company's activities are through the company's own members, by an issue of ***shares*** or through long term loan creditors, by an issue of ***debentures.*** The money raised from shares is *capital*, which the company cannot generally reduce by returning it to members; but that raised on debentures is a *debt* which the company can redeem at any time subject to the terms of the debentures. The income earned from shares is called dividend which can be paid out of distributable profits; but that earned from debentures is called interest which can be paid out of profits or capital.

(a) Shares. A share does not, as its name implies, make the holder an owner of the company's assets **(Macura v. Northern Assurance Co (1925));** but it gives him certain rights in the company (e.g. the right to dividend, and to a say in the democratic process of the company). Its principal liability is to pay, on call or by pre-determined instalments, any balance outstanding on it. Basically, there are three types of shares: ordinary shares, preference shares and deferred shares.

Ordinary shares confer a right to the equity in the company (i.e. a share in the surplus assets in a winding up of the company), a right to a dividend when one is declared, and to attend and vote at general meetings. Section 89 confers a statutory pre-emption right on ordinary shares, giving ordinary shareholders a right to be offered new ordinary shares for cash (other than those which are to be issued under an employee share scheme) before such shares can be offered to outsiders. The offer must remain open for 21 days. An allotment which contravenes section 89 is not invalid; but the aggrieved shareholders may bring an action within two years for compensation against the company and the directors in default. Members may waive their statutory pre-emption rights by passing a special resolution to that effect. In addition, a private company may expressly exclude such rights in its constitution. Unless otherwise stated, all shares issued by a company are presumed to be ordinary shares and rank equally.

Preference shares give preference over all other shares either as to dividend, repayment of capital, or both. Where they carry a fixed rate on dividend, it is implied that they are ***cumulative*** (i.e. arrears of dividend are accumulated and must be paid before a dividend is paid on other shares, as long as the company is a going concern - **Webb v. Earl (1875)**). Preference shares are not preferential as to capital repayment in a winding up; but if such a right is expressly given, the shares are presumed to confer no right on surplus capital since all the rights relating to capital would have become exhausted as a result of the express provision dealing with capital (**Scottish InsuranceCorp. v. Wilson & Clyde Coal Co (1949)**). Preference shares carry the same voting rights at general meetings as ordinary shares unless such rights are expressly excluded.

Deferred shares are also known as management or founders' shares and they often carry multiple votes; but their right to a dividend and repayment of capital is deferred until ordinary shareholders are paid a fixed percentage.

Protection of Class Rights. Class rights are special or preferential rights given to a class of shareholders where the shares are divided into different classes. They are usually attached to preference shares rather than ordinary shares. The protection given to class rights takes two forms. The first relates to the procedure which is necessary to vary the rights, and the second is for any dissenting shareholder to apply to the courts for the cancellation of the variation. The procedure which has to be used for the variation varies according to whether the class rights are set out in the memorandum, the articles or elsewhere **(s.125).** If the class rights are in the memorandum and neither the memorandum nor the original articles contain a method by which the rights attached to the shares can be varied, then the consent of all the shareholders of the company (not just the preference shareholders) is required. If the class rights are in the articles or elsewhere and no variation clause is contained in the articles, the rights can only be varied if either the holders of three-quarters, in nominal value, of the affected shares consent in writing to the variation, or an extra-ordinary resolution passed at a separate general meeting of the holders of that class sanction the variation.

In the event of the appropriate procedure being followed, dissenting shareholders of the affected class holding at least 15 per cent of the relevant shares can apply to the courts within 21 days of the giving of the consent or the passing of the extra-ordinary resolution to have the variation cancelled **(s.127).** The courts may cancel the variation if they are satisfied that the variation would unfairly prejudice the affected class. If the courts are not so satisfied, they must confirm the variation. The company must send a copy of the court order to Companies Registry within 15 days.

Payment for Shares. The general rule is that shares may be paid for in cash or in a non-cash consideration. However, if the company is a public company special rules apply. The non-cash consideration cannot be services **(s.99);** and where it is assets, there must be a proper valuation of the assets by the company's auditor to ensure that the value of the assets is not less than the nominal value of the shares together with any premium payable on those shares **(s.103).** The auditor must also prepare a valuation report for the company within six months before the shares are allotted. For breach of sections 99 and 103, the allottee will have to pay to the company the amount of the discount in cash with interest. In addition, a public company cannot accept future assets for its shares unless there is an undertaking that the assets will be transferred to the company within five years of the allotment **(s.102).**

No company, whether public or private, is allowed to issue its shares for a consideration which is less than their nominal value **(s.100).** If the shares are issued at a discount the allottee will have to pay to the company the amount of the discount in cash with interest. Any subsequent purchaser, with knowledge of the discount, will also be liable. Section 100 is not infringed where a company issues its shares to underwriters at a discount to underwrite the issue as long as conditions set out in section 97 are observed. Also a private company can issue its shares in exchange for overvalued assets and the courts will not interfere with the transaction in the absence of fraud **(Re Wragg (1897)).**

A company may, without any special powers in its articles, issue its shares at a premium (i.e. for a sum greater than their nominal value). By section 130, a sum equivalent to the premium must be transferred into a special account known as the *Share Premium Account.* This account is treated as a capital account and it cannot be used to pay a dividend. However, it may be applied in paying for fully paid bonus shares given to members; writing off preliminary expenses, or the expenses of, or the commission paid or discount allowed on, an issue of shares (i.e. shares to underwriters at a discount) and debentures of the company; providing for any premium payable by the company on the redemption of shares and debentures.

Procedure for Allotting Shares. Directors must observe certain procedures before they can issue shares. They must ensure that the authorised share capital has not been exceeded. If the company has already issued shares up to its authorised capital a shareholders' meeting is required to increase the capital **(s.121).** As directors do not have implied power to issue shares, they must obtain authority from the shareholders. This authority may be found in the articles or it may be conferred on the directors by ordinary resolution **(s.80).** In any event the authority can last for only five years at a time unless renewed by the shareholders in general meeting. A private company can elect to opt out of the provision that authority given to directors to issue shares is subject to a five year maximum period. It was held in **Russell v. Northern Bank Development Corp.** that where shareholders bind themselves by a shareholder agreement as to how they should exercise their power to issue shares any party to the agreement may institute injunctive proceedings to enforce the agreement.

Directors who wish to issue ordinary shares for cash to outsiders must ensure that ordinary shareholders waive their statutory pre-emption rights by special resolution before the shares are allotted **(s.89).** Where the shares to be issued are partly paid and the company is a public company, at least a quarter of the nominal value of the shares and the whole of any premium payable on them must be paid up before the shares can be allotted **(s.101).** The amount paid up on the nominal value of the shares is called *paid-up share capital* and the amount outstanding is known as *uncalled share capital.* A company can by special resolution decide that the uncalled capital shall be called up only when the company goes into liquidation in which case this capital is known as *reserve capital.*

Within two months of an allotment of shares the company must issue the shareholder with either a ***share certificate*** or a ***share warrant (s. 185).*** A share certificate is evidence only of title to shares and its owner becomes a member of the company when his name is entered in the register of members. Only two statements in a share certificate are of legal significance (i.e. as to who is the holder of the shares, and the amount paid up on them). These statements prevent the company from denying their accuracy in favour of an innocent party. For example, the statement that the named person is the holder of the shares is a representation by the company that, at the date of issue, that person has a good title to the shares (**Dixon v. Kennaway & Co (1900)**). A share warrant is a document of title. It is not very common in the United Kingdom and can be issued only if the articles authorise it and the shares are fully paid up.

Transfer and Transmission of Shares. Transfer is the voluntary conveyance of shares by a shareholder; transmission arises by operation of law, for example, on the death or bankruptcy of a shareholder his shares automatically pass to his personal representatives or his trustee in bankruptcy, although they do not become members of the company until their names are put on the register of members.

A transfer of shares has to be in writing, properly stamped and registered by the company before the transferee can become a member of the company. This written document is called an instrument of transfer and it may be in the form prescribed by the company's articles or, if it relates to fully paid shares, as provided by the Stock Transfer Act 1963. The instrument of transfer should show the names and addresses of the parties, the nature and number of shares, the date of the transfer and the consideration being paid (if relevant). For registration purposes, the instrument of transfer and the share certificate must be sent to the company. If the company is satisfied with the documents, it will enter the transferee's name on the register of members and issue him with a new share certificate.

Where the shareholder is not transferring all of his shares in the share certificate to one transferee, the transferor himself will send the documents to the company for registration and a procedure known as ***certification of transfer*** will then apply. This procedure requires the company to retain the share certificate and to return the instrument(s) of transfer to the shareholder with the words *'certificate lodged'* endorsed on the instrument(s). The shareholder then delivers the instrument(s) to the transferee(s) for stamping and presentation to the company. By section 184, the company's certification on the instrument(s) is a representation by the company only that the transferor has a *prima facie* title to the shares. Thus, if the company fraudulently or carelessly makes a false certification, it will be liable to a purchaser who in good faith acts on the false certification.

Section 183(4) gives both the shareholder and the transferee a statutory right to enforce registration of a transfer, if necessary by applying to the courts to rectify the register of members under section 359. However in certain cases the directors must, and in other cases may, refuse to register the transfer. The directors *must* refuse to register the transfer if it is not properly stamped **(s.183),** or if it infringes a pre-emption clause. The directors *may* refuse to register the transfer if the articles give them a discretion to do so. Such a discretion has to be exercised by resolution passed at a directors' meeting before the company can refuse to register the transfer. Thus if there is equality of voting at a board meeting when considering the issue of registration of a particular transfer, the transfer must be registered **(Moodie v. Shepherd Bookbinders Ltd (1949)).** Also, the directors must convene the board meeting within a reasonable time. By requiring the company to notify the transferee of any refusal to register the transfer within two months of the deposit of the documents for registration, section 183(5) implies that 'two months' is a reasonable time and that any act outside this period will be invalid for undue delay unless it is not possible for the directors to exercise their power earlier **(Re Swaledale Cleaners Ltd (1968)).** The power to refuse to register a transfer must be exercised in good faith and for the benefit of the company otherwise a successful application will be made to the courts to order registration. Unless the directors have given a reason for refusing to register a transfer, the courts will not interfere with the exercise of their discretion.

There is no implied warranty by the shareholder that the transfer would be registered **(London Founders Association v. Clarke (1888));** so unless the transferee bought the shares 'with registration guaranteed' he does not have any contractual remedies against the shareholder for failure to obtain registration. In addition, the company is under a statutory duty to continue to deal with the shareholder because his name is still in the register of members unless the courts direct otherwise **(s.360).**

Where a transfer is forged the transfer is a nullity and the title of the shareholder whose signature is forged on the instrument of transfer is not affected. Therefore, he can compel the company to put his name back on the register of members, if the company has registered the transfer. An innocent third party who obtains registration for a forged transfer to himself cannot rely on the new share certificate issued to him by the company since he obtained it by presenting a forged transfer;

but if he transfers the shares to another innocent transferee the second transferee can make the company liable on the new share certificate; although the company in turn will be entitled to an indemnity from the person who submitted the forged share certificate for registration.

In **Sheffield Corp. v. Barclay (1905)**, **B** sent to the corporation for registration a transfer of stock which stood in the names **T** and **H.** The transfer was a forgery because **T** had forged **H's** signature on the transfer form. **B** was ignorant of the forgery. The corporation duly registered the transfer. **B** transferred the stock to third parties to whom share certificates were issued. The corporation was estopped from denying that those registered were in fact stockholders. **H** subsequently discovered the forgery and compelled the corporation to buy him an equivalent amount of stock and pay him the missing dividends with interest. The court held that **B** had to indemnify the corporation for any damages that it paid out even though he was unaware of the forgery, because he submitted the forged transfer.

A shareholder may mortgage his shares as security for a loan by transferring his shares to the lender (mortgagee) with provision that the shares should be re-transferred to him (mortgagor) once the loan is paid off. It will be a legal mortgage if the transfer is registered by the company. It will be an equitable mortgage if the shareholder deposits his share certificate with the lender together with a blank transfer (i.e. a proper instrument of transfer but with the transferee's name left blank, such name to be filled in by the transferee only if the shareholder defaults with the loan). An equitable mortgage can also be effected by the shareholder simply depositing his share certificate with the lender (no instrument of transfer is prepared); but such a mortgage is rare because the lender has to apply to the courts for power to sell the shares in the event of default by the shareholder.

Register of Members. This register must include the following matters: the names and addresses of members, number of shares or stock, the amount paid as consideration, and the date when each person was entered on the register. The register and not the share certificate is the document of title to shares; and it must be available for inspection during office hours. Members may inspect it without a charge, and other persons on payment of a fee. If a member has at least five per cent of the nominal value of the voting capital he must be put also on a register called *Register of Substantial Shareholding* where the company is a public company.

(b) Debentures. A trading company has implied power to borrow money for trading. In exercising this power the company can issue debentures and debenture stock to persons prepared to lend it money and can charge its assets as security. A debenture is indivisible and usually provides for repayment at specific dates. Debenture stock constitutes one composite debt. It can be transferred in fractional amounts, and is often made repayable in the event of the winding up of the company or by its default. For isolated transactions, such as obtaining a loan from a bank, the company simply will issue single debentures. But with larger public issues, the debentures are issued in series, all ranking equally with each other. Debenture stock and debenture issued in series are usually issued by trust deed, whereby the assets charged as security are transferred by the company to trustees for the benefit of the lenders.

The normal trust deed would include provisions dealing with the following matters: appoint and powers of the trustees; description and terms of the debentures or debenture stock; the type of security and circumstances in which it will be enforced; the obligations of the company. A trust deed has certain advantages. It enables the security to be by way of a specific mortgage or charge on the company's land , rather than just by way of a floating charge. By giving the security to trustees, the prohibition by the Law of Property Act 1925 that a legal interest in land cannot be vested in more than four persons is thus circumvented. Also, a trustee with necessary powers can intervene promptly in the event of default by the company.

There are various types of debentures. Debentures can be in ***registered*** form, transferable by a duly stamped instrument of transfer like shares, or payable to ***bearer,*** in which case they are negotiable instruments and coupons are attached to them representing right to interest. Debentures may be issued as ***redeemable*** or ***perpetual*** debentures. If redeemable, they will be redeemed according to the terms of issue. Redeemable debentures may be re-issued but their date of redemption on re-issue cannot be later than the date of the original debentures. If perpetual, the loan is repayable only by default of the company or in the event of a winding up; and they will not be invalid simply because the date of repayment is postponed for too long a time **(s.193).** Debentures may be issued on terms that they can be converted into shares at fixed dates or at the option of the debenture holder. The attraction of such an investment is that it allows the debenture holder to switch his debenture to shares while the option to convert exists. Nevertheless, debentures issued at a discount cannot be made immediately convertible into paid up shares of the full par value, since this would indirectly constitute issuing shares at a discount **(Mosely v. Koffyfontein Mines (1907)).**

When issuing secured debentures, a company may charge all or any of its undertaking or property including its uncalled capital (unless converted into reserve capital) as security for the loan. The charge may be a fixed or a floating charge or a combination of both. A fixed charge is a mortgage of fixed assets such as the company's freehold and leasehold property, fixed plant and machinery, and goodwill. A fixed charge will prevent the company from dealing with the security without the concurrence of the debenture holder. A floating charge is a charge on unspecified assets such as the company's undertaking and after-acquired stock. The charge simply 'floats', and will become a fixed charge when it crystallises. Crystallisation takes place when the company ceases to carry on business or the chargee intervenes.

A floating charge is not as advantageous as a fixed charge for various reasons. A fixed charge on property already subject to a floating charge will have priority over the floating charge unless the fixed charge was made expressly subject to the floating charge, or the floating charge contained a provision that no subsequent charge will have priority over it and the creditor with the fixed charge had notice of that provision. Debts such as taxes and employees' wages are preferential when the company is in receivership and must be paid before debts secured by a floating charge **(s.40 Insolvency Act).** A floating charge created by an insolvent company within one year before the company goes into liquidation to secure an existing debt can be set aside by the liquidator **(s.245 Insolvency Act).** If the person to whom the floating charge was given was connected with the company the period is extended to two years and it makes not difference that the company was solvent when it created the charge. Other disadvantages of a floating charge are that it does not cover assets which the company is acquiring under a hire purchase agreement; assets seized and sold by the sheriff in execution of a judgement obtained by an unsecured creditor against the company; assets in the possession of the company which are subject to a reservation of title clause **(Aluminium Industrie BV v. Romalpa Ltd).**

Despite its vulnerability, a floating charge may nevertheless be a useful security to its holder. Only a creditor secured by a floating charge can appoint an administrative receiver (see later). Moreover, a floating charge ranks ahead of ordinary unsecured debts. From the company's point of view a floating charge is more advantageous than a fixed charge since it allows the company to use the assets charged until crystallisation of the charge.

Registration of Charges. Charges created by a company on its property are required to be registered in the company's own register of charges **(s.411)** and, if they fall within the ambit of section 395, with the Registrar of Companies. With the latter, the charge must be registered within 21 days of its creation otherwise it is void against the company's secured creditors, administrator, and liquidator, though the advance itself is not affected and becomes immediately repayable. It is the duty of the company to send the necessary particulars of the charge to the Registry for registration; but in practice, the chargee himself will do so to ensure registration within the prescribed time.

A charge can only be registered outside the prescribed time with leave of the courts **(s.404).** However, the courts will only allow for late registration if the omission is accidental, or due to inadvertence or some other sufficient cause, or is not of a nature to prejudice the creditors or shareholders, or on grounds that it is just and equitable to grant relief. An application for late registration is not normally granted if the company is in liquidation or is insolvent and on the verge of liquidation or if the chargee, having discovered his charge is not registered, delays his application for late registration in order to see which course would be to his advantage.

The effect of late registration is to make the charge valid from the date of its creation subject to the right of the courts to impose such conditions as seems just and convenient. It is standard practice for the courts to attach a 'proviso' to a late registration order protecting rights of intervening secured creditors. The wording of the 'proviso' usually only protects rights acquired against the company's property during the extension period (i.e. between the end of the 21 days within which the statute requires registration and the date of actual registration). A subsequent chargee is protected notwithstanding that he had knowledge of the unregistered charge before his charge was acquired. If the subsequent charge was created and registered within the statutory time limit allowed for registration of the first charge (i.e. within 21 days), the subsequent charge does not obtain priority by reason of the 'proviso'.

For registration purposes, a charge has to be accompanied with a brief summary showing the date of creation of the charge, the amount secured, the property to which the charge applies, and the person entitled to it. Additional particulars may be included but this does not make them known by constructive notice to anyone unaware of them **(Wilson v. Kelland (1910)).** On registration of the charge, the Registrar will issue a certificate of registration. This certificate will be conclusive evidence that the requirements of the Act as to registration have been complied with, and that the prescribed particulars on the register have been entered by the Registrar; but it is no authority that the contents of those particulars submitted for registration are accurate.

Remedies of Debenture Holders. The remedies of a debenture holder where the company defaults with the loan will depend on whether the debenture holder is secured or not. If he is unsecured, he may sue for the sum due together with interest on it, and if the judgement is unsatisfied he can levy execution against the company. As an alternative to the above remedy, he can petition for a winding up order of the company on grounds that the company is unable to pay its debts. If he is secured, the debenture holder has additional remedies. He may take steps to enforce the security and exercise any power conferred by the debenture on him (e.g. the power of sale and the appointment of a receiver). Alternatively, he may apply to the courts for the appointment of a receiver.

Receivers. A receiver is a person appointed to take possession of property which is subject to a charge and to deal with it primarily for the benefit of the holder of the charge. Once a receiver is able to pay off the creditors whom he represents he must vacate office and the company can continue business as before.

The courts have power to appoint a receiver on the application of any secured creditor if the principal sum or interest is in arrears, or the company is being wound up, or the security is in jeopardy (e.g. the company is threatening to dispose of its entire undertaking). Where the security is the company's business the courts will provide the receiver with power to manage the business or appoint a manager to assist him; but will do this only if the creditor seeking the appointment is secured by a floating charge. Court appointed receivers to enforce a charge are rare since most debentures or trust deeds contain express power to make one.

A receiver or manager of the whole (or substantially the whole) of the company's property appointed out of court by or on behalf of creditors secured by a floating charge is called an *administrative receiver.* An administrative receiver has statutory powers to manage the company. Only a person qualified to be an insolvency practitioner can be appointed an administrative receiver. To be an insolvency practitioner a person must be qualified under the rules of a recognised public body to act as such and must have proper insurance bonding. An ordinary receiver need not be an insolvency practitioner.

The appointment of an administrative receiver will depend on the terms of the debenture. Many debentures contain a list of events which would entitle the debenture holder to appoint one, such as where the company defaults with the principal sum or interest . A receiver who decides to accept an appointment must do so not later than the end of the next business day after receiving the document of appointment. The appointor must then notify Companies Registry of the appointment within seven days. In addition, an administrative receiver must inform the company forthwith of his appointment, and all known creditors within 28 days, and must receive a statement of affairs in respect of the company within 21 days.

An administrative receiver is an agent of the company unless and until the company goes into liquidation **(s.44 IA)** or until the creditors whom he represents are paid in full; so his appointment does not result in the automatic dismissal of the company's employees. However, the directors' powers over the security are suspended but they still remain in office and so are liable to file annual returns and documents at Companies Registry.

An administrative receiver (as well as the company) is personally liable on contracts he makes for the company during his receivership. However, the administrative receiver can contract out of this liability. An administrative receiver is not liable on existing contracts made by the company before his appointment unless he adopts them after re-negotiations. In the case of existing employment contracts, nothing he does or does not do during the first two weeks of his appointment will be taken into account when deciding whether he had adopted such contracts **(s.37 IA).**

Within three months after his appointment, an administrative receiver must prepare a report for the company's creditors stating the circumstances leading to his appointment, what he has done and intends to do about the company's property and business, the amount of preferential debts payable and the prospects of other creditors.

An administrative receiver is under a duty to pay off preferential debts of which he had notice, before any payment can be made to the debenture holders whom he represents **(s.40**

IA). Remuneration, expenses and indemnity also take priority over the debenture holders. Only the courts can remove an administrative receiver from office; but he may resign on giving notice.

(iv) Maintenance of Capital. A limited company has its capital to back its credit and while the company is allowed to use this capital freely for trading, the law will only permit it to return capital to members if certain procedures (principally for the protection of creditors) are followed. One procedure which requires the courts' consent, namely, section 135 has already been considered (see alteration of capital clause in the Memorandum of Association). Other procedures which do not require the courts' involvement are discussed below.

Section 159 allows a company, if so permitted by its articles, to issue shares which are redeemable or liable to be redeemed at the option of either the company or the shareholder. However, the shares must first be fully paid up, the company must have in existence issued shares which are non-redeemable, and the redemption must be effected on the terms set out in the company's articles.

Section 162 enables a company, if authorised by its articles, to purchase its own shares (whether redeemable or not) subject to the same rules as apply to redemption except that the terms of the purchase need not be set out in the company's articles. However, the company must obtain permission from its members before it can effect the purchase. For an 'off-market' purchase members must give permission by special resolution. Before the resolution is passed, a copy of the proposed purchase contract must be made available for inspection by the members at the company's registered office for at least 15 days immediately preceding the meeting and at the meeting itself. For a 'market' purchase (i.e. where the shares are being bought off a recognised exchange) permission is given by ordinary resolution. The resolution must state the maximum number of shares that may be purchased and the price range for the shares.

The company must finance the acquisition from distributable profits or the proceeds of a fresh issue of shares. However, a private company which does not have enough profits/proceeds of a fresh issue may make up the shortfall out of capital as long as it satisfies the conditions contained in section 171, such as that the articles must authorise the use of capital in this way, the shareholders must sanction by special resolution the use of capital to effect the purchase, the directors must make a declaration of solvency backed by an auditor's report confirming their view that the company has enough assets to pay its debts in full for at least a year, and creditors must be given details of the proposed capital payment and an opportunity to inspect the declaration of solvency and special resolution. Dissenting members and creditors can apply to the courts within five weeks from the date of the special resolution to set aside the resolution. The use of capital in this way is called *permissible capital payment*.

Section 151 makes it unlawful, subject to exceptionc, for a company to give financial assistance to a third party to purchase its shares or shares in its holding company unless the assistance is an incidental part of some large purpose and is given by the directors in good faith for the benefit of the company. Financial assistance includes any loan, guarantee or indemnity, security, release, and any other financial assistance which materially reduces the net assets of the company. It makes no difference whether the assistance is given before or at the same time as the acquisition of the shares.

A public company can give financial assistance lawfully in the following cases : a loan by a money lending company in the ordinary course of business to a customer even though the customer uses it to purchase the lender's shares; a loan to employees other than directors to enable them to own shares in the company; and the provision of money by the company for the purchase of its shares under an employee share scheme. In addition, a private company can give financial assistance freely as long as it complies with the procedure and timetable set out in sections 155 to 158. The members must approve of the financial assistance by special resolution, and any member(s) who hold at least 10 per cent of the share capital and who did not vote for the resolution can apply to the courts within four weeks to cancel the resolution. In addition, the directors must make a declaration of solvency; the assistance must be given out of distributable profits if it would otherwise reduce the book value of the company's net assets; and the assistance must be given within eight weeks of the declaration of solvency being made, or within such longer time as the courts, in dealing with any objection, may fix.

If unlawful financial assistance is given then criminal sanctions are imposed on the company and on those directors who are knowingly party to the breach. Loans made by the company cannot be recovered since the transaction would have been unlawful **(Selangor Rubber Estates v. Cradock (1967))** and any guarantee or security given in connection with the prohibited transaction will be invalid **(Heald v. O'Connor (1971)).**

Section 263 prohibits a limited company from declaring a dividend except out of profits available for distribution. In determining whether it has distributable profits, the company must satisfy the *realised profits* test. This test provides that the 'profits available for distribution' will be the amount by which the company's accumulated realised profits (revenue and capital) exceed its accumulated realised losses (revenue and capital). Any provision in the accounts (e.g. for bad debts, or for depreciation of a fixed but wasting asset) is to be treated as a realised loss. However, a provision for depreciation of a fixed asset need not be treated as a realised loss if the decrease in value of that asset is compensated for by an overall increase in the value of all the other fixed assets. Unrealised profits can only be used to pay for fully paid bonus shares issued to members.

A public company is further prohibited from declaring a dividend if the effect of the distribution will reduce the company's net assets to below the aggregate of its called up share capital and its undistributable reserves (e.g. share premium account, capital redemption reserve and revaluation reserves). The effect of the *net assets* test as laid down in section 264 generally means that a public company must make good both its realised and unrealised losses before it can declare a dividend; while a private company need only make good its accumulated realised losses.

If the company is an investment company and its constitution prohibits the company form distributing capital profits, section 265 lays down special rules for the distribution of trading profits. The company may make a distribution out of its accumulated realised revenue profits less it accumulated revenue losses (whether realised or unrealised) and only then if the effect of the distribution would not reduce the assets to less than one and a half times the aggregate of its liabilities. An investment company is a public company, whose shares are quoted on a recognised exchange and whose business consists of investing its funds mainly in securities with the aim of spreading investment risk. If the company is an insurance company all amounts shown in the profit and loss account are treated as realised when determining whether there are profits available for distribution.

A member who receives an unlawful distribution and who knows or ought to know that it comes out of undistributable funds is liable to repay the amount he has received **(s.277).** If that amount cannot be recovered from the member, then the directors in default will have to pay the amount with interest.

The question of declaration and payment of a dividend is usually dealt with by the articles. Where statutory articles are adopted, Article 102 gives the directors the sole power to decide whether a dividend should be declared and, except for an interim dividend, it has to be sanctioned by the members. A dividend so declared and approved becomes an enforceable debt from the date of the meeting.

Finally, section 142 requires a public company which suffers a serious capital loss to summon an extra ordinary general meeting within 28 days to consider the company's financial position and whether it should be re-registered as a private company. 'Serious capital loss' means that the company's net assets have been reduced by losses to half or less of the amount of its paid up capital.

(v) Meeting and Procedure. 'Meeting' implies the coming together of two or more persons. Thus as a general rule a single person cannot constitute a meeting **(Re London Flats Ltd (1969)).** The general rule is subject to four exceptions. The DTI may direct that one member present, whether personally or by proxy, can constitute a meeting **(s.367);** the courts have similar power **(s.371);** a single member can hold a class meeting if he is the only member of a class of members left; and in a single member private company that member can hold a meeting. The Companies Act recognises two types of members' general meetings: the annual general meeting and extra ordinary general meetings.

The annual general meeting (AGM) has to be held once every calendar year **(s.366)**, although a private company may, by elective resolution, opt out of this requirement. The first AGM of the company must be held not later than 18 months after incorporation. In all other cases, not more than 15 months can lapse between such meetings. The normal business transacted at the meeting includes the declaration of a dividend, consideration of the financial statements, the election of directors in place of those retiring and the appointment of the auditor. A member holding at least five per cent of the total voting shares of the company can compel the company to include any special item on the agenda but he must give at least six weeks notice **(s.377).** If a company fails to hold an AGM, the DTI acting on the application of a member may compel the company to do so.

An extra ordinary general meeting (EGM) may be convened by the directors whenever they think fit; but they must convene one within 28 days if the auditors request one, or if the net assets of a public company fall to half or less of the company's paid up capital. Minorities holding at least 10 per cent of the paid up capital can require the directors to call an EGM and if the directors fail to send out notice of the meeting within 21 days of the date of the requisition being served on them, the requisitioners (providing they represent more than half of the total voting shares of the company) may themselves convene the meeting within three months of the requisition date **(s.368).** Where the requisitioners do not represent more than half of the total voting strength they will have to apply to the courts to convene the meeting. The courts have power to order an EGM and to hold and conduct the meeting as they see fit **(s.371).** In **Re El Sombrero Ltd (1958),** the company had three members of whom two were directors holding ten per cent of the shares. The articles provided for a quorum of two members. The majority shareholder wanted to call a meeting under section 368 to remove the directors, but they frustrated his efforts by refusing to attend such a meeting. He therefore made an application to the courts to call a meeting and to dispense with the need for a quorum. The application was granted.

To enable members to exercise their powers at a general meeting, the directors must send notice of the meeting to each member who is entitled to attend and vote. Notice need only be sent to the UK address of the member. Failure to serve notice to a member entitled thereto will invalidate the proceedings of the meeting **(Young v. Ladies Imperial Club (1920)).** To mitigate the harshness of the rule that failure to serve notice even to one member will invalidate the meeting, Table A Article 39 provides that any accidental failure to give notice of the meeting or the non-receipt of notice by a person entitled to it will not invalidate the meeting. Most companies either adopt Article 39 or include in their articles a similar provision. In **Re West Canadian Collieries Ltd (1962),** the failure to serve notice on some members happened because the address plates of those members were not put in the addressograph machine. The court held that it was an accidental omission within the articles of the company and so did not invalidate the meeting. However in **Musselwhite v. C.H. Musselwhite & Son Ltd (1962)** failure to send notice of a general meeting to some members, because the directors erroneously believed that they were no longer members, was held not to be an accidental omission, within an article of the company similar to Article 39, but a mistake of law. So the meeting was invalid.

The notice must specify the time and place of the meeting and the general nature of the business to be transacted. Where the meeting is the annual general meeting the notice must specify this; and where the meeting is convened to pass a special or extra ordinary resolution, or an ordinary resolution requiring special notice, the notice must specify either the text or the entire substance of the resolution **(Re Moorgate Mercantile Holdings Ltd (1980)).** The length of notice depends on the type of meeting to be summoned and the type of resolution to be passed. An annual general meeting requires at least 21 days notice and any other meeting at least 14 days notice, unless a special resolution is to be passed in which case 21 days notice is required. Shorter notice is permitted for an AGM if all the members entitled to attend and vote agree, and for any other meeting if a majority in number of members holding 95 per cent of the voting shares agree. A private may, by elective resolution, reduce the percentage required to sanction shorter notice to not less than 90 per cent.

Exceptionally, special notice is required to be given to the company by a member if he intends to propose a resolution to remove a director or auditor from office or to re-appoint a director of a public company who is over the age of 70 years. Special notice means 28 days notice and it must be given to the company which then may give 21 days notice of that resolution to members. The company cannot be compelled to circulate the resolution to members (and thus it will not be included on the agenda for the annual general meeting) unless the member complies with section 372. In **Pedley v. Inland Waterways Association Ltd (1977),** the plaintiff wanted to propose an ordinary resolution to remove the director at the annual general meeting. He gave the company secretary 28 days notice of the resolution he intended to propose but as the plaintiff did not hold at least five per cent of the voting shares, the secretary did not circulate the resolution. The court held that the plaintiff would have to comply with section 377 before he could compel the company to include his resolution for circulation.

Even though proper notice is given for a meeting, matters transacted at the meeting will only be valid if the meeting is properly conducted. This means that there must be a quorum for the meeting; a chairman must be appointed to preside over the meeting; decisions must be fairly reached, if necessary by resolution, after adequate discussion; and voting must be conducted properly.

The quorum is the minimum number of persons entitled to attend and vote and who are actually present in person or by proxy at the time when the meeting proceeds to business. Unless the articles state otherwise, a quorum for all company meetings (apart from a meeting of a single member private company) is two persons present in person. Article 41 provides that if within half an hour after the meeting is due to start a quorum is not present, the meeting is adjourned to the same day, time, and place in the next week (or to such other time and place as the directors may determine). If during the meeting a quorum ceases to be present the meeting stands adjourned in the same way as if there was no quorum at the beginning of the meeting. However, business transacted before the meeting becomes inquorate remains valid **(Re London Flats Ltd).**

A member who is unable to attend the meeting in person has a statutory right to appoint another person as his proxy to attend and vote on his behalf **(s.372).** The proxy must be appointed in writing in accordance with the company's articles; but the articles cannot require the instrument appointing the proxy to be deposited more than 48 hours before the meeting. Where a company invites proxies by issuing proxy forms, it has to issue them to all members, and not just to those members who are expected to support the directors. Unless the articles provide otherwise, a proxy cannot vote on a show of hands. Moreover a proxy can only speak at a meeting if the company is a private company. Where a proxy is general (i.e. given a discretion as to how to vote) the person holding the proxy form can vote as he thinks fit; but if he holds a special proxy form (i.e. is instructed to vote in a particular way) he cannot abstain. A corporate member will usually appoint a representative rather than a proxy, since the former has power to make on-the-spot decisions, to vote on a show of hands and to speak at the meeting even if the company is a public company.

Voting in the first instance is by a show of hands; and each member will have one vote only, irrespective of how many shares he holds. Where voting is by poll (i.e. a card vote) the number of voting shares held by a member will determine his number of votes. The articles usually will set out the provisions for a poll but any provision which excludes the right to demand a poll at a general meeting, other than on the election of the chairman or the adjournment of the meeting, will be void **(s.373).** Similarly, any provision that a poll may be allowed only if the requisitioners exceed five members, or hold more than one-tenth of the paid up capital will be void.

The chairman of the general meeting is usually the chairman of the board of directors. However, if there is no chairman to act, the members may appoint one from amongst themselves **(s.370).**

A company must keep a written record of the proceedings of all general and directors meetings and enter them in special books, called the *minute books*. Once the minutes are signed by the chairman at the same or the next succeeding meeting, they are evidence of the proceedings. The minute book of the general meeting must be kept at the registered office and be open to inspection by members without a charge. The company must produce copies to members on request, but there is a charge for this service

(vi) Officers of the Company. Every company must have directors, a secretary and an auditor. A director may act as secretary but a sole director may not. An auditor is an officer of the company under certain provisions of company legislation (e.g. s.727), although he is not included in section 744 in its definition of the term 'officer'.

(a) Directors. These are the persons responsible for the day to day running of the company. Section 282 stipulates a minimum of one director for private and two for public companies.

For certain purposes, a director includes what is known as a 'shadow director'. A shadow director is someone who is not actually appointed as a director (so he has no right to attend board meetings) but on whose instructions the appointed directors are accustomed to act. Professional advisers such as lawyers and accountants and holding companies which give instructions to directors of their subsidiaries are not normally shadow directors. The following are some of the statutory provisions which apply to both formally appointed directors and shadow directors: any service contract given to a director and capable of exceeding five years (where the company's ability to terminate is limited) is not binding on the company unless it is approved by the members **(s.319);** a copy of a director's service contract must be made available for inspection by members at the office where the register of members is kept **(s.318);** substantial property transactions (i.e. transactions exceeding £100,000 in value, or 10 per cent of the company's net assets subject to a minimum value of £2,000) between the company and its directors must first be approved by the members otherwise they are voidable at the option of the company unless restitution is not possible, or rights have been acquired by innocent third parties for value, or the transaction is affirmed by the company in general meeting within a reasonable time **(s.320);** and loans to directors are prohibited unless they are to enable the directors to perform their duties and are approved at the next general meeting or the loans do not exceed £5,000 per director **(s.330).**

The company's first directors are named in the articles, or alternatively, the articles may give the subscribers to the memorandum power to make an appointment. However the first appointment is made, it is not effective unless the persons concerned are named in the statement of directors and secretary and give their written consent to act as such when the documents necessary for the formation of the company are delivered to the Registrar **(s.10).** If the persons appointed as first directors are different from those named as directors in the statement, their appointment will be void; and those named in the statement will be treated as if they were appointed as first directors **(s.13).** The subsequent appointment of directors is governed by the articles.

Table A provides that all the directors must retire at the first annual general meeting of the company, but at every subsequent annual general meeting one-third of the directors must retire and stand for re-election. Directors with service contracts are not subject to retirement by rota. The board of directors has the power to appoint a new director whether to fill a casual vacancy, or as an additional board member, but such an appointment must be confirmed by the members at the next annual general meeting. Public company directors elected in a general meeting must be voted on individually unless the meeting has previously unanimously agreed to waive the rule **(s.292).** Third parties may treat the acts of a director whose appointment is procedurally defective as if they were those of a properly appointed director **(s.285).**

There are various ways in which a directorship may terminate. If statutory articles are adopted by the company Article 81 states that a director is disqualified from holding office on becoming of unsound mind, becoming absent from board meetings for more than six months without permission, or by resigning from office by notice in writing to the company. A public company director must retire at the first annual meeting held after his 70th birthday **(s.293)** unless the articles or the members, by ordinary resolution, allow him to continue. If the articles require the directors to hold shares in the company, this requirement must be satisfied within two months of their appointment or such shorter time as the articles may decide, otherwise the directors must vacate office immediately **(s.291).** Directors who were permitted by the articles to assign their office, lose office once an assignment is made and is sanctioned by special resolution by the members **(s.308).** Members also have a statutory right to remove directors by ordinary resolution (see later). The courts have wide power under the Company Directors Disqualification Act 1986 to disqualify directors from taking part in the management of a company or being concerned in the promotion, liquidation or receivership of a company. In some cases disqualification can last for up to fifteen years. The Act gives the courts a *discretion* to disqualify a director in the following cases: where a director has been convicted on indictment of a company offence (e.g. fraud); where there have been persistent breaches of company legislation, most notably in not delivering accounts and making annual returns; where there has been fraudulent trading or any other fraud or breach of duty in relation to the company which is revealed in a winding up; where a director has been convicted summarily on at least three occasions within a period of five years for failing to make annual returns to the Registrar. The courts *must* make a disqualification order if, during insolvency proceedings, the official receiver on behalf of the Secretary of State applies for one against a person involved in the management of the insolvent company and the courts are satisfied that the conduct of that person makes him unfit to be concerned in the management of a company **(s.6).** A disqualified person commits an offence (punishable by up to two years' imprisonment) if he acts in contravention of a disqualification order without leave of the courts.

Members control over the board. The directors' powers to manage the company are contained in the articles, and where statutory articles are adopted, Article 70 gives the directors general powers of management. The most effective control by members is to remove the directors from office by ordinary resolution **(S.303);** but the directors concerned have a right to defend themselves both by written representations which have to be circulated to members and by addressing the meeting at which the resolution is to be proposed. Section 303 overrides any clause in the articles aimed at entrenching the position of the directors; but a number of factors restrict its use. If the directors hold shares in the company they may enter into an agreement with other shareholders (a shareholder agreement) as to how each party to the agreement will vote in general meeting. Such an agreement will be upheld by the courts **(Russell v. Northern Bank Development Corp. Ltd).** Again, the articles may contain weighted voting rights which give an effective voting power far greater than the number of shares held by an individual would normally allow. In **Bushell v. Faith (1969)**, a company had three members, all of whom were directors holding 100 shares each. The articles provided that in the event of a resolution being proposed at a general meeting of the company for the removal from office of any director, each of that director's shares will carry the right to three votes per share. A motion to remove on of the directors was proposed; two directors voted in favour and the director in question against. The votes were thus 200 for, and those against 300. The court held that it was permissible to have weighted voting rights, and directors could be removed only if the resolution was carried. In this instance, the resolution was defeated. Finally, the removal of a director of a very small private company may be a ground to wind up the company under the 'just and equitable' principle of section 122 (1)(g) **(Ebrahimi v. Westbourne Galleries Ltd (1973))** so that this may make members think twice before exercising their power to remove that director from office.

Publicity concerning directors. A company must keep a *Register of Directors and Secretary* at its registered office. This register should contain particulars of these officers including any other directorship held by them for the past five years. The Registrar of Companies has to be notified of any changes within 14 days. A *Register of Directors' Interest in Shares and Debentures* in the company must also be kept and any changes in interest must be notified in writing to the company within five days. 'Interest' includes a director's spouse's and child's (under 18) interest. These registers must be made available for inspection for at least two hours a day. Also copies of directors' service contracts must be made available for inspection by the members at the company's registered office.

Non-contractual payment of compensation to directors for loss of office has to be disclosed and approved by members.

Nature of directors' duties. Directors' duties to the company are three-fold. As organs of the company, the courts will treat their mental state and act as acts of the company. So where statutory duties (e.g. filing annual returns and keeping proper accounts) are imposed on the company the directors, as well as the company, will be liable for non-compliance. As agents of the company the directors are under a duty at common law to exercise care and skill when managing the company. The common law principle was laid down in **Re City Equitable Fire Insurance Co (1925)** which established three propositions. First, a director is entitled to exhibit no greater care and skill when managing the company than can be expected from a person of his knowledge and experience. Second, a director is not required to give his full-time attention to the company's affairs unless he has a service contract to manage the company. Third, when the management of the company is lawfully delegated to others, a director will not be liable for their negligence provided that the delegation was in good faith. In equity the directors are fiduciaries and therefore they must show a high standard of integrity and honesty towards the company in their dealings with it or on its behalf. This duty has to some extent been modified and clarified by legislation and it covers two separate areas; the exercise of directors' powers in good faith for the benefit of the company and secret profits by directors.

The directors must use their powers for the purposes for which they were conferred, and in what they believe to be in the best interest of the company. Thus they will be in breach of their duty if they act *ultra vires*, or if they use their powers improperly to secure an advantage for themselves or for a third party or for a certain section of the members at the expense of the company. In **Hogg v. Cramphorn (1966)**, the directors issued new shares on trust for the company's employees to prevent a take-over which was supported by the majority of members. The new issue was declared void by the courts because the directors were motivated by self interest. In **Bamford v. Bamford (1969)**, in similar circumstances, the issue was upheld because it was ratified by a general meeting, the holders of the new issue of shares not voting thereat. The directors' duty of good faith is owed to the members collectively, not individually **(Percival v. Wright (1902)).** In exercising their powers for the company's benefit, the directors must take into account the interests of employees and the members in general **(309),** and in the case of employees *ex gratia* payments may be made to them on the transfer of the business, even though it is not in the interest of the company to make such payments **(s.719).** This power cannot be exercised without members' approval and should not prejudice creditors' interest.

If directors make a profit during the period of their directorship they must return the profit to the company unless it is disclosed at a members meeting and a resolution is passed permitting them to keep it. In **Regal (Hastings) Ltd v. Gulliver (1942)**, a company which owned a cinema formed a subsidiary to buy two more cinemas, with a view of selling all three. The directors subscribed for shares in the subsidiary, and therefore greatly benefited when the subsidiary was sold later at a profit. The directors were ordered by the court to return the profit. Where directors use information acquired during their directorship to make a profit after they cease to be directors, they must also return the profit to the company. In **Industrial Development Consultants v. Cooley (1972)**, the managing director of a company resigned and took up a contract which his company was unable to acquire. The court held that he was accountable to his former company for the profit.

Directors may vote on any transaction in which they have an interest when it comes before a general meeting; but if they hold the majority of shares their action may be attacked by dissenting shareholders on the ground that it is fraud on the minority. In **Cook v. Deeks (1916)**, the directors negotiated a contract on behalf of the company and later took up the contract themselves. At a general meeting, they used their majority shareholding to obtain a resolution declaring that the company had no interest in the contract. The court held that the contract in equity belonged to the company, and the directors in using their voting powers to vest the contract to themselves had perpetuated a fraud on the minority.

Directors who are in breach of their duties towards the company can apply to the courts for a full or partial indemnity. The courts have power under section 727 to give such indemnity when the directors had acted honestly and reasonably and with regard to all the circumstances of the case. Furthermore, while any provision in a company's articles which excludes directors' liability for negligence, breach of trust or statutory duty is void **(s.310),** a company may lawfully include in its articles a provision to the effect that the company will meet the costs incurred by its directors for breach of duty **(s.310(3)).** Artiles 118 contains a provision giving an indemnity on these terms. This provision can be relied on by the directors as long as they succesfully defend an action against them or they obtain an indemnity from the courts under section 727. The company can also purchase indemnity insurance on behalf of the directors in respect of any liability the directors may incur for breach of duty. Such insurance must be disclosed in the directors' report.

(b) Secretary. The directors usually have power to appoint the secretary **(Art. 99)**; but the first secretary of the company is invariably appointed by the promoter. The secretary of a public company must be suitably qualified for his post (e.g. he must be a qualified lawyer, or accountant from one of the chartered bodies, or a chartered secretary) and the directors must ensure that he has the requisite knowledge and experience **(s.286).** Particulars of the secretary must be included in the register of directors and secretary and in the annual returns; and whenever there is a change of secretary, notice must be given to the Registrar of Companies within 14 days.

The secretary is an officer of the company **(s.744);** so many of the duties imposed by company legislation on 'officers' also affect him. Thus, for example, he has to sign the annual returns and accompanying documents, and to keep an make available registers, such as the register of directors and secretary.

The secretary has the authority to bind the company for contracts connected with the administrative side of the company's affairs. In **Panorama Development Ltd v. Fidelis Ltd (1971),** the defendant company's secretary hired cars from the plaintiff ostensibly for the defendant's business, but in reality he used the car for his own purposes. It was held that the company was liable to pay for the hire charges.

(c) Auditor. The directors have power to appoint the first auditor of the company and to fill casual vacancies. An auditor so appointed holds office until the next annual general meeting where he must put himself up for re-appointment. If the company does not appoint an auditor, the Secretary of State may appoint one for the company. A person can be appointed as auditor only if he holds an appropriate qualification (e.g. a chartered or certified accountant's qualification) and if he has no connection with the company (e.g. as its employee, secretary or as a partner or an officer of the company) which would compromise his independence. An auditor may be removed from office by the general meeting or he may resign in writing. If he resigns, his resignation notice must include either a statement that there are no circumstances connected with his resignation he counsiders should be brought to the notice of the members or creditors of the company or a statement of such circumstances. Where such circumstances exist, the statement must be sent within 14 days to every member and creditor. A copy must also be filed at Companies Registry. The auditor can require the directors to convene an extra-ordinary general meeting to consider the reasons for his resignation.

The primary duty of an auditor is to report to the members on the accounts. His report must specifically state whether the accounts have been properly prepared in accordance with the Companies Act, and whether, in his opinion, they give a true and fair view. Such an opinion is a personal one; the auditor does not guarantee the accuracy of financial statements. However, he must 'bring to bear on the work he has to perform that skill, care and caution which a reasonably competent, careful and cautious auditor would use' - per Lopes LJ in **Re Kingston Cotton Mill Co (1896).** In addition, it is the auditor's duty to carry out such investigations as will enable him to form an opinion on matters such as whether adequate returns for the purpose of the audit have been received from branches not visited by him and whether he has received all the informaton and explanations which he considers necessary for the purpose of the audit.

An auditor owes his duties to the company and to the shareholders as a body, and not to individual shareholders either as shareholders or as potential investors of the company **(Caparo Industries plc v. Dickman (1990)).**

(vii) Remedies of Shareholders. It is a cardinal principle of company law that minority shareholders cannot sue for wrongs done to their company or complain of irregularities in the conduct of it internal affairs. An action on behalf of the company has to be brought by the board of directors. If the directors refuse to act , for example, because they themselves are the wrongdoers, the members in general meeting can institute proceedings as long as a special resolution is passed at the meeting to bypass the directors. This is known as the ***Rule in Foss v. Harbottle (1853).*** In **Pavlides v. Jensen (1956)**, a minority shareholder brought an action against the company's directors alleging that as a result of their negligence in undervaluing the company's land during the sale of it to outsiders, the company suffered a loss. The court held that an action was not maintainable because the proper plaintiff was the company itself, and not members individually; and as the sale was *intra vires* and no fraud was alleged; it could be ratified by the company in general meeting.

The ***Rule in Foss v. Harbottle*** is subject to some common law exceptions. An individual member can apply to the courts for an injunction to prevent the directors from performing acts which are *ultra vires* the company. Also wrongful acts which require the approval of more than a simple majority to make them valid, such as the passing of a special resolution, cannot be ratified. In **Baillie v. Oriental Telophone Co (1915)**, directors wished to increase their fees, and called a meeting at which a special resolution was required. Although the correct majority was obtained, the notice of the meeting was insufficient. The court allowed a member to institute legal proceedings to prevent the directors from acting on the resolution. Again, a member whose personal rights have been infringed or are about to be infringed by the company under majority control may bring an action to enforce those rights **(Pender v. Lushington).** Finally, acts by the majority who control the company are not ratifiable and legal proceedings may be brought by individual members, if those acts amount to fraud on the minority. 'Fraud' means improper motive and not just common law deceit.

The following are examples of fraud on the minority: expropriation of the company's property; expropriation of other members' property; an issue of shares to harm the minority; and a negligent act by the majority which benefits them at the expense of the minority. In **Daniels v. Daniels (1978)**, the company, which was controlled by its directors (husband and wife), bought land for £4,250 and later resold it at the same price to the lady director. She resold it for £120,000 five years later. In an action by a minority member against the directors for gross negligence, the company argued that since the minority was not alleging fraud by the majority no action could be brought on behalf of the company to recover the loss because of the rule in **Foss v. Harbottle**. However, Templeman J held that the action would be allowed since negligence by the directors and controlling shareholders resulted in one of them obtaining a benefit from it, and this was fraud in the wider sense.

The action brought by an individual member under the above exceptions may take the form of a *derivative action,* a *personal action* or a *representative action*. It is a *derivative action* where the wrong is done to the company. This allows the member to sue on behalf of the company to enforce rights derived from it. However, the courts will insist that the member should satisfy certain procedural requirements, such as, that the wrong should involve some element of fraud on the company; the defendants and their friends must be in control of the company; the company must be made nominal defendant with the wrongdoers in order to be bound by the judgement; and it must be in the interest of justice to dispense with the general rule requiring suit by the company. It is a *personal action* where a member wishes to assert his own rights against the company; and it is a *representative action* where the wrong is done to the member and others by those controlling the company. A *representative action* enables members to associate together and pool resources to bring the action in the name of a member. They will all share in the proceeds, and the costs will be reduced accordingly.

The Alternative Remedy. Section 459 allows a member to petition the courts for relief on grounds that the company's affairs are being or have been conducted in a manner which is unfairly prejudicial to the interest of it members generally or to the interest of some of the members (including the petitioner) or alternatively, that some actual or proposed act or omission of the company is or would be so prejudicial.

This section is used to obtain relief by an aggrieved member and is an alternative to a petition to wind up the company on the *'just and equitable'* ground under **section 122 (1)(g) of the Insolvency Act** because of fraud or oppression. The courts can grant any relief including an injunction against the wrongdoers, an order requiring the company or the majority shareholders to purchase the petitioner's shares, an order regulating the company's affairs in future, and an order authorising the petitioner to start a derivative action on behalf of the company.

The term 'unfairly prejudicial' is not statutorily defined. It includes isolated acts or omissions which are discriminatory to minorities, such as where a misleading letter is sent by the chairman of the company urging members to accept an offer in which they, the directors, have a financial interest while ignoring a much more favourable alternative offer **(Re A Company (No. 008699 of 1985) (1986)).** The petitioner must be unfairly prejudiced in his capacity as a member and not in any other capacity, such as a director. In **Elder v. Elder & Watson (1952)**, the petitioners who were members and former employees were refused the alternative remedy because they were petitioning over their dismissal from employment by the company. In considering whether conduct is unfairly prejudicial to the petitioner, the petitioner's own bad conduct in relation to the company is ignored **(Re London School of Electronics Ltd (1986)).**

(viii) Public Regulation of Companies. There are various bodies which seek to regulate companies, such as, the Council of the Stock Exchange which lays down rules for the admission of securities to be dealt with on the Stock Exchange (such rules are legally enforceable under the Financial Services Act); the Securities and Investment Board set up under the Financial Services Act to grant recognition to specific self-regulatory organisations so as to enable their members to carry on investment business; and the Financial Report Review Panel set up under the Companies Act 1989 to make application to the courts in respect of corporate accounts which do not meet the requirements of company legislation. However, by far the most important regulatory body is the DTI which regulates commerce in the United Kingdom. The DTI carries out tasks mainly by way of investigations and by consenting to prosecutions for insider dealing.

The DTI has statutory powers to investigate both the affairs of the company and the ownership of the company. It *may* investigate the company if it suspects that the company's affairs are being carried on in a manner which is likely to be prejudicial to members or fraudulent to the creditors, or if the board of directors is in breach of its duty or if it has been withholding information **(s.432).** It *must* investigate the company's affairs if minorities holding at least ten per cent of the company's issued share capital, or at least 200 members request it and justify their application**(s.431).** The applicants may have to deposit a security for costs. The DTI can also investigate the ownership of shares in, or debentures of, a company if it has good reasons to do so **(s.442)** and minorities can compel it to do so (unless their request is vexatious) by satisfying similar conditions to those under section 431. The investigation is carried out by inspectors who have wide statutory powers. On the inspectors' findings, the DTI may institute civil proceedings in the company's name; or petition for the winding up of the company; or for some other remedy for unfair prejudicial conduct; or for a disqualification order against the directors.

Insider dealing. This arises when a person who by virtue of his connection with the company knowingly uses unpublished price-sensitive information to buy or sell the company's shares (or shares of another company with which his company has been negotiating) in open market. The Criminal Justice Act 1993 prohibits this kind of dealing by insiders. 'Insider' is limited to individuals, not companies. It includes not only directors but also other officers (such as the secretary and the auditor), employees professional advisers and public servants (e.g. officers of regulatory agencies) whose relationship with the company is such that they would be expected reasonably to have access to confidential corporate information.

The Act prescribes three ways in which the offence of insider dealing can be committed, namely, if the individual **deals** in the price-sensitive securities; if he **encourages** another person to deal in the securities; and if he **discloses** the information to another person otherwise than in the proper performance of the function of his employment, office or profession. It is a defence to the dealing and encouragement offences that the individual did not expect the dealing to result in a profit or the avoidance of a loss; or had reasonable grounds to believe that the information had been disclosed widely enough that those dealing without the benefit of it would not be prejudiced; or would have done what they did whether or not they had the information. It is a defence to the disclosure offence that the individual did not expect anyone to deal upon disclosure of the price-sensitive information.

The Criminal Justice Act does not contain any civil remedies, only criminal penalties.

Chapter 13

Employment Law

Introduction

Employment law regulates the relationship which arises when one person supplies his services to another for a payment. This relationship is based on contract between the two parties. The contract may take one of two forms. It may be a contract *for* service where the person supplying the service is called an 'independent contractor' and where the employer is not generally liable for his torts, nor is he liable to him under the unfair dismissal and redundancy provisions, for national insurance contributions, and for common law duties similar to those implied in a contract in favour of employees. Or it may be a contract *of* service where the person supplying the labour is called an 'employee', worker or servant and it is this type of contract which we will be considering.

Various pieces of legislation also affect the employment relationship, much of this legislation aimed at protecting employees where the common law has failed as an adequate means of control over the economically stronger contractual party. Such pieces of legislation include the anti-discrimination statutes, and the Employment Rights Act 1996.

I The Contract of Employment

(I) Identifying the Contract

The courts have developed three main tests to determine whether a contract of service exists: (a) the **control** test; (b) the **organisation** test; (c) the **multiple** test.

(a) The Control Test. This test states that a person is employed under a contract of service if the employer controls the manner in which the work is done. This test is very useful in identifying a simple contract of service involving unskilled labour (as with domestic servants) but not where the worker has some degree of independence (as with airline pilots).

(b) The Organisation Test. Also known as the 'integration' test, this test was expounded by Lord Denning in **Stevenson, Jordan Harrison Ltd. v. Macdonald & Evans (1952)** when he said 'under a contract of service a man is employed as part of the business and his work is done as an integral part of the business, whereas under a contract for service, his work although done for the business is not integrated into it but is only accessory to it.' This test has its usefulness where the person employed is highly skilled. Thus in **Cassidy v. Min. of Health (1951)** full-time medical staff of a hospital were held to be employees even though they had a certain degree of independence in doing their work, with the result that the hospital was vicariously liable for their negligence. The organisation test has its weakness in that it fails to take into account cases where an employee is required to provide some of his tools and where he is paid on a productivity basis.

(c) The Multiple Test. Also known as the 'mixed' test it states that in order to determine whether a contract of service exists, several factors have to be considered: the employer's power to appoint and dismiss, the manner of payment of wages, the right to control the method of doing the work, whether the worker has invested his tools with a view to make a profit or risk a loss, and what the contract says. This test allows the courts to determine the economic reality of the situation and it was used in **Ready Mixed Concrete Ltd. v. Ministry of Pensions & National Insurance (1968)** where lorry drivers as a condition of employment were required to purchase their employers' lorries on hire purchase terms and, at their own costs, to maintain them and were paid on a piecework basis over and above guaranteed minimum earnings. They had to pay their own tax and national insurance contributions. The court held that they were independent contractors despite the fact that they were required to wear the company's uniform and had guaranteed earnings.

The multiple test has been used in recent years in connection with persons supplied by employment agencies and the like on a temporary basis with the result that such persons are classified as employees of the agencies, employees of the clients, or independent contractors.

(ii) Characteristics of the Contract

The general principles of contract law apply to contracts of employment.

(a) Agreement. There must be an agreement on the essential terms. However, not all the essential terms have to be decided by the parties themselves. A great many are made through collective bargaining between employers and trade unions and incorporated in the employee's contract through agency rules (i.e. the union as an agent of its members), and by express incorporation (e.g., a job applicant being employed on terms set out in the staff handbook which invariably includes collective agreements). Certain terms (e.g., equal treatment between a man and a woman) are implied by legislation and cannot be excluded.

(b) Form. In general no particular form is required for the contract; but if an employee does not have a written contract, he must be given a **written statement** of his main terms of employment not later than two months after his employment commences **(s.1 ERA).**

(1). The Written Statement. All employees normally working for at least eight hours a week are entitled to it provided that they have been in employment for at least four weeks continuously with their employer. However, certain categories of employees, such as registered dock workers. merchant seamen, persons employed by their spouses, and persons working outside Great Britain (unless temporarily) are not entitled to it.

The written statement must include the name of the parties, the date when the employment commenced, whether any period of past employment is to be counted towards the present employment (this is important for redundancy and unfair dismissal), the rate or scale of remuneration or the method of calculating it, provisions (if any) for sickness and sick pay, holidays and holiday pay, pension rights, any collective agreement directly affecting the terms and conditions of employment, (for temporary employees) the expected date when the employment is to end, and where the employee is required to work outside the UK for more than one month the length of period and the currency in which he is to be paid. If not included in the written statement, the employer must attach to it a note specifying any disciplinary powers he may wish to rely on, and grievance procedures.

The written statement is only evidence of the contract so that it may be contradicted **(Owens v. Multilux Ltd. (1974)).** If the employer fails to provide the employee with a written statement of his terms of employment, the employee must go to an industrial tribunal for a declaration as to his contractual rights. A written statement supplied to the employee by the tribunal has contractual effect and so it cannot later be contradicted by the parties.

Where the terms of the contract are varied (either by agreement or because the employer reserves power in the contract to vary the terms unilaterally and that power is exercised reasonably) the employer must give the employee written notice of the change within one month.

(2). Itemised payslip. Every employee is entitled to one. It must set out his gross and net pay, fixed and variable deductions and the reasons for them. An employer who fails to provide one or who does not provide one in the prescribed form is liable in damages to the employee **(Davis v. Roath Labour Club (1978)).** The amount of damages is equivalent to the value of the deductions subject to a maximum of 13 weeks deduction.

(c) Consideration. The consideration provided by the employer for the employee's service is called 'wages' or 'salary'. It may take the form of a lump sum, and even payment in kind (e.g. food and lodging). The Employment Rights Act permits the employer to pay wages directly into the employee's bank account, or by cheque, postal or money order and this can be done without having to obtain the employee's prior written consent.

Although common law does not require consideration to be adequate, various pieces of legislation tend to set a minimum wage for employees. Thus an employee who has contractually agreed to take a low wage may nevertheless claim to be underpaid under the various anti-discrimination statutes. These include:

(1) **The Equal Pay Act 1970.** It implies an equality clause in a contract requiring equal treatment in terms of pay, holiday, sick pay and other contractual provisions between a man and a woman in the same employment and doing similar work or work given equal value under a job evaluation exercise undertaken by the employer or an industrial tribunal. The Act does not cover any special treatment accorded to a woman in connection with pregnancy or childbirth. Moreover it is a defence for the employer to show that the less favourable treatment is genuinely due to a material difference (other than sex) between the two employees (e.g. skills, experience, qualifications, market forces).

The provisions of the Act may be enforced by an individual civil action in an industrial tribunal either during the employment or within six months of leaving the job. However arrears of pay can only be recovered for the two years preceding the date of reference to the tribunal.

(2) Treaty of Rome, Art 119. The Article requires 'equal pay for equal work' between men and women. 'Pay' includes pensions directly paid by the employer **(Barber v. Guardian Royal Exchange Assurance Group ECJ (1990)),** but the work must be identical and not just broadly similar as with the Equal Pay Act. The comparison may be made between an employee presently employed and one formerly employed by the employer to do the same work. In **Macarthys Ltd. v. Smith (1980),** a stockroom manageress who was paid £50 a week claimed that her male predecessor had been paid £60 a week to do the same work. Her claim under the Equal Pay Act failed because, under the Act, the comparison had to be made between employees presently employed; however, her claim under Article 119 succeeded.

(iii) Restrictions on Freedom to Contract

When considering job applicants for work, an employer has to take account of the various anti-discrimination statutes. The Race Relations Act 1976 makes it unlawful for him to discriminate between job applicants and/or in their terms and conditions of employment on grounds of race, colour, nationality ethnic or national origin. The Act does not cover discrimination in employment in private households; nor does it cover discrimination on grounds of religion unless the religious factor was a distinctive characteristic of a racial group (as in **Mandla v. Lee (1983)** where a 'no turban' requirement at a private school was held to be indirect discrimination against a 13 year old Sikh boy). It is a defence under the Act to show that the race requirement is a genuine occupational qualification for the job (e.g. as in the employment of Chinese waiters in a Chinese restaurant).

The Sex Discrimination Act *1975* makes it unlawful to discriminate in employment on grounds of sex or marital status. Thus to refuse to employ a woman because she might become pregnant or because she is pregnant is unlawful direct discrimination. However to refuse to employ a pregnant woman because she will be unable to carry out the work might not be unlawful. The comparison has to be made between her treatment and that of a man who would be unavailable at the critical time, whether for medical or other reasons. (c.f. **Webb** v. **EMO Air Cargo (UK) Ltd. 1992).** The Sex Discrimination Act does not cover discrimination on grounds of pay. It is a defence to show that the sex status of the person is a genuine occupational qualification for the job, for example, for reasons of decency or privacy (as in the case of a single sex establishment such as schools and prisons) or for reasons of physiology (as in the employment of a model). Furthermore, trivial acts of discrimination are ignored. In **Peake v. Automotive Products Ltd. (1977),** a male employee complained that he had been discriminated against by his employers because they had allowed his female colleagues to leave five minutes earlier than men to avoid the rush at the rush at the factory gates. The Court of Appeal dismissed the complaint as being too trivial to be unlawful.

Both the Race Relations Act and the Sex Discrimination Act cover three types of discrimination; **direct discrimination** (i.e. refusing to employ the job applicant because of his race or sex); **indirect indiscrimination** (i.e. imposing an unreasonable condition for the job knowing that the likelihood of the applicant and his race or sex being able to satisfy the condition is significantly smaller than other job applicants); and **discrimination by victimisation** (i.e. refusing to give the applicant a job because he had previously complained to a tribunal that his former employer had breached the anti-discrimination statutes). In **Price v. Civil Service Commission (1978)** it was held to be indirect discrimination against women, for the Civil Service to impose an age limit on applicants wishing to join the service at an executive grade since women who by reason of marriage will frequently be above the upper age limits and would be disqualified.

The provisions of the two Acts may be enforced by an individual civil action for damages in an industrial tribunal. As a result of the European Court of Justice ruling in **Marshall v. Southampton and SW Hampshire Area Health Authority (No.2) (1993)** the damages may be substantial where there is a finding of unlawful discrimination on grounds of the complainant's sex. An alternative procedure exists whereby the complaint can be investigated by the Commission for Racial Equality (in the case of racial discrimination) or by the Equal Opportunities Commission (in the case of sex discrimination) with a view to obtaining an injunction. The relevant commission can also apply to the High Court for a judicial review that any decision or act of the government or arm of the government is discriminatory. in **R v. Sec. of State for Employment, ex parte Equal Opportunities Commission (1994),** the House of Lords upheld a claim brought by the EOC which alleged that the provisions of the Employment Protection (Consolidation) Act 1978 which required part-timers working for between eight and sixteen hours a week to work for five years instead of two years before they could qualify for redundancy payments and protection against unfair dismissal, discriminated against women who formed the majority of part-time workers and contravened European Union Law.

The Disability Discrimination Act 1995 requires an employer who employs a minimum number of employees (usually twenty) to employ a quota of three per cent or more handicapped persons where suitable work is available. Non-compliance with the Act can lead to a fine. However, the Act is hardly ever observed.

The Rehabilitation of Offenders Act 1974 makes it unlawful to refuse to employ a rehabilitated offender by reasons that he has a conviction which is spent. For a conviction of up to 30 days imprisonment the conviction is spent after seven years; but for a sentence exceeding 30 months, the conviction can never be spent. Where a conviction is spent there is no legal or contractual obligation to disclose the conviction. The Act does not provide any civil redress and certain employees are removed from its scope by order of the Secretary of State for Employment.

(v) Terms of Contract

The express terms of the contract will state any particular rights and duties of the parties, but there are also a number of rights and duties implied at common law and statute during the employment and these are discussed below.

(a) Duties of the Employer

(1) To pay the agreed remuneration. At common law the employer has to pay the agreed remuneration if the employee is available for work even though no work is provided or the employee is suspended from work for indiscipline. This rule is subject to a contrary intention. If the employee is unavailable for work through sickness and there is not contractual provision for sick pay, the courts usually make a distinction between hourly paid workers and salaried staff. With the former, there is a presumption that they are not entitled to remuneration if they do not work **(Brown v. Crumlin Valley Colleries Ltd. (1962)).** With the latter, there is a presumption in favour of remuneration unless the contrary is shown. In **Orman v. Saville Sportswear Ltd. (1960),** where a production manager was absent from work after a heart attack, the court implied a term that during his illness he was entitled to his wages of £30 per week together with the production bonus of £20 which he could reasonably have expected to earn had he worked.

The common law rule for payment of remuneration is itself supplemented by statutory provisions. The Employment Rights Act prohibits deductions from wages unless authorised by statute (e.g. for PAYE and national insurance) or by a term of the worker's contract or because the worker has given previous written consent. In any event deductions in respect of cash shortages or stock deficiency cannot exceed 10% of gross pay (where the employee works in the retail trade). Deductions to recover overpaid wages though, are permitted. Unauthorised deductions may result in the employer forfeiting any claim he may have against the employee. The employee can go to an industrial tribunal to recover the deductions.

An employee with four weeks continuous service who is laid off work by his employer has a statutorily implied right to be paid his remuneration. If he is laid off because there is not work available for him, then provided it is not due to a strike in the industry or he does not refuse suitable alternative work from his employer, he is entitled to guaranteed wages for up to twenty days a year **(s.28).** If he is laid off because the nature of his work constitutes a health risk (e.g. under the Health and Safety at Work Act 1974), he is entitled to be paid his full wages for up to 26 weeks whilst suspended from work **(s.64).** If instead of suspending the employee on medical grounds the employer dismisses him, the employee may bring an action for unfair dismissal though he does not have the normal two years continuous service to qualify for protection against unfair dismissal. An employee who is incapable of working because of disease or disablement is not entitled to remuneration during suspension on medical grounds; he should claim social security benefits.

A female employee with at least 26 weeks service with her employer, whether full-time or part-time, who is unable to work because of pregnancy is entitled to six weeks maternity pay at the higher rate and a further twelve weeks at the lower standard rate whilst absent. She can take her maternity leave at any time after the start of the eleventh week before the baby is due. Maternity pay at the higher rate is 90 per cent of her earnings. She also has a right to get back her job or a suitable alternative one if she was working for at least two years with the employer and satisfies further conditions (e.g. she must return to work not later than 29 weeks after child birth, she must have indicated to her employer before going on maternity leave that she intended to return to work and confirm this in writing within 14 days if her employer asked for such confirmation during the three weeks before the end of her maternity leave). She has to give the date of her intended return but the employer can postpone this date for another four weeks. An employee with less than two years service at the beginning of the eleventh week before the expected week of child birth, whether full-time or part-time, is entitled to 14 weeks maternity leave and for her contract of employment to continue unless she resigns or is dismissed **(s.71).** A pregnant employee, irrespective of her length of service with her employer is entitled to be paid her wages if she is unavailable for work because of ante-natal care **(S.55).**

(2) To indemnify the employee. The employer has to indemnify his employee for all liabilities and expenses properly incurred in the course of his employment.

(3) To provide for the safety of his employee. The employer has to take reasonable care to ensure the health and safety of his employee at work. This duty arises both in contract and tort and will be considered further under 'Occupational Safety'.

(4) To provide work. This is a negative duty on the employer in that he is under no general duty to provide work; as long as he pays the agreed remuneration, the employee cannot complain **(Turner v. Sawdon (1901)).** However, in three cases payment of wages is not enough, and the employer must provide some work: in contracts with commission or piece workers where the consideration is the agreed rate and an implied obligation to provide a reasonable amount of work **(Turner v. Goldsmith (1891));** in contracts with skilled workers where the consideration is a salary and an implied obligation to provide a reasonable amount of work to maintain skills **(Langston v. AUEW (1974))**; and with actors where the consideration is a salary together with the opportunities of becoming better known **(Marbe v. George Edwards (Daly's Theatre) Ltd. (1928)).**

(5) To provide references. This is also a negative duty on the employer in the sense that there is no legal obligation on him to give a reference or testimonial to the employee. The duty is a moral one. If the employer does give a reference it has to be accurate because if it is better than the employee deserves, and it induces some other person to employ him the employer will be liable for professional negligence to the person relying on the reference **(Hedley Byrne v. Heller & Partners (1964)).** If on the other hand, it is a bad reference the employer may be liable to the employee in the tort of defamation subject to the defence of qualified privilege. In **Spring V. Guardian Assurance plc (1994)** the House of Lords held that a duty of care was owed also to the subject of the reference, so the writer could be liable to him for professional negligence.

(6) To allow time off work. By reason of the observance of public holidays by employers. there is a duty implied by custom in an employment contract for the employer to provide for public holidays with pay. This is subject to a contrary intention. The Factories Act 1961 also requires the employer to allow his female employees and other young persons employed in a factory days off work with pay on Christmas Day, Good Friday and all bank holidays. This statutory right cannot be excluded by contract.

The Employment Rights Act requires the employer to allow his employee reasonable time off with pay to find another job if he is given notice of redundancy, and without pay to carry out his public function if he holds a specified public office (e.g. as a justice of the peace, member of a tribunal, member of a local council or of the governing body of an educational establishment). The employer has to allow an employee who is an official of a recognised trade union reasonable time off with pay to carry out his trade union duties and without pay to attend trade union activities if he is a member of such a union.

(b) Duties of the Employee

(1) To obey lawful and reasonable orders. The employee is under a duty of obedience towards his employer and must carry out all orders which are within the terms of his contract. Orders which are unlawful or wholly unreasonable need not be obeyed. In **O'Brien v. Associated Fire Alarms Ltd. (1968),** it was held that an employee who lived and worked in Liverpool was entitled to refuse an order from his employer to work in Barrow-in-Furness (some 120 miles away!). However, if there is a mobility clause in the contract of employment, the exercise of this clause by the employer is not subject to reasonableness **(White v. Reflecting Roadstuds Ltd. (1991)).** In **Pepper v.Webb (1969),** a gardener refused to put in some plants and told his employer 'I couldn't care less about your bloody greenhouse and your sodding plants.' The court held that the employer's order was reasonable and justified his action in dismissing the gardener.

(2) To be ready and willing to work. An employee will be in breach of this duty and the employer can terminate his contract if the employee withdraws his labour through strikes **(Simmons v. Hoover Ltd. (1977)).**

(3) To exercise due care and skill. In **Lister v. Romford Ice & Cold Storage Ltd. (1957),** the House of Lords held that there was an implied term in a lorry driver's employment contract that he would exercise reasonable care when going about his employer's business.

(4) To serve his employer honestly and faithfully. This is also known as the duty of fidelity and its scope is wide and far reaching. It embodies the obligation not to damage the employer's property maliciously or to misappropriate it, not to disclose confidential information unless it is in the public interest to do so (e.g., as in **Initial Services Ltd. v. Putterill (1968)** where it was in the public interest to disclose an arrangement by a former employer to maintain prices contrary to the Restrictive Trade Practices Acts); not to misuse the employer's trade secrets (for breach of this duty an action may be brought against the employee and any third party to whom the secret is given); not to accept bribes, secret commissions or gifts from third parties; and not to keep any benefit arising out of his work.

The common law rule on benefits obtained in the course of employment is particularly important in the case of inventions and copyright. An invention made by an employee during work belongs to the employer if the invention is sufficiently related to the employee's trade (as with research workers, engineering draughtsmen and directors). The invention belongs to the employer notwithstanding that the employee only exploits it after his employment ceases **(Triplex Safety Glass Co. v. Scorah 1938).** Section 40 of the Patents Act 1977 now permits the courts to apportion the benefit of an invention between the employer and employee in certain cases (e.g., if the invention is of outstanding benefit to the employer). The law on copyright is the same as with inventions. The copyright belongs to the employer if the employee made the work in the course of his employment. Where published work consists partly of material belonging to the employer, he may prevent such material from being used (as in **Stevenson, Jordan & Harrison Ltd. v. Macdonald & Evans (1952),** where an assignment undertaken by an accountant for his employer was used by the accountant for his book on business management).

The duty of fidelity also requires the employee to work only for his employer in the employer's time. However, there is no implied obligation to work exclusively for the employer. The employee may utilise his spare time as he pleases but if he uses it to work for a rival employer, his employer may prevent him from doing so if it is shown that confidential information might be disclosed. In **Hivac Ltd. v. Park Royal Scientific Instruments Ltd. (1946),** manufacturers of midget valves for hearing aids were able to obtain an injunction restraining a rival employer from employing their employee on Sundays because of the possibility of their 'know-how' being disclosed.

An ex-employee is free to go into competition with his former employer unless he contractually agreed not to do so and the restraint was reasonable or he solicited the employer's customers to transfer their business to him while he was still employed with his former employer (**Sanders v. Parry** (**1967**)).

(v) Termination of the Contract

The contract of employment may be terminated by operation of law or by the parties themselves.

(a) Termination by law. The contract automatically comes to an end on the liquidation of a company and through frustration. Frustration arises where some event occurs after the employment begins, which makes performance impossible or purposeless. Such event may include the incapacity of the employee and also when he has to serve a substantial prison sentence (as in **Hare v. Murphy Bros. (1973),** where the employee was imprisoned for 12 months). In the case of sickness, several factors have to be taken into account, such as the terms of the contract including any provision as to sick pay, the length of time the employment is likely to last in the absence of sickness, the position the employee holds in the employment, the nature of the sickness and the length of service already provided by the employee (**Marshall v. Harland & Wolf Ltd.** (**1972**)).

(b) Termination by the parties. The contract may be brought to an end by agreement, by notice, without notice, as a result of unfair dismissal and through redundancy.

(1) **By agreement.** This agreement may be implicit from the terms of employment such as where the contract is to last only for a limited period (i.e. a fixed term contract) or for the duration of the job (i.e. a task contract). Fixed term contracts for two or more years which are not renewed will amount to a dismissal for the purposes of unfair dismissal and redundancy. 'Task' contracts are not fixed term contracts for such purposes.

(2) **By notice.** At common law either party may terminate the contract lawfully by giving reasonable notice to the other party. What amounts to reasonable notice will depend on the employment in question. Generally, the more exalted the employment, the longer the period. Section 86 of the Employment Rights Act lays down minimum periods of notice, but these will not apply if a longer period is given by custom or by express agreement. An employee with at least four weeks continuous service is entitled to at least one week's notice, and after two years employment to at least two weeks notice; thereafter to an additional week for each year of continuous employment up to a maximum of 12 weeks. The employer is only entitled to one week's notice. Section 86 does not apply to certain employees (e.g., civil servants, and registered dock workers).

An employer who provides proper notice may still be liable in damages for unfair dismissal and redundancy.

(3) **Without notice.** This is *prima facie* a breach of contract, unless there are circumstances which the law regards as sufficient to justify it. Where the employer terminates the contract this is known as **summary** dismissal and if it cannot be justified, the employee may bring an action for **wrongful** dismissal. In considering conduct which justifies summary dismissal, Lord Evershed MR in **Laws v. London Chronicle Ltd. (1959)** said 'The question must be whether the conduct complained of is such as to show the servant to have disregarded the essential conditions of the contract.' In this

case, a journalist who left a meeting at the request of her immediate superior but against the orders of the chairman and was summarily dismissed, was held to have been dismissed wrongly because of the conflicting orders given to her.

(4) **Unfair dismissal** This is dismissal contrary to statute; and the action is brought in an industrial tribunal for damages. The employee must prove that he has been in continuous employment with the employer for a minimum period (at present, two years) unless he was dismissed because of his membership or non- membership of a trade union, or (in the case of a female employee) was dismissed on grounds of pregnancy, or was dismissed for carrying out legitimate health and safety activities in which case this service requirement does not apply. The employee must also prove that he was dismissed. Dismissal arises : (x) where the employer terminates the employee's contract with or without notice; or (xx) in the case a fixed term contract for two or more years, where the term expires without the contract being renewed; or (xxx) where the employee terminates his contract with or without notice in circumstances which would entitle him to do so without notice (i.e. constructive dismissal).

The 'unfairness' of the dismissal is found in the reason for the dismissal. Certain reasons are automatically unfair and the tribunal has no choice in the matter, such as where a female employee is dismissed because of a reason connected with pregnancy or where her maternity leave is ended by redundancy and the employer does not offer her alternative employment when there is a suitable vacancy; an employee dismissed for reasons of trade union membership; an employee unfairly selected for redundancy; an employee selected for dismissal on grounds of race or sex; and an employee (not just a safety representative) dismissed for legitimate health and safety activities. Some reasons are automatically fair reasons for a dismissal and the tribunal has no jurisdiction to consider whether the dismissal is unfair, namely, an employee dismissed on grounds of national security, and an employee dismissed while on strike or taking part in any other form of industrial action as long as all other employees so participating are also dismissed and none is re-engaged within three months of the dismissal. In other cases, there is only a presumption of 'unfairness' in the dismissal so that the employer can rebut it.

The employer is given five reasons under sections 98 to justify the dismissal: the employee's lack of capability (e.g. lack of academic qualification or professional competence); the employee's misconduct; redundancy; statutory grounds (e.g. restrictions imposed by the Immigration Act); and other substantial reasons (e.g. refusal of employee to accept changes in his contract as part of a business reorganisation where there is a good sound business reason for the re-organisation and the changes in the terms of the employment are the only sensible way of dealing with the problem). Unlike wrongful dismissal, where subsequently discovered reason may be relied on by the employer to justify the dismissal, with unfair dismissal the employer can only rely on the reason known to him at the time of the dismissal. Thus in **W.Devis & Son Ltd v. Atkins (1976)**, where an employer dismissed his employee for refusing to implement the employers's purchasing policy and subsequently discovered that the employee was guilty of dishonesty, the House of Lords prevented the employer from relying on the dishonesty to justify the dismissal.

An employer who is to defend successfully an action for unfair dismissal must not only show that the reason was one justifying the dismissal but also that he acted reasonably in the circumstances. Thus a dismissal for ignoring a 'no smoking' ban at the workplace will still be unfair unless the employer shows that before introducing the ban there was full consultation, clear communications, sufficient 'forewarning' and proper disciplinary procedures to enforce it. Similarly a dismissal for redundancy will be unfair unless the selection was proper, the consultation was adequate and the employee was offered alternative work if such work was available. ACAS codes of practice require the employee to be given warnings before dismissal for misconduct (depending on the gravity of the misconduct). Other established procedures at the workplace should also be followed.

An action for unfair dismissal must be brought within three months after the dismissal and the tribunal can recommend re-instatement (i.e., that the employee should be taken back on his existing contract), re-engagement (that the employee is allowed back to work but on a new contract) or award damages against the employer. The damages awarded may fall under four headings: (a) a *basic award.* Minimum two weeks' pay and calculated by the length of service (up to 20 years service) in the same way as with redundancy payments (see later). This award may be reduced if the employee's conduct contributed to his dismissal, (b) a *compensatory award* which is such sum as the tribunal considers just and equitable in all the circumstances based on the financial loss suffered as a result of the dismissal. This award may be reduced if the employee failed to take reasonable steps to mitigate his losses, (c) an *additional award* which is a form of punitive damages where the employer fails to comply with a request from the tribunal to re-instate or re-engage the employee, and (d) a *special award* which is granted where the employee is dismissed because of his membership or non-membership of a trade union and the tribunal, at the employee's request, orders re-instatement or re-engagement and the employer refuses to comply with such order.

Certain employees are not protected against unfair dismissal, These include employees who have reached retirement ages (unless they are dismissed for trade union reasons), employees employed by their spouse, employees ordinarily employed outside Great Britain, and employees under fixed term contracts for two or more years who have agreed in writing to 'contract-out' of such protection.

(5) **Redundancy.** This means that there is no work available for the employee as defined by his contract of employment. Under the State Scheme for redundancy compensation as governed by The Employment Rights Act, an employee who is made redundant and who satisfies certain conditions is entitled

to redundancy compensation from his employer; and if the employer is unable to pay the compensation by reasons of insolvency, the State will meet that payment out of the National Insurance Fund.

The employee must have been in continuous employment with his employer for at least two years and working for a minimum of 8 hours a week. The rules for determining 'continuous employment' are the same as with unfair dismissal so that continuity of service is not broken by a change in job with the same employer; engagement of the employee by an associated employer; periods of absence from work due to sickness of less than 26 weeks; stoppages due to strikes although they will reduce the number of weeks calculation of redundancy compensation (see later); and working temporarily abroad with the employer's consent for not more than 26 weeks. A change in ownership of the business from one person to another does not break the continuity of employment and rights of the employee against the old employer are preserved against the new employer **(Transfer of Undertaking (Protection of Employment) Regulations 1981).**

The employee must have been dismissed, laid off or placed on short time because of the cessation or diminution of work in order to qualify for redundancy compensation. 'Laid off' means that the employee is not provided with any paid work during a normal working week; 'placed on short time' means that the employee is provided with less than half his normal work a week. An employee who is laid off or placed on short time for four consecutive weeks or for any six of the last thirteen weeks may give notice in writing of his intention to claim redundancy compensation if there is no reasonable prospect of normal work resuming.

An employee who satisfies the above conditions may be disqualified from receiving redundancy compensation if his employer could have terminated his employment because of his misconduct (e.g., if he is dismissed for redundancy whilst on strike, as in **Simmons v. Hoover Ltd.** (**1977**)**);** and also if he unreasonably refuses an offer of suitable alternative employment by his employer. An employee who accepts alternative employment may, within four weeks of taking it, claim his redundancy payment if the new employment turns out to be unsuitable.

Certain employees are not protected by the redundancy payment provisions. These include employees over the retirement age, Crown employees and employees covered by a collectively agreed scheme exempted by order.

Redundancy compensation is assessed according to the employee's age, earnings capacity and length of continuous service in weeks. From the age of 41 to 65, the employee is entitled to one-and-a-half weeks' pay (subject to a statutory limit) for each year of completed service up to a maximum of 20 years. In other age groups similar provisions apply except that the week's pay changes (i.e., if the employee is 22 to 40 it is one week's pay a year, and if he is 21 and under, it is half a week's pay a year. Where the employee is made redundant in the year of retirement there is a reduction in his total entitlement by one-twelfth for each month of the year he has worked.

An employer has a duty to consult a recognised trade union as soon as possible which is not less than 90 days before the dismissals take effect if 100 or more employees have been made redundant within a period of 90 days or less, or 30 days if 10 or more employees are being made redundant over a 30 day period. Even if only one employee is affected the union must be consulted. Consultation involves the employer telling the union the reasons for the proposed redundancies, the number and description of the employees affected, the total number of employees of that class employed, and the proposed methods of selecting and carrying out the dismissals. Failure to consult the union may result in the union applying to an industrial tribunal for a protective award in the form of wages for the employees affected. Consultation need not take place if there are special circumstances which render it not reasonably practicable for the employer to do so (e.g. such as the employer's insolvency). The employer must also notify the Department of Employment of proposed redundancies. The notice is the same as that for trade unions. If proper notice is not given to the Department of Employment, the employer may be subject to a fine.

An action for redundancy payments must be brought by the employee in an industrial tribunal within six months of being made redundant.

II Occupational Safety

The legal protection which attempts to ensure occupational safety comes from the common law and legislation. Set standards of care are imposed by common law on employers to protect their employees from industrial injury and disease. However, these standards are based on what reasonable employers would do at any given time and so fail to meet new risks which often emerge in an industrial society. Accordingly, parliament has found it necessary to legislate in this area; the main statutory protection coming from the Health and Safety at Work Act 1974 and the Factories Act 1961.

(i) Common Law Protection

Various common law torts come into operation where industrial injury and disease result from work activities. These include the tort of negligence and strict liability.

(a) **Negligence.** An employer owes a duty to his employee to take reasonable care, so that the employee can carry on his work without unnecessary risk **(Smith v. Baker 1891).** This duty is owed to each employee individually. However, an experienced worker dealing with a familiar and obvious risk may not reasonably need the same attention or the same precautions as an inexperienced worker who is likely to be more receptive of advice or admonition. In **Qualcast (Wolverhampton) Ltd. v. Hayes (1959),** the House of Lords held that employers were not responsible in negligence to an experienced worker who was splashed on the foot with molten metal whilst not wearing protective spats. The employers had provided spats but did not order or advise the plaintiff to wear them.

An employer is under no obligation to find out any particular defect of an employee unless he ought to know of the person's particular defect. Thus, in **James v. Hepworth & Grandage (1968),** where the employers were unaware that the plaintiff worker was illiterate and could not read their notice on the use of safety equipment, the court held that they were not negligent in failing to make special provisions for him.

The employer's duty at common law extends to take proper care of his plant, equipment. premises and access thereto. The employer must provide a safe system of work. This includes care for the manner of doing the job and proper instructions to staff (e.g. warning of danger and supervision where appropriate). An employer who sends his employee to work elsewhere still owes him a duty to take reasonable care not to expose him to unnecessary risk.

(b) **Vicarious Liability** In certain circumstances the law will impose liability on one person for the torts committed by another. This is known as vicarious liability. The most common example of vicarious liability arises where there is an employer and employee relationship. In such a relationship an employer will be liable for the torts of his employee if those torts were committed within the course of employment.

An employer will be vicariously liable where his employee does an authorised act in an unauthorised manner. In **Century Insurance Co. Ltd. v. Northern Ireland Road Transport Board (1942),** an employee of the defendants, who was a petrol tank driver, was transferring petrol from a tanker when he lighted a cigarette and then threw away the lighted match which caused a conflagration, damaging the plaintiff's property. The defendants were held liable for the careless act by their driver. Intentional wrongful acts committed by an employee (e.g. assault and fraud) are not generally within the course of employment and so the employer will not be vicariously liable where the employee commits such acts. However, employees who are employed as 'bouncers' at a discotheque and employees who take reasonable steps to protect their employer's property can make the employer vicariously liable for assaults on third parties. So too can an employee who commits a fraud while acting within the scope of his actual or ostensible authority. In **Lloyd** v. **Grace. Smith & Co. (1912),** the managing clerk of a firm of solicitors was allowed to undertake conveyancing work unsupervised. He fraudulently induced the plaintiff to transfer his cottages into his name and then disposed of them for his own benefit. The House of Lords held that the firm was vicariously liable for his fraud.

Where a driver deviates from an authorised route so it can be said that he is on an entirely new and independent journey, he is regarded as being on a 'frolic of his own'. In such a case an employer will not be vicariously liable for the negligence of the employee. Whether or not an employee is on a 'frolic of his own' is a question of degree of deviation from his authorised route. In **Storey v. Ashton (1869)** an employee, after completing his deliveries, deviated from an authorised route to visit his brother-in-law. His negligence caused a road accident. It was held that he was on a frolic of his own as he was on an entirely new and independent journey which had nothing to do with his employment. But in **Williams v. A &H Hemphill Ltd. (1966)** an employee was driving some boys home and made a considerable detour because the boys wanted to follow some girl guides. The bus on which they were travelling was involved in an accident. It was held by the court that the driver was still within the course of his employment as at the time of the accident the boys were still on the bus. Lord Pearce referring to **Storey v. Ashton** said that the case may have been decided differently if, at the time of the accident, the driver was carrying some cargo belonging to his employer.

An employer will not be able to avoid liability if he expressly prohibits the mode or manner of doing an authorised act **(Limpus v. London General Omnibus (1862)).** Where, however, an employer expressly prohibits the doing of an act he may be able to avoid liability. In **Twine v. Beans's Express (1946),** a driver of a van, contrary to express instruction, gave a lift to an unauthorised person who was killed as a result of the driver's negligence. The Court of Appeal held that the employers were not vicariously liable for the driver's carelessness. The basis of the court's decision was that the driver in giving a lift to an unauthorised person was doing an unauthorised act (i.e. he was doing an act outside the scope of his employment). On the other hand, in **Rose v. Plenty (1976)** a milkman who allowed a child to ride on his milk float, even though he was prohibited by his employers to do so, was held to be acting within the course of his employment when the child was injured by the milkman's negligence because the use of the child was for the benefit of the employers' business. The Court of Appeal decided that the milkman was doing exactly what he was employed to do, namely, delivering milk; he was only doing it in an unauthorised manner.

An employer who lends his employee to another employer remains vicariously liable for the torts of that employee unless control of the employee has passed to the temporary employer. In **Mersey Docks & Harbour Board v. Coggins and Griffith Ltd. (1947),** the Harbour Board hired out a crane and driver to the defendants. The contract provided that the crane driver was to be the employee of the defendants, but the Board would continue to pay his wages and had the power to dismiss him. The House of Lords held that the Board was still the employer of the driver and so was vicariously liable for his negligence which resulted in injury to a third party.

A clause transferring liability from the permanent employer to the temporary employer even though the permanent employer retains control of the loaned employee, is to be treated as an exemption clause and as such is subject to the

provisions of the Unfair Contract Terms Act 1977 (**Phillips Products Ltd. v. Hyland** (**1987**)).

Finally, it should be noted that although an employer is not generally liable for the torts of his independent contractor, he will however be liable where strict liability is imposed by law (**Rylands v. Fletcher** (**1968**)); where the independent contractor is employed to do work on the highway; where the employer was negligent in hiring the independent contractor; and where the work is 'extra hazardous involving special danger to others' (**Sumner v. William Henderson & Sons Ltd.** (**1964**)).

(c) **Defences to negligence** The two main defences are (1) consent (*volenti non fit injuria*) and (2) contributory negligence.

(1) **Consent .**This defence operates to negate what would have been a tort committed by the defendant. It must be proved by the defendant that the plaintiff voluntarily consented to the risk of injury and agreed (expressly or impliedly) to give up his right to sue him in respect of the injury suffered. Mere knowledge of the risk is not sufficient for the defence to apply (**Dann v. Hamilton 1939**).

Due to the inequality of the relationship between employer and employee the defence of consent by an employer is unlikely to succeed where an action is brought against him by his employee. In **Smith v. Baker (1981),** an employee had worked for some time in a quarry in which it was the practice to swing large blocks of stone over the heads of the workmen. He never objected to working under such conditions even though he must have known that it was dangerous. When he was injured by a falling stone, he was able to make his employers liable; their defence of consent failed. However where the employer is not in breach of any of his duties and is only vicariously liable for his employee's breach of duty consent may be a defence. In **ICI Ltd. v. Shatwell (1965)** two employees of the defendants disregarded safety measures in the face of express prohibition by the defendants and statutory regulations. As a result one of the employees was injured whilst testing detonators. The House of Lords held that since the two employees were aware of the risk of injury by explosion the defendants could plead consent.

The defence will fail where the plaintiff acts under a legal or moral obligation **(Hayes V. Harwood *1935*).** In **Ogwo v. Taylor (1988)** a fireman suffered serious burns despite wearing protective clothing after he entered the roof space of the defendant's house to control a fire started by the defendant's negligence. Lord Bridge said that even if the defendant was to raise the defence of consent it would fail in the case of a professional fireman as it would be utterly repugnant to our notion of contemporary justice.'

Where the plaintiff sustains injury in consequence of acting in the belief that there is a real source of danger when in fact no such danger exists, the defence of consent is likely to succeed **(Cutler v. United Dairies (1933)).**

Consent is no defence to an action by a passenger against the driver of a motor vehicle for injuries suffered as a result of the driver's negligence **(Road Traffic Act 1988).**

(2) **Contributory negligence.** This is where the plaintiff and the defendant are each partly at fault for the damages the plaintiff has suffered. In such a case the damages recoverable will be reduced to such extent as the courts think just and equitable **(S.1(1) Law Reform (Contributory Negligence) Act 1945).**

Where the risk of injury is foreseeable and the plaintiff by his careless conduct exposes himself to that risk, he will be guilty of contributory negligence. In **Jones** v. **Livox Quarries Ltd. (1952)** a truck collided into the back of a traxcavator. The Court of Appeal held that it was foreseeable that the plaintiff could be injured by a vehicle colliding into the back of the traxcavator, so the plaintiff's damage was reduced accordingly.

The standard of care required of the plaintiff is that of the objective reasonable man. He will be guilty of contributory

negligence 'if he ought reasonably to have foreseen that if he did not act as a reasonable, prudent man, he might be hurt himself (per Denning L J in **Jones v. Livox Quarries Ltd.** 1952). In **Froom v. Butcher (1975)** the plaintiff whose car was involved in a collision with another car was not wearing a seat belt at the time of the accident. Had he been wearing a seat belt his injuries would have been prevented or lessened. The Court of Appeal reduced the plaintiff's damages accordingly because of his contributory negligence.

The plaintiff will not be guilty of contributory negligence where the defendant's negligence causes him to act under a real sense of danger, even though subsequently the plaintiff's course of action is proved to be wrong **(Jones v. Boyce 1816).**

Whether a child can be guilty of contributory negligence is dependent upon his or her age. In **Gough V. Thorne (1966)** Lord Denning said that 'a very young child cannot be guilty of contributory negligence. An older child may be; but it depends on the circumstances. A judge should only find a child guilty of contributory negligence if he or she is of such age as reasonably to be expected to take such precautions for his or her own safety...'

(d) **Strict liability.** The modem doctrine of strict liability for the escape of dangerous substances has its origin in the leading case of **Rylands v. Fletcher (1868)** where Blackburn J, said that 'a person who for his own purposes brings onto his land and collects and keeps there anything likely to do mischief if it escapes, must keep it at his peril, and if he does not do so is prima facie answerable for all the damage which is the natural consequence of its escape.' In that case the defendant rnillowners who had constructed a reservoir on their land, were liable for the acts of independent contractors when the water leaked and flooded a neighbour's mines.

(e) **Defences to strict liability.** The four main defences **are, consent, default of the plaintiff, act of a stranger, and act of God. Act of God** arises where an escape is caused through natural causes and without human intervention in 'circumstances which no human foresight can provide against, and of which human prudence is not hound to recognise the possibility.'

(ii) Statutory Protection

A person injured by another's breach of duty imposed by statute may be able to treat the breach as a tort giving rise to a claim for damages, subject to the following conditions being satisfied:

(1) **The Statute must allow for civil redress.** An action for damages by an injured worker will be available only if it was the intention of Parliament that there should be a civil remedy. Parliament may provide a penal (i.e. criminal) remedy in which case it is presumed that this is the only remedy unless the duty created by the statute was for the protection of a particular class of the community of which the plaintiff was a member rather than to protect the public generally. In **Groves** v. **Lord Wimborne (1898)** the court held that the duty to fence dangerous machinery under the Factories Act was designed to protect workers in a factory so that a boy working in an iron works, who was injured when his arm was trapped in unfenced cog-wheels, could recover damages under the section even though the breach also involved a fine.

(2) **The right kind of damages must be suffered.** The plaintiff must next show that he suffered the kind of injury that the statute was intended to prevent and that the duty was absolute.

(3) **The breach must have caused the injury.** If the injury would have happened even if the breach did not occur, the action will fail. In **McWilliams** v. **Arrol & Co. Ltd. (1962),** the plaintiff's husband, a steel erector fell to his death. A safety

belt would have prevented the fall but the employers did not provide one; and it was not the practice of steel erectors to wear safety belts, even on work on this type. The employers were held not liable for the deceased's death because on the evidence, it was highly improbable that he would have worn a belt had one been provided.

(a) Defences to breach of statutory duty. Consent (or *volenti*) is no defence where the duty is imposed on the employer and he has breached that duty (**Wheller v. New Merton Board Mills Ltd. (1933)).** However if the employer is only vicariously liable for his employee's breach of statutory duty, consent may be a defence **(ICI Ltd. v. Shatwell (1965)).** Contributory negligence is a defence subject to the Law Reform (Contributory Negligence) Act on the apportionment of damages. In **Uddin v. Associated Portland Cement Manufacturers Ltd. (1962),** a workman was injured during working hours where he had no authority to go, when he tried to catch a pigeon. He had leaned across a dangerous revolving shaft which was unfenced and his clothing became caught on one of the studs. The employers were held to be in breach of section 14 of the Factories Act 1961 but the damages recovered by the employee were reduced by 20 per cent for his contributory negligence.

(b) The Health and Safety at Work Act 1974. This Act only permits a penal remedy but a conviction for breach of its provisions may be used in evidence in any subsequent civil action for damages (e.g. in the tort of negligence). The Act sets up a Health and Safety Commission and a Health and Safety Executive. The function of the Commission is to improve existing health and safety statutes and it may approve and issue codes of practice which if not followed may be used in evidence in criminal proceedings. The Executive has the responsibility of enforcing the health and safety provisions.

Unlike other health and safety statutes, the Act imposes obligations not on premises but on people. It affects all persons who, by their work activities, may endanger health and safety. Thus the Act is wide enough to cover persons engaged at all stages of production.

An employer owes a duty to his employees and other persons who would be affected by his undertaking. To his employees, he is under a general duty to take steps to secure their health, safety and welfare at work. This obligation is discharged by providing, for example, a safe system of work, adequate instructions to staff, adequate supervision by competent personnel and written information of his safety policy. Safety representatives may be appointed from amongst employees and if they so request. the employer must set up a joint safety committee which will review existing safety measures and recommend improvements. To non-employees, such as members of the public, the employer must conduct his business so as to ensure that such persons are safe and not exposed to risks to their health and safety.

An employee, whilst at work. has to take reasonable care for the health and safety of himself and of others who may be affected by his acts or omissions. Moreover, he must co-operate with his employer in carrying out the provisions of the Act. Manufacturers, suppliers, installers and designers of articles used at work must ensure that the articles are so designed and constructed as to be safe when properly used. Occupiers and owners of premises used for work activities must make sure that the premises are safe in every respect.

The provisions of the Act are enforced by factory inspectors who can issue improvement notices requiring breaches to be remedied, and prohibition notices requiring work activities to cease until steps are taken to improve safety standard, and they can seize and render harmless all articles or substances which they reasonably believe can cause serious personal injury. The inspectors can prosecute offenders in a magistrates court.

(c) The Factories Act 1961. Generally the Act applies to protect all person working in a factory whether or not employed by the employer. Factory means any premises where manual labour is employed in any process for, or incidental, to making any article; or the altering, repairing, ornamenting, finishing, cleaning or washing or the breaking up or demolition or the adoption of any article for sale; or slaughtering animals or confining them prior to slaughter. The manual labour used to make the article etc. must be used for the purpose of gain. A place can only be a factory if manual labour is substantially performed there and is not incidental to the business. This is particularly important where premises are used for both manual and non-manual labour (e.g. a shop which sells wreaths and crosses and has a room at the rear to manufacture them).

General health provisions are contained in Part I of the Act (such as those relating to cleanliness, overcrowding and medical provisions).

Part II of the Act deals with fencing and other provisions. Three categories of machinery are required to be fenced: the **prime mover** (i.e. all moving parts and flywheels of any machine which provides mechanical energy from any source) must be securely fenced **(s.12)**; transmission machinery (i.e. any device such as a pulley or driving belt by which the motion of the prime mover is carried to the productive machine or appliance) must also be securely fenced unless it can be shown to be safe because of its position or construction **(s.13);** and all **dangerous parts** of all other machinery must be fenced unless they are safe by their position or construction **(s.14).** A part of machinery is dangerous if it is a possible cause of injury to anybody using it. The duty to fence a dangerous part of a machine does not extend to dangerous material in the machine. So in **Eaves v. Morris Motors Ltd. (1961)** where a workman injured his finger on a sharp, rough edge of a bolt which he was milling, the Court of Appeal held that the bolt was not part of the machine and so could not be covered by the duty to fence.

By Section 16 of the Act, all such fencing is required to be of substantial construction, regularly maintained and kept in position. This fencing is only necessary whilst the machine is in use. Apart from the fencing provisions, the other important safety provisions are that floors, passageways etc. are required to be of sound construction and properly maintained and to be kept as free from obstruction or slippery substances as is reasonably practicable (**s.28);** and that there should be safe access to every place of work as is reasonably practicable (**s.29).**

The Factories Act imposes both criminal and civil liability for breach of its provisions.

Chapter 14

Law of Tort

Introduction

Although the law of tort is extensively and largely judgemade, the courts have not given a settled judicial definition and the matter has been left to learned authors. Salmond defines a tort as 'a civil wrong for which the remedy is a common law action for unliquidated damages and which is not exclusively the breach of a contract or the breach of a trust or other merely equitable obligation.'

A tort differs from a contract in that the duties are fixed by law rather than by the parties themselves. Further, in tort, the duty is towards persons generally; in contract, it is towards a specific person or persons. Nevertheless, the same facts may create alternative liability in tort or in contract.

Each tort has its own special defences; but in addition, certain general defences apply to all torts. These general defences include **consent** (discussed more fully later); **mistake** (a mistake of law is no defence, but a mistake of fact may be, where the reasonableness of conduct is in question); **inevitable accident** (this is some external occurrence which could not have been foreseen or prevented by the precautions which a reasonable human being would have been expected to take, as in **Stanley v. Powell (1891)** where a pellet from the defendant's gun most unexpectedly glanced off a tree and accidentally hit the plaintiff); **necessity** (only available as a defence where the defendant has inflicted a small harm to prevent a greater harm for which neither the plaintiff nor the defendant was responsible, as in **Cope v. Sharp (1912)** where the defendant trespassed on an adjoining land and started a fire as a fire-break to prevent the spread of a larger fire to his employer's land); and **statutory duty** (a statute authorising an act which would normally be a tort).

Some of the most important torts will now be examined, even if only in outline.

1. Negligence

This tort will arise where the defendant by his careless conduct causes damage to person or property and the circumstance is one where the law recognises a duty to take reasonable care on the part of the defendant. Three basic ingredients are present in this tort : (a) a duty of care; (b) breach of this duty; and (c)consequential damage.

(a) Duty of Care. Whether or not a duty of care exists in a particular case is a question of law. The traditional approach has been to recognise a duty of care situation only in certain specified circumstances such as in the case of road accidents and in the course of employment. Then in **Donoghue v. Stevenson (1932),** the landmark for the modern approach, Lord Atkin introduced the neighbour principle for determining the existence of a duty of care in any given situation. This principle provides that a duty of care exists whenever there is foreseeability of harm to the plaintiff and a relationship of nearness or 'proximity' in time and space between the parties.

The neighbour principle was taken further by Lord Wilberforce in **Anns v. Merton London Council (1978),** where he propounded a two-stage test in order to determine whether or not a duty of care exists. This test is based on whether the harm suffered was reasonably foreseeable between the parties so that a *prima facie* duty of care arises, and whether there were any considerations which ought to negate, reduce or limit its scope. Such considerations refer to policy factors and they include the floodgate argument (i.e.whether by recognising a duty of care in a novel situation would lead to a 'flood' of claims in court), who is in a position best to bear the loss (this may weigh heavily against parties who are or should be covered by insurance), the judicial role of the judges to apply the law rather than to make it (especially if by making law it would be going against the trend of statutory provisions), and practical considerations which affect the day to day provision of goods and services (of particular importance in the case of the medical profession and liability for medical negligence).

The use of policy factors by the courts when deciding whether to recognise a new duty of care situation is not a new practice but has been a major consideration since **Donoghue v. Stevenson.** In **Thorne v. University of London (1966),** a student attempted to sue his examiners alleging negligence on their part in marking his examination scripts. However, the Court of Appeal refused to recognise a duty of care on the examiners, holding instead that this was a purely domestic matter of the University and for which the courts had no jurisdiction . Similarly, in **Rondel v. Worsley (1969)**,
a client attempted to sue his barrister alleging negligence in the conduct of the client's case in court. The House of Lords held that the barrister could not be sued in negligence since this would otherwise lead to numerous retrials by dissatisfied clients (this immunity for barristers does not extend to out of court matters such as pre-trial acts or omissions - **Saif Ali v. Sydney Michell (1978)**). The two-stage test changed the way in which the courts used the neighbour principle. Previously, the neighbour principle was used to recognise new duty of care situations only where there were good policy reasons for doing so. Now the courts would use the neighbour principle for

creating new areas of liability unless there were policy reasons for excluding it. The use of the neighbour principle in this way has led to a rapid expansion of new duty of care situations and thus the area of negligence.

More recently, Lord Wilberforce's two-stage test has been criticised for being too broad in placing too much emphasis on foreseeability of harm, at the expense of the nature of the relationship between the parties. The end result being that cases where liability should be excluded will now satisfy the first limb of the test. In addition, the test has been criticised for too much reliance on policy to negate the duty. Further, many senior judges have refused to use the test in cases not involving physical injury to person.

Alternative tests have been suggested to determine the existence of a duty of care in novel `situations. In **Caparo Industries plc v. Dickman (1990),** Lord Bridge offered a three-stage test based on foreseeability of harm to the plaintiff, a relationship of proximity between the parties, and the situation must be one where the courts consider it *fair, just and reasonable* to impose a duty of a given scope. Another test which has the support of some English judges is the incremental approach which requires each novel claim to be dealt with on its own merits. This approach takes the view that different claims create different problems which are not susceptible to a simple approach based only on foreseeability of harm. A claim for economic loss, for example, creates different problems from a straight forward claim for physical injury to person, so that special rules should be developed within the category in which the claim falls. The incremental approach was put forward by Brennan J. in **Sutherland Shire Council v. Heyman (1985)** where he said "It is preferable that the law should develop novel categories of negligence incrementally and by analogy within established categories, rather than a massive extension of a *prima facie* duty of care restrained only by indefinite considerations..."

The situations examined by the courts in determining whether or not a duty of care exists are well documented. A manufacturer of a product owes a duty of care to the ultimate consumer of his product, to take all precautions necessary to ensure his product is reasonably safe. Failure to do so which results in the product causing injury to person or damage to other property will render the manufacturer liable for the loss inflicted by his careless act. Such loss includes *consequential economic loss* i.e. financial loss which is the consequence of injury to person (loss of earnings) or damage to property (loss of profits). In **Donoghue v. Stevenson,** a customer bought a bottle of ginger beer for a friend. After the friend had consumed some of the ginger beer she discovered the remains of a decomposed snail in the bottle and became very ill. She successfully sued the manufacturer for negligence. Lord Atkin ruled that a manufacturer whose product is intended to reach the ultimate consumer in a form in which it leaves him with no reasonable possibility of intermediate examination owes a duty to the consumer to take reasonable care. This is the narrow ratio of **Dongohue v. Stevenson.**

If the defective product does not cause physical injury to person or damage to other property but rather damage to the product itself, so that the product has a lower value than it should or costs money to repair i.e.*defective product economic loss*, such loss is not normally recoverable under the **Donoghue v. Stevenson** principle. In **Murphy v. Brentwood District Council (1990),** the plaintiff claimed £35,000 from the council as compensation from the reduction in value of his house as a result of defects in the design which the council had approved. The action was brought under the neighbour principle, but it failed because the defects did not cause damage to other property.

The common law rule on product liability has been extended further by legislation. The Consumer Protection Act 1987 imposes strict liability (i.e. liability even though there is no breach of duty) on a producer who supplies a defective product which is intended for private use or consumption and which causes damage while in consumer use. A 'producer' is any person who manufactures or processes a defective product or who hold himself out as producing the product by putting his name or trade mark on it. A person who imports a defective product from outside the European Union can also incur liability. So too can a retailer who refuses to identify the person who supplied him with the product. 'Product' means goods (e.g. growing crops, substances and ships) and electricity, and it includes a product which is comprised in another product whether by virtue of being a component part or raw material or otherwise. It excludes a building supplied by way of a creation or disposal of an interest in land and agricultural produce which has not undergone an industrial process. A product is defective if its safety to person or property is not such as one would generally be entitled to expect. The defect may be attributable to the way in which the product is sold or packaged, as well as to any instructions and warnings given as to its use.

Part 1 of the 1987 Act imposes civil liability on the producer and it allows the wronged party to claim damages for personal injury, though damage to other property is only recoverable if the loss exceeds £275. However, economic loss (other than consequential economic loss)is not recoverable. Furthermore, the producer is provided with various defences, such as , that he did not supply the product in the course of his business or with a view to make a profit; the product was not defective when it was supplied; the defect was a result of compliance with a European obligation or domestic legislation; and that the state of the art at the time was not such that the producer of a similar product would have discovered the defect while the product was still under his control.

Liability under Part 1 does not depend on there being a contract between the producer and the consumer. If there is a contractual relationship between the parties it remains more advantageous for the consumer to bring an action under the Sale of Goods Act for breach of the implied condition as to satisfactory quality. Liability under the Sale of Goods Act is strict; it does not provide the wrongdoer with any statutory defences, and all types of economic loss are recoverable in a contract action.

There is no general duty of care for **acts** which cause *'pure economic loss'* i.e. financial loss such as loss of profit which is not a direct consequence of damage to property. In **Spartan Steel & Alloys Ltd. v. Martin & Co. Ltd. (1973),** the defendant carelessly cut through the power cable leading to the plaintiff's factory. The power was cut off for some fourteen hours which resulted in molten metal in a furnace valued at £368 being damaged. The plaintiff recovered £368 for actual damage to the metal and an additional £400 for loss of profits which would have been earned on the resale of the metal had it not been damaged (*consequential economic* loss). However, loss of general profits which would have been made had the factory not been shut down (*pure economic loss*) was not recoverable since there was no damage to the factory itself.

There are however two instances where pure economic loss has been recovered : in **Junior Books Ltd. v. Veitchi Co. Ltd (1983),** and in solicitor/beneficiary cases where the beneficiary loses a gift under a will as a result of the solicitor's negligence (**Ross v. Caunters (1980)** and **White v. Jones (1995)**). In **White v. Jones,** the House of Lords justified the courts' willingness to impose liability on solicitors for careless conduct resulting in pure economic loss to third parties on the basis that such third parties would not otherwise have any remedy against negligent solicitors. In **White v. Jones**, the solicitors were instructed by a client to change her will in favour of the plaintiff but failed to do so with the result that the plaintiff was denied a gift under the will after the client's death. The House of Lords held that the solicitors owed the plaintiff a duty of care, but not under the **Donoghue v. Steveson** principle; but rather on the basis of an assumption of responsibility by professionals to undertake a task under the **Hedley Byrne & Co. Ltd. v. Heller & Partners Ltd. (1964)** principle (see below).

There is a duty of care for **statements** which cause pure economic loss. This duty was recognised in 1964 in **Hedley Byrne & Co. Ltd. v. Heller & Partners Ltd.** which derives its status from rules based on a special relationship between the parties. In **Hedley Byrne,** a bank negligently gave a reference regarding the creditworthiness of one of its customers to an advertising firm. The House of Lords held that but for a disclaimer notice protecting the bank from liability, the bank would have been liable in negligence for losses incurred by the firm when the firm gave credit to the customer in consequence of the reference. Lord Devlin said that the duty of care imputed on the bank was the result of a special relationship which existed between the bank and the advertising firm.

There are various formulations as to what constitutes a special relationship (see, for example, Lord Oliver in **Caparo Industries plc v. Dickman (1990),** and Neill LJ in **James Mc Naughton Papers Group Ltd. v. Hicks Anderson & Co. (1991)**), the net effect being that a special relationship will exist if (1) the statement maker is a person who has or professes to have special knowledge or skill. He need not be a professional person. In **Chaudhry v. Prabakar (1989),** the Court of Appeal imposed liability on the defendant under **Hedley Byrne** even though he was not a professional, but only professed to have knowledge about motor cars after he carelessly recommended an unroadworthy car as suitable for the plaintiff to purchase from a third party ; (2) the statement maker assumes responsibility for the statement. In **Williams v. Natural Life Health Foods Ltd (1998),** the House of Lords (through Lord Steyn) said that 'assumption of responsibility' does not depend on the state of mind of the statement maker, but rather whether the recipient of the statement could reasonably conclude from the words or actions of the statement maker that the latter is assuming personal responsibility. Thus, the test of assumption of responsibility appears to be objective, rather than subjective; and (3) there is reasonable reliance on the statement by the recipient of the statement. The requirement of 'reasonable reliance' confines liability to careless statements made on a business or formal occasion, thus excluding careless statements made in a casual or off-handed way (i.e. in a situation where it is clear that what was said was not intended to be taken seriously). It also means that the statement maker must know that the statement will be relied on by the recipient of the statement. In **Spring v. Guardian Assurance plc (1994),** the House of Lords held an employer liable to his former employee under **Hedley Byrne** after he gave a careless reference about the employee to a prospective employer resulting in the employee failing to get the job he sought. Lord Goff said that there was an assumption of responsibility by the employer to the employee for the reference and reliance by the employee on the exercise by the employer of due care and skill in respect of its preparation.

The special relationship discussed above will invariably arise where the parties deal with each other directly; but it can also arise where the recipient of the statement passes on the information to a third party if that party had commissioned the statement (as in **Smith v. Eric Bush 1989)**) or if the statement was made for his benefit (c/f **Caparo Industries plc v. Dickman)** in which case a special relationship and thus a duty of care will exist between the statement maker and the third party. In **Caparo,** the plaintiffs who were relying on the annual accounts of their company made a successful take-over bid for the company. The company turned out to be less profitable than the accounts indicated; so the plaintiffs brought an action under **Hedley Byrne** alleging that the accountants had prepared the accounts negligently. The House of Lords held that even if the accountants were negligent they owed no duty of care to the plaintiffs since the accounts were intended for the benefit of the shareholders as a body and not specifically for individual shareholders. Moreover, the purpose of the audit was to comply with the provisions of the Companies Acts and not to encourage share purchase in the market or to be a guide to the making of investment decisions.

In recent years, the courts have been extending the **Hedley Byrne** principle to cover careless **acts** by professionals, so that it would appear that pure economic loss may now be recovered whenever a professional assumes responsibility for a task and performs that task carelessly. The extension of the **Hedley Byrne** principle brings into question its relationship with the *fair, just and reasonable* stage of Lord Bridge's three-stage test in **Caparo Industries plc** for a duty of care. In **Williams v. Natural Life Health Foods Ltd,** Lord Steyn said that 'once a case is identified as falling within the extended **Hedley Byrne** principle, there is no need to embark on any further inquiry whether it is *just, fair and reasonable* to impose liability for economic loss.' Stuart-Smith LJ in **W v. Essex County Council (1998)** also supports this view but only in relation to pure economic loss cases.

There is a duty of care not to cause nervous shock by careless conduct. 'Nervous shock' means recognised psychiatric injury, such as mental illness or a personality change, and not simply grief or horror or fear of harm **(Hicks v. Chief Constable of South Yorkshire Police (1992)).** In **McLoughin v. O'Brian (1983),** Lord Wilberforce set out three elements that a nervous shock claim should possess before a duty of care can exist in favour of the plaintiff.

The first element requires that the plaintiff must come within the recognised class of persons who the law will protect. The following fall within the recognised class: a person who suffers nervous shock by seeing the negligent conduct and fearing for his own safety **(Dulieu v. White (1901)**) or for the safety of his property **(Attia v. British Gas plc (1988)** **);** and a person who suffers nervous shock by reason of physical injury or peril to a third party with whom he has close ties based on love and affection (**Boardman v. Sanderson (1964)).** Third party ties based on love and affection have to be proved unless the relationship is one of parent and child, husband and wife or fiancees **(Alcock v. Wright (1991)).** A spectator or bystander does not fall within the recognised class unless he is a rescuer (**Chadwick v. British Railways Board (1967),** or he is actively involved in the activity from which the negligent conduct arises **(Dooley v. Cammell Laird & Co. (1951)),** or he has no choice in being present at the scene of the disaster (c.f. **Bourhill v. Young (1943)**) which is so horrific that even a reasonably strong-nerved person would have been so shocked (*obiter* per Lords Keith and Ackner in **Alcock v. Wright).** A primary victim (i.e. a person who fears for his own safety) can recover for nervous shock, notwithstanding that shock was not foreseeable to him and that he did not sustain any physical injury, as long as the circumstances are such that physical injury to him was foreseeable **(Page v. Smith (1995)).** However, a secondary victim (i.e. a person who fears for another's safety) can recover for nervous shock only if it was reasonably foreseeable that he would suffer from shock. Thus secondary victims who are abnormally sensitive to shock will not be owed a duty of care. In **White and other v. Chief Constable of South Yorkshire (1998),** The House of Lords indicated that even though the police and the fire services are hardened to events which can cause an ordinary person distress, this does not prevent them from pursuing claims for nervous shock.

The second element requires that the plaintiff must be in the danger zone at the relevant time or else come on the scene within the immediate aftermath. If the plaintiff goes to the danger zone or to the hospital or morgue and sees the horrific results within two hours this can be within the 'immediate aftermath' (as in **McLoughin v. O'Brian** where the plaintiff went to the hospital within two hours of a motor car accident, in circumstances which were distressing and learnt that one of her children had died and saw her husband and other children who were severely injured waiting to be attended to by the medical staff); but not if he goes some eight hours later when the victim had already been cleaned up (as in **Alcock v. Wright** where following the Hillsborough Stadium disaster, when 95 football spectators were crushed to death, the plaintiff suffered nervous shock after identifying his brother-in-law's body at the mortuary at midnight, eight hours after the accident).

The third element requires that the shock must be caused through seeing or hearing first hand the distressing event or its immediate aftermath. Hearing it through third parties is not enough **(Ravenscroft v. Rederiaktiebolaget Transatlantic (1991));** nor is seeing it through live television coverage **(Alcock v. Wright).** However, perception through television is not ruled out altogether; for instance a situation in which a live television broadcast of children travelling in a hot air balloon suddenly bursting into flames may give rise to an action (per Lords Ackner and Oliver in **Alcock v. Wright).**

There is no general duty to prevent third parties (i.e.strangers) from deliberately causing harm to another person or to his property. In **Smith v. Littlewoods Organisation Ltd (1987)**, the owners of a disused cinema carelessly left it unlocked, whereby vagrants entered the building and set light to it thus causing damage to neighbouring buildings. It was held that the owners of the cinema were not liable for the damage caused by the vagrants. Similarly, in **Topp v. London Country Bus (South West) Ltd (1993)**, the defendants left their minibus unlocked and unattended with the key still in the ignition some way from a pub. A third party stole the bus and caused an accident in which the plaintiff's wife was killed. It was held that the defendants owed no duty of care to the plaintiff's wife for the injury caused by the act of the third party as it was not reasonably foreseeable that a stranger would steal the bus since the bus was parked in a remote area.

In **Smith's** case, Lord Goff identified four instances where a duty of care for third parties' wrongful acts will be imposed. The first will arise where there is a special relationship between the plaintiff and the defendant (as in **Stansbie v. Troman (1948)**, where the plaintiff gave the defendant control of their premises to decorate it, and the defendant carelessly left the premises unattended so that a thief got in and stole the plaintiff's property); the second situation arises where there is a special relationship between the defendant and the third party (as in **Home Office v. Dorset Yacht Co Ltd (1970)**, where employees of the Home Office who were in a position of control over a group of borstal boys, carelessly failed to supervise the boys who caused damage to the respondent's yacht; the third situation will arise where the defendant presented the third party with the means to commit the wrong in circumstances where it was likely that the third party would do so (as in **Haynes v. Harwood (1935)**, where the defendants left their horses unattended in a street and a boy caused the horses to bolt thus creating a danger to members of the public. Here, the plaintiff was injured while trying to stop the horse); the final situation arises where the defendant knew that the third party was creating a danger on his property and failed to take adequate steps to abate the danger.

(b) Breach of duty. Once it has been established that the defendant is under a duty of care, the next step is to prove that he was in breach of that duty. The standard of care expected of the defendant is that of the objective reasonable man. Where he is a member of a class or group with defined skills, he is required to act as a reasonable member of that class or group (e.g. doctors or motorists). The law, however, will not create sub-classes or groups which would have the effect of producing a variable standard of reasonable care, and would mean uncertainty and difficulty in arriving at fair and consistent decisions. In **Nestleship v. Weston (1971),** a learner driver panicked and caused injury to a friend who was giving her driving lessons when the car mounted the pavement and struck a lamp post. The Court of Appeal held that the standard of care required of a learner driver was the same as the standard required from an experienced driver, the standard being that of a reasonably competent and experienced driver and that in the circumstances the learner driver was liable.

In considering how a reasonable man would have acted in the position of the defendant, the courts will take account of the following factors:

(i) *The degree of likelihood of the risk occurring.* If the risk is small then a reasonable man would not be expected to take precautions against it happening. In **Bolton v. Stone (1951)**, the plaintiff was standing on a highway and was struck by a cricket ball hit out of a cricket ground. The House of Lords held that although such an event was foreseeable the defendant was not in breach of duty, as the likelihood of injury to a person in the plaintiff's position was very slight (in thirty years, the ball had only left the ground on six occasions).

On the other hand, if the likelihood of the risk of harm occurring is great then a reasonable man would be expected to guard against it happening. In **Miller v. Jackson (1977)**, a housing estate was situated near a cricket ground. On numerous occasions during a two year period cricket balls were hit from the ground and on to the property of those living in the estate, causing damage to property. The defendant cricket club was held to be in breach of duty in not taking adequate precautions as the risk of harm to person or property was great.

(ii) *The magnitude of the risk.* If the harm to be inflicted is serious should the risk materialise, then a reasonable man will be expected to take the appropriate measures to prevent such harm occurring, notwithstanding that the risk is small. In **Paris v. Stepney Borough Council (1951)**, the plaintiff, a one-eyed welder working for the council, was completely blinded when a piece of metal flew into his eye. The plaintiff 's work involved some risk of injury to his eye but the likelihood of injury was too small to require the council to provide the other two-eyed workers with goggles. Nevertheless, the House of Lords held that the council was in breach of its duty to the plaintiff for not providing him with goggles, as it was aware of his disability and that if the risk materialised it would result in the plaintiff losing his sight altogether.

(iii) *The cost of precautions.* If the costs outweigh the benefits derived from eliminating the risk, then failure to do so would not amount to negligence. In **Latimer v. AEC Ltd (1953)**, a factory floor became slippery after heavy rain caused a flood. This in turn resulted in oil in the factory spreading over the floor. Despite the employers taking all reasonable steps to make the floor safe, it still remained slippery causing the plaintiff to slip and sustain injury. The House of Lords held that the employers were not breach of duty to the plaintiff since the risk of injury was very slight and it would be unreasonable to expect the employers to shut down the factory in the circumstances.

If the cost of precautions is small, then measures to eliminate the risk will be required to be undertaken. In **Haley v. London Electricity Board (1965)**, a hole was dug in the pavement by the defendants who warned sighted persons of the hole, but failed to take adequate measures to warn blind persons even though the cost of such measures was small. The defendants were held liable when the plaintiff, who was blind, fell into the hole and became deaf as a result.

(iv) *Emergencies.* Where the defendant is faced with an emergency the standard of care will be adjusted to take account of the dilemma in which he finds himself. In **Watt v. Hertfordshire County Council (1954),** a fireman was injured when the driver of a rescue truck braked suddenly and the jack which was in the truck fell on him.The rescue truck was not equipped to carry the jack but it was the only truck available at the time to answer an emergency, where a woman was trapped under a heavy lorry, and the jack was essential to save the woman's life. The court held that the council was not negligent because it had taken a reasonable risk in an emergency. On the other hand, in **Ward v. London County Council (1933)**, a council was held liable when the driver of one of its fire engines drove through a red traffic light when hurrying to the scene of a fire. In doing so, the driver of the fire engine collided with the plaintiff's car. Here, the emergency had to be balanced against the risk to road users.

Normally, a person who alleges that another person's conduct is below the standard of a reasonable man must prove such an inference unless the rule *res ipsa loquitur* (the thing speaks for itself) applies. This rule shifts the burden of proof from the plaintiff on to the defendant. To rely on *res ipsa loquitur* the plaintiff must show that the thing which caused the damage was under the control of the defendant and that the nature of the accident was such that it would not have occurred in the ordinary course of events without the presence of negligence (**Cassidy v. Ministry of Health (1951)).**

(c) Consequential damage. Even though the defendant is in breach of duty, he will not be liable unless the damage suffered by the plaintiff is the result of his breach (*causation in fact*) and the damage is not too remote (*causation in law*).

(1) *Causation in fact.* The 'but for' test is generally employed by the courts that requires the plaintiff to prove on

the balance of probabilities that the defendant's breach caused the damage he has suffered (or materially increased the risk of the damage occurring). If the damage would have occurred regardless of the breach the defendant will not be liable. In **Barnett v. Chelsea & Kensington Hospital (1969)**, a night porter died of arsenic poisoning after the defendant hospital failed to give him proper medical attention. The hospital was able to avoid liability by proving that the porter's death was not caused by their failure to examine him, as he would have died anyway.

Where damage to the plaintiff is attributable to successive causes the decisions of two cases must be considered. In **Baker v. Willoughby (1970)**, it was held that the defendant will be liable where his own negligence causes injury to the plaintiff and the supervening act is a crime or a tort. In the case itself, the plaintiff suffered leg injuries from a road accident due to the defendant's negligence. The injuries affected his mobility and his earning capacity. Before the trial, the plaintiff suffered a second injury to the same leg when he was shot in a robbery, resulting in amputation of the leg. The defendant argued that his liability to the plaintiff had diminished by the supervening event. However, the House of Lords rejected this argument. Lord Reid stated that the plaintiff was not being compensated for the injury itself but the loss he had suffered as a result of the injury. Thus, the shooting had not diminished the plaintiff's pain and suffering or the loss of his earning capacity.

Conversely, in **Jobling v. Associated Dairies (1982)**, it was held that the liability of the defendant would be reduced if the supervening event is the consequence of a physical disability which occurs independently of the negligence. In the case itself, the plaintiff suffered injury as the result of the defendants' breach of statutory duty which affected his earning capacity. Before the trial, the plaintiff was found to be suffering from a crippling disease totally unconnected to the defendant's tort which prevented him from working altogether. The House of Lords held that the defendants were only liable for the reduction in the plaintiff's earning capacity up to the time he became incapacitated by the disease.

Liability of the defendant is limited where part of the damage resulting from his breach was caused by intervening independent acts (*Novus actus interveniens*).

There are three categories of *novus actus interveniens*:

(a) **Intervening act of nature.** Where an intervening act of nature occurs independently of the defendant's breach and causes damage, then generally the defendant will not be liable. In **Carslogie Steamship Co. v. Royal Norwegian Govt. (1952)**, the plaintiffs'' ship was caught in a storm while at sea and was extensively damaged. The ship would have been able to avoid the storm if it had left the port earlier, but it was delayed in port for repairs after an earlier accident caused by the defendants' negligence. The plaintiffs sued the defendants to recover the costs incurred for the repairs caused by the storm damage. However, the House of Lords held that the defendants were not liable for such damage because the storm had broken the chain of causation.

(b) **Intervention of the plaintiff.** The defendant will not be liable where the further damage suffered by the plaintiff is the result of his (i.e.the plaintiff's) own intervention in terms of his careless conduct which breaks the chain of causation **(McKew v. Holland (1964)).**

(c) **Intervention of a third party**. The defendant will not generally be liable for damage caused by the intervening act of a third party unless the defendant's negligence causes the third party to act involuntarily **(Scott v. Shepherd (1733)).**

(ii) *Causation in law.* In addition to the requirement that the damage suffered by the plaintiff must be the result of the defendant's breach, the plaintiff must also show that the damage is not too remote. The damage will not be too remote if it is foreseeable that that kind of damage would result from the breach. In **The Wagon Mound (No.1) (1961),** the defendants negligently discharged oil into the sea. The oil spread to the plaintiffs' wharf where wielding operations were being carried out; it ignited and caused damage to the plaintiffs' wharf and ships. The Privy Council held that the defendants were not liable for the damage because damage by fire was not foreseeable (at the time, it was not known that oil could ignite on water).

Once the kind of damage the plaintiff has suffered is foreseeable, it is irrelevant that the extend of the damage was not foreseeable. This is because of the 'egg-shell skull' rule which states that the wrongdoer must take the victim as he finds him. In **Smith v. Leech Brain & Co Ltd (1962),** the deceased, a labourer, worked with molten metal and was not supplied with any safety equipment, such as a shield, from his employers. As a result of a colleague's negligence, he was burnt on the lip by molten metal. It was found that the deceased had a disposition to cancer and that the burn was a causal factor in triggering off his death from cancer. It was held that his employers, were liable for his death as injury from burns was foreseeable.

As long as the damage is foreseeable it does not matter that the manner of its occurrence is not foreseeable. In **Hughes v. Lord Advocate (1963),** a manhole was carelessly left uncovered by employees of the Post Office with only a canvas shelter over it and lighted paraffin lamp placed around it. A young boy who was held not to be a trespasser knocked one of the lamps into the manhole. The lamp exploded and the boy was severely burned. The court held that the Post Office was liable as burns from the lamp was a foreseeable cause of the injury, and it was not important that the events leading to the injury was unforeseeable i.e. it was not foreseeable that a lamp could explode.

Defences to Negligence. The specific defences to negligence, namely contributory negligence and consent, have been fully dealt with in Chapter 13. So too was the doctrine of vicarious liability.

II Liability for Defective Premises

An occupier of premises is under a duty of care towards persons who come on to his premises. This duty is imposed by statute, namely, the Occupiers' Liability Acts 1957 and 1984. The 1957 governs the liability of an occupier where the person who comes on his premises is a visitor (i.e. he is on the premises lawfully), and the 1984 Act where the person on premises is a trespasser.

An occupier is any person who has a sufficient degree of control over the premises to put him under a duty of care towards those who come lawfully on to them. He need not be the owner of the premises. It is possible for there to be more than one occupier of the premises. 'Premises' means any fixed or moveable structure including any vessel, vehicle or aircraft.

By virtue of section 1 (2) of the 1957 Act, a visitor is any person who is on the premises with the occupier's permission. If the visitor has been given express permission, such permission may be limited by time, space or purpose. Therefore a visitor who exceeds his limited permission becomes a trespasser. A person may also have the implied permission of the occupier to be on the premises. It remains a question of fact whether a person has such implied permission. In **Robson v.**

Hallett (1976), the court held that a person who enters premises for the purpose of communicating with the occupier is regarded as having the occupier's implied permission to be on the premises. However, once the occupier has made it clear to the visitor that permission to be on the premises has been revoked, the visitor will become a trespasser if he does not leave the premises within a reasonable time. Further, the occupier's knowledge of unauthorised persons regularly entering his premises is not sufficient to make them visitors with the occupier's implied permission. This is so unless positive steps have not been taken by the occupier to let them know that they are not permitted on the premises. Such steps could take the form of a notice stating '*no canvassers, hawkers, or circulars*', or as in **Edwards v. Railway Executives (1952)** by repairing fences whenever children break them to gain access to the occupier's premises.

The 1957 Act provides that an occupier of premises owes a 'common duty of care' to all his visitors. Thus he is required 'to take such care as in all the circumstances of the case is reasonable to see that the visitor will be reasonably safe in using the premises for the purposes for which he is invited or permitted by the occupier to be there' **(s.2 (2)).** The courts will consider various factors as laid down in the 1957 Act to determine whether the occupier has discharged his common duty of care, in particular the degree of care to be expected from the visitor as well as the nature of the danger.

The Act provides that the occupier must be prepared for children to be less careful than adults. Where a professional is employed to come on the premises to do work of a specific nature, the occupier can expect that person to guard against any special risks ordinarily incidental to the work **(s.2 (3)(b)).** In **Roles v. Nathan (1963),** two chimney sweeps were killed by fumes while attempting to seal up a sweep hole in the chimney of a coke-fired boiler while the boiler was still alight. The court held that the occupier was not liable for the deaths. Lord

Denning said 'when a householder calls in a specialist to deal with a defective installation on his premises, he can expect the specialist to appreciate and guard against the dangers arising form the defect.'

The 1957 Act also makes provision for defence whereby the occupier may be able to avoid liability by showing that he is covered by one of the defences under the Act. It is a defence for the occupier to warn the visitor of the danger on the premises, though such a warning will only absolve the occupier's liability if it is sufficient to make the visitor reasonably safe **(s.2 (4)(a)).** It is a defence for the occupier to show that the damage suffered by the visitor was the result of the faulty execution of structural work to the premises by an independent contractor. Such a defence, however, will be based on the occupier showing that he had acted reasonably in entrusting the work to the independent contractor and had taken steps to ensure that the contractor was competent and thus doing the work properly. The occupier will not be liable to a visitor for any loss which results from a risk voluntarily undertaken by the visitor. The occupier may plead contributory negligence where the occupier is in breach of his common duty of care to the visitor and the visitor himself is careless of his own safety. In the last resort and subject to the Unfair Contract Terms Act (in relation to business liability), the occupier may exclude his liability to the visitor by a contractual or non-contractual notice.

The Occupiers' Liability Act 1984 requires an occupier to give a trespasser such protection as is reasonable in all the circumstances of the case if the occupier is aware of the danger and has reasonable grounds to believe that the trespasser is in or may come within the vicinity of the danger **(s.1 (3)).** The occupier can discharge this duty by taking reasonable steps to warn of the danger or to discourage persons from taking the risk **(s.1 (5)).** Unlike the 1957 Act where the loss recoverable by visitors extends to damage to property as well as personal injury, trespassers are only protected under the 1984 Act for personal injuries.

III Defamation

Defamation means the publication of a statement which tends to lower the plaintiff in the estimation of right thinking members of society generally or which brings him into hatred, ridicule or contempt or which tends to make such people shun or avoid him. Defamation may take two forms : libel and slander. Libel is a defamatory statement in a permanent form (e.g. in writing or as in a picture or on stage). Slander is a defamatory statement published in a transient form (e.g. in speech or by gestures).

Generally the two torts are governed by the same rules but libel can also be a crime if the statement tends to provoke a breach of the peace. Libel is always actionable without proof of special damage. 'Special damage' means loss which is capable of being estimated in money (e.g. loss of hospitality; but not loss of friendship). Slander is only actionable on proof of special loss unless the slander imputes that the plaintiff has committed a criminal offence punishable with imprisonment; or is unfit to carry on this trade or profession; or suffers from a contagious or infectious disease; or (in the case of a woman)is of loose morals.

To establish a claim for defamation, the plaintiff must show three things : (a)the statement is defamatory; (b) it refers to the plaintiff; (c) the statement was published.

(a) **Defamatory statement.** The statement is defamatory only if it causes the plaintiff's reputation to suffer in the eyes of right thinking members of society. So even though an allegation that the plaintiff has reported his club for illegal gambling may result in the plaintiff being thought less well of by members of the club, the statement would not be defamatory because it would not be so regarded for a 'good and worthy subject of the king to report a crime (**Byrne v. Deane** (**1937**)). The views of the average 'good and worthy subject of the king' may change with the passing of time. In **Shaw v. Akram (1981)**, it was held to be defamatory to say that the plaintiff had insulted the Muslim religion. However, a light-hearted comment is not likely to be construed as defamatory. Nor is a statement made in the heat of the moment. In **Fields v. Davies (1955),** the defendant called the plaintiff, a married woman, 'a tramp'. The court held that it was not defamatory but mere vulgar abuse as it was so unsuited to be construed as otherwise by those who heard it, considering the obvious temper of the defendant at the time.

Where it is not obvious from the words themselves that the statement is defamatory, the statement may be defamatory because the words have a latent and secondary meaning which is defamatory (a *false innuendo*) or because the words are combined with extrinsic facts known only to the persons to whom the statement is communicated, making the statement defamatory (a *true innunendo*). An innunendo must be specifically pleaded and proved by the plaintiff. In **Tolly v. Fry & Sons Ltd (1931),** the defendants included a cartoon of the plaintiff, a well known amateur golfer, in an advertisement for chocolate. This was done without the plaintiff's consent. The plaintiff alleged that the advertisement was defamatory because it implied that the plaintiff was prostituting his amateur status, by accepting payment for the use of his name and photograph. The House of Lords held that the advertisement was capable of being so construed as explained by evidence from fellow golfers who testified for the plaintiff that they believed that he had compromised his amateur status.

In **Lewis v. Daily Telegraph Ltd (1964),** the plaintiff alleged that a headline in the defendants' newspaper which read

'Fraud Squad Probe City Firm' (which was factual) was defamatory because it implied that the plaintiff was suspected of fraud by the police. However, the court held that the words were not in their ordinary meaning defamatory; and as the plaintiff did not plead additional facts to establish defamation by innunendo, his action failed.

It is no excuse, subject to the defence of innocent publication (see post), that the defendant was unaware of the extrinsic facts which made an innocent statement defamatory. In **Cassidy v. Daily Mirror (1929),** the defendants published a picture of the plaintiff's husband and a young woman with a statement that they had been engaged. This information was supplied to the defendants by the plaintiff's husband. The plaintiff argued that the photograph and the statement contained an innunendo to those who knew her that she was not married to her husband and was accordingly, 'living in sin' with him. The court held that the report in the paper was capable of being so construed as explained by evidence from the plaintiff's friends who said that they were given that impression.

(b) **Reference to plaintiff.** This requirement is satisfied if the plaintiff is referred to by name, and it makes no difference that the defendant intended to refer not to the plaintiff but to a third party to whom the statement was true or to a fictitious person. In **Newstead v. London Express Newspaper Ltd (1940),** the defendants published a statement that 'Harold Newstead, a thirty year old Camberwell man' had been convicted of bigamy. This was true of Harold Newstead, a self-confessed bigamist, but untrue of the plaintiff who had the same name, about the same age and also lived in Camberwell. The court held that the plaintiff could recover damages for the defamation. Similarly in **Hulton v. Jones (1910),** the defendant published a humorous article describing immoral conduct of one Artemus Jones. The article was intended to be fictitious but friends of the plaintiff, a barrister, thought that the article referred to him. The House of Lords held that as reasonable people believed that the article referred to the plaintiff, he could recover damages.

If the plaintiff is not referred to by name he can still sue as long as the statement refers to him by implication **(Morgan v. Odhams Press Ltd (1971)).** If the defamatory statement refers to a class which is large,then in general no member of that class can sue unless he can show that the defamation was particularly referable to him.

Where the statement is published innocently, the defendant may avoid liability to pay damages if he is willing to make an offer of amends **(s.4 Defamation Act 1952).** An *offer of amends* means an offer to publish a suitable correction and apology and to meet the plaintiff's costs and expenses reasonably incurred as a result of the publication. The statement is published innocently if either the publisher did not intend the statement to refer to the plaintiff and had no reason to believe that it might refer to him (as in **Newstead v. London Express Newspapers Ltd**); or the words were not defamatory on the face of them and the publisher did not know of the circumstances where they might be understood to be defamatory of the plaintiff (as in **Cassidy v. Daily Mirror**). If the offer is refused then the publisher has a defence if he proves that the statement was published innocently, that the offer was made as soon as possible and, if the publisher was not the author of the statement, that he statement was written by the author without malice.

(c) **Publication by the defendant.** This means communicating the defamatory statement to a person other than the plaintiff himself or the defendant's spouse. If the recipient does not understand the statement or realise that it refers to the plaintiff there is no publication **(Sadgrove v. Hole (1901)).** Also, there is no publication if a third party gets to know of the defamatory statement through his own wrongful act which is not caused by the defendant's negligence. In **Huth v. Huth (1915),** a defamatory letter was sent by the defendant to his wife in an unsealed envelope addressed to her and her inquisitive butler read the letter. The court held that there was no publication to the butler since it was not his duty to read the mail. However, in **Theaker v. Richardson (1962)**, where the defendant sent a defamatory letter to the plaintiff, a local councillor, in a manila envelope similar to the type used for election address, and the plaintiff's husband read it believing it to be an election address, the court held that there was publication to the husband.

Every defamatory statement repeated is a fresh publication and constitutes a separate cause of action. Thus in the case of a book there is a series of publications; author to publisher, printer and publisher, and finally the distributor (e.g. bookseller, library) when the book is sold. However, the distributor will not be liable for publication made by him if he proves that he was unaware of the libel contained in the book or journal and there was no reason for him to know that the matter was defamatory (**Sun Life Assurance Co of Canada v. W.H. Smith & Son Ltd (1934)).**

Defences to defamation. Several defences are available. If the plaintiff consented to the publication,, he cannot complain. If the defendant can show that the statement is substantially true he can plead **justification** even though he made the statement with malice. Section 5 of the Defamation Act provides that where the words complained of contain two or more distinct charges against the plaintiff the defence of justification will not fail simply because the truth of each charge is not proved and if the charge not proved does not materially injure the plaintiff's reputation having regard to the true charges.

The defendant can plead **privilege** where the statement was made on a privileged occasion. Statements made in Parliament have absolute privilege and are fully protected. So too, are statements made during the course of judicial proceedings in the UK and in reports of such proceedings if they are accurate, fair and contemporaneous with the proceedings. Official communications between officers of the State in the course of their official duties, and communications between solicitors and their clients made in connection with litigation, are equally protected. Some other occasions (e.g. fair and accurate reports of parliamentary proceedings whether or not they are contemporaneous; reports of foreign proceedings which are of legal interest to the English public; statements made in the discharge of a legal or moral or social duty where the recipient has an interest in receiving them; statements made in the protection of an interest; and professional statements between solicitor and client) only attract qualified privilege (i.e. they are privileged only if they are made without malice or without the intention that they should injure the other person's reputation).

In **Watt v. Longsdon (1930)**, the defendant received a report that the plaintiff, an overseas director of his company, was dishonest and leading an immoral life. He showed the report to the chairman of the company and to the plaintiff's wife.The report proved to be false. It was held that communication of the report to the chairman was covered by qualified privilege since there was both an interest in making and receiving it. However, communication to the plaintiff's wife was not protected by qualified privilege since the defendant had no duty to inform the wife of the allegation. In **Osborn v. Boulter (1930)**, a publican complained to the brewers who supplied him with beer that it was of a poor quality. The brewers dictated a letter to their typist defending the beer and stating that they had heard rumours that the poor quality of the beer was due to the watering of it by the publican. It was held that the letter was privileged because it was written as part of the brewers' business in protecting the business.

Finally, if the alleged defamatory statement was only comment on a matter of public interest and it was fair and made in good faith, the defendant may plead **fair comment.** For comment to be fair it must be based on facts. In **London Artist Ltd v. Littler (1969)**, the defendant published a letter alleging that the reason why a successful play closed down was because the plaintiff had plotted to close the play by enticing the four leading performers to terminate their contract. The defence of fair comment failed because the defendant could not prove an inportant fact, namely, that the plaintiff plotted to close the play. The defendant need not prove all the alleged facts. It is sufficient if on the facts proved his comment was fair **(s. 6 Defamation Act).** The defence of fair comment is defeated by malice (i.e. evil motive).

IV Torts Against Goods.

A person who wrongly interferes with goods may be liable in the tort of **trespass to goods** if the interference is direct and physical and the goods are in the possession of another.This tort usually arises when goods which are in the physical possession of another person are removed or damaged. If the interference amounts to a denial of the true owner's title to the goods (e.g. where a non-owner sells goods to a buyer, or refuses to return the goods to the true owner) liability will arise in the **tort of conversion.**

The Tort (Interference of Goods) Act 1977 gives the courts a discretion to grant the plaintiff damages or an order for the return of the goods or their value, and to grant the defendant an allowance for improving the value of the goods where he acted under a mistaken but honest belief that the goods belong to him.

Remedies in Tort

The main remedies in tort are damages and injunction. Damages in tort are always unliquidated as the purpose is to put the plaintiff in the position he would have been in had the tort not been committed. In the case of personal injuries, damages may be awarded under various headings such as loss of earnings (both actual and future), loss of amenity (i.e. loss of ability to engage in activities which the plaintiff enjoyed before the injury); pain and suffering and medical expenses. In awarding damages, the courts will make deductions for tax (e.g. PAYE) and social security benefits received. Special damage (e.g. medical expenses and damage to clothing must be specifically claimed). Where the tort is actionable *per se* (without the need for any damage to be suffered, as in the case of trespass) and the plaintiff has not suffered any actual damage, the courts may award nominal damages. Where the courts want to punish the defendant, in addition to compensating the plaintiff, they may award exemplary damages. Exemplary damages are awarded only in limited circumstances such as in the case of oppressive, arbitrary and unconstitutional acts of pubic officials, or where the defendant's conduct has been calculated to make a profit for himself even after paying damages to the plaintiff.

An injunction may be granted by the courts to prevent the defendant from continuing some tortuous act (e.g. as in the case of nuisance).

Effect of Death

Under the Law Reform (Miscellaneous Provisions) Act 1934 as amended, on the death of a person all causes of action (except defamation) whether as defendant or plaintiff survives against or for the benefit of the estate. Damages which can be recovered by the estate where death comes after injury will include medical expenses, funeral expenses and damages for loss of earnings up to the date of death (but not for loss of income in respect of any period after death).

Under the Fatal Accident Act 1976 dependants of the victim can also sue for any monetary loss which they have suffered as a result of his death. Damages for bereavement may be awarded to a spouse for the loss of a spouse and to parents for the loss of a child.

Limitation of Actions

A claim for damages for personal injuries (including death) becomes statute barred after three years from the date when the action could first have been brought (unless the cause of action was concealed by fraud , mistake or where the plaintiff was under a disability in which case the courts can extend the period **(Limitation Act 1980).**

An action for property damage becomes statute barred six years after the date when the damage occurred and not when it was discovered. However the Latent Damage Act 1986 provides that in the case of latent defects an action for negligence resulting in property damage can be brought within three years from when the plaintiff knew or ought to have known of the defects, notwithstanding that the six year period has passed as long as the action is not brought later than fifteen years from the date of the defendant's breach of duty

Chapter 15

Examination Technique

Introduction

We know from experience that most students work very hard, but that very many fail to do justice to themselves in the examination. We firmly believe that this is because many do not know what is expected of them, and are not familiar with the technique of writing specific answers in response to specific questions.

General

Students should bear the following general points in mind:

1. Read the instructions in the question paper carefully. Do not assume they are the same as last year's .

2. Read **all** the questions carefully before starting to write the answers. Do not worry if your mind goes completely blank when you first read them. You might even feel that you cannot answer a single question. Re-read the questions, and you will be pleasantly surprised to discover that there are some you can answer. Once you start writing you will recall things you learnt a long time ago, which were stored somewhere in the deep recesses of your memory.

3. Do the easiest question first, but not before you have read the others. To start by answering your easiest question calms your nerves, and gives you all-important confidence.

4. You **must** budget your time and allocate almost equal time to each question. However, it is not unusual to spend a little more time on your first answer. You will find that your writing speed improves with time. You should allow yourself ten to fifteen minutes to spare at the end for a final check-up on all answers.

5. Plan your answers in rough outline before you begin writing. Write down all the points you wish to discuss, and the names of relevant cases. As soon as you think of another point, write it down before it escapes your memory. It is perfectly reasonably to make rough notes on your examination script. You need not be anxious about the examiner noticing your sketch. In our experience, it creates a favourable impression on the examiner; it is a sign of an orderly mind.

6. Do not answer a question any part of which you do not understand.

7. Answer the question asked, and not the one you hoped to find. It is a mistake to assume that the mention of a topic in the question is an invitation for you to write everything you know about that and other related subjects. You must answer the question asked, and no other. Pages of irrelevant material are a waste of your valuable time, earn no marks and may annoy the examiner.

8. Remember that the examiner has prepared a marking scheme allocating marks to different parts of the question. It is essential that you answer all the questions you are required to answer. You must not spend a disproportionate amount of time on any question or part of it. You must answer all parts of the question even if it is in note form. Remember - no answer, no marks !

9. It is in your interest to get the examiner on your side. It should not come as a surprised to you that examination scripts are marked under pressure and in a hurry. Examiners have to meet the deadline set by the examination bodies. Try to help the examiner by writing neatly. Make use of headings and sub-headings and underline important parts of your answer. Examiners hate dull-looking unbroken long essays.

10. We know that it is far easier said than done, but if at all possible check over answers at the end. You may have missed out the important negative which is vital to your answer.

Use of Cases

Do not be over-anxious about the number of cases you will have to encounter and remember. They are intended to illustrate the legal principles stated, and are not meant to be committed to memory in their entirety. As a rule, it is sufficient to cite one case to support a legal point.

Of course, it looks better if you can remember the names of the cases, but it is not essential to remember all of them. You are expected to remember names of only important and well-known cases. If your memory is not good, don't despair. It is sufficient to say 'in a well-known case'; if you know it, it must be well-known. The examiner is interested in finding out whether you understand the principle established in a particular case, and does not expect you to relate the facts of the case in great detail. Resist the temptation to retell the 'story' in your own humorous and irresistible style, even if your tutor does so in class; the examiner has heard it before. However, you must give sufficient facts to make sure of the decision.

It is permissible to invent hypothetical cases to illustrate your point as long as you make it clear that they are your own invention. Do not pretend that they are facts of some recent fictitious case.

Always underline case names and references to statute.

Answering Problem Questions

This type of question is meant to test your ability to apply basic legal principles to factual situations. Many candidates fail because they do not display their knowledge sufficiently and leave too much unsaid.

You should identify the legal points involved, explain the relevant principles, and apply them to a given set of acts and come to a conclusion. You must come to a conclusion; but it need not be a definite one. It is permissible to suggest alternatives, and make reasonable assumptions about additional facts or other information. Many problems are deliberately set with scope for agreement on both sides.

Remember it is the reasoning that earns marks, not a good guess at the right conclusion. The examiner wishes to see your reasoning set out in the script. You earn good marks even if you reach the 'wrong' conclusion i.e. different from that of the examiner.

If you are asked to advise one of the parties, there is no need to write a personal letter with all of the unnecessary details. You should so it in the form of a note or memorandum concluding 'John Smith is advised ...' or 'It is submitted John Smith is likely to succeed...' Clever answers like 'John Smith is advised to consult his solicitors' should be avoided. Extra-legal advice regarding an individual's moral obligations etc. should be avoided. Answers based on common sense are unlikely to earn many marks. The examiner expects legal advice, supported by legal authority.

Firm grip of the facts is essential. If the facts are complicated, you may draw diagrams (which you can cross out afterwards) to understand the problem exactly.

Students must accept facts given. It is not very clever to criticise the examiner by suggesting or implying that the facts are insufficient, or that the question could have been better drafted. Similarly, it is not desirable to sound patronising by saying 'It is a good question,' etc.

Chapter 16

Questions and Answers

Question 1: **(a)** The Sea Transport Company chartered the vessel *Aphrodite* to the Coalheare Company, 'expected ready to load on 1st January at the port of Southampton.' On 1st January *Aphrodite* was at Panama and she subsequently called at New York. She reached Southampton on 23rd March. The Coalheare Company wish to repudiate the contract.

Advise them.

(b) Smithson offered to sell his car to Jenkins. 'It's a good car in first rate condition.' Smithson honestly believed this to be true, but the car's engine was in fact seriously defective. Jenkins asked Smithson whether he would permit Pry , a mechanical engineer, to inspect the car on his behalf. Smithson agreed to this. Pry made a careless inspection and reported that the car was in excellent condition. Jenkins bought the car and has now discovered the defects.

Advise Jenkins.

(ICSA)

Answer: **(a)** This question is concerned with the relative importance of contractual terms. Was the term 'expected ready to load on 1st January at the port of Southampton' a condition, a warranty or an innominate term? If it is a condition, the Coalheare Company will normally be entitled to repudiate the contract and also claim damages for any loss they have suffered. Or alternatively, they may continue with the contract and simply bring a claim for damages. If it is a warranty, they can only claim damages and must continue with the contract. If it is an innominate term, Coalheare Company will have to wait until some time after the breach to see whether it has a serious effect on the contract. Then, only if the breach deprives them of a substantial benefit of the contract can they terminate the contract. A term is only treated an innominate term if it is impossible to label it as a condition or a warranty.

In the problem, although the parties have not expressly classified the term as a condition, it is plain that they intended it to give a right to terminate if it was breached, because the contract is a mercantile contract and in such contracts provisions as to time are usually of the essence of the contract. In a similar case, **Bunge Corp v. Tradax Exports SA (1982),** the House of Lords held that a provision requiring the buyer to give the seller 15 days' notice of the ship's readiness to load a cargo of Soya bean meal was intended as a condition and gave the seller a right to terminate when shorter notice was given.

Nevertheless, the Coalheare Company may not now be able to terminate the contract. They ought to have acted promptly and by waiting until 23rd March, they are by their conduct treating the condition as an *ex post facto* warranty. They must therefore continue with the contract and claim damages for the delay.

(b) As against Smithson, Jenkins may have difficulty in obtaining a remedy. He cannot rely on the Sale of Goods Act I979 which offers protection against defective goods sold since, in a private sale, the rule is *caveat emptor* (let the buyer beware). Nor can he obtain a remedy under the Misrepresentation Act 1967 because he was not induced by the untrue statement by Smithson as to the car's condition to enter into the contract of sale, but relied on his own expert, Pry, who wrongly confirmed Smithson's statement (**Attwood v. Small**

(1838)). His only chance of success is to prove that Smithson's statement constituted a collateral contract between Smithson and himself (**Andrews v. Hopkinson (1957)**).

As against Pry, Jenkins may be able to recover damages either in contract (if Pry was paid to carry out the inspection) or in the tort of negligence (if Pry carried out the inspection as a favour to Smithson).

Question 2: Explain with reasons whether or not the following are valid and enforceable agreements:

(a) where the agreement contains a clause excluding the jurisdiction of the courts;

(b) where a lease is granted with an option to renew on terms to be agreed later by the parties;

(c) where a transport concern agrees to take all its petrol from a particular garage without reference to price but with a clause providing for arbitration in the event of a dispute arising;

(d) where an offer to sell goods states that the offer will be deemed to have been accepted unless there is notification to the contrary.

(CIMA)

Answer: **(a)** An agreement is only a contract if the parties intend it to be legally binding. It is common practice, therefore, for parties to include a clause in their agreement to show that they do not intend the agreement to have contractual effect. This may be necessary with commercial agreements since the courts presume such agreements to be legally binding unless the parties clearly indicate otherwise.

Words such as 'Gentleman's Agreement' and 'Binding in Honour only' have been accepted by the courts to rebut the presumption in favour of legal relations. But, in general, the courts would not accept any form of words which seek to oust their jurisdiction and will declare clauses of this type illegal and void on grounds of public policy (**Baker v. Jones (1954)**). Nevertheless it is always a question of construction as to whether a clause is intended to oust the courts' jurisdiction or simply intended to make the agreement legally unenforceable. In **Rose and Frank v. Crompton (1925),** a marketing agreement included a clause which stated 'this arrangement is not entered into....as a formal or legal agreement and shall not be subject to the legal jurisdiction in the Law Courts.' The court held that the clause simply meant to make the agreement legally unenforceable.

In the problem, if the clause is construed as in **Baker v. Jones** it will be void; but if it only intends to make the agreement legally unenforceable as in **Rose and Frank v. Crompton**, it is valid and the courts will only intervene if the arbitration is improperly performed.

(b) The lease is valid but the option to renew on terms to be agreed later by the parties appears to be void on grounds of uncertainty of terms. In **Courtney & Fairbairn Ltd v. Tolaini Bros (Hotels) Ltd (1975),** it was held that an agreement to negotiate is too uncertain to have any binding force.

(c) An agreement does not have to be worked out in meticulous detain in order to be complete. Thus, a contract for the sale of goods is often complete as soon as the parties have agreed to buy and sell, the remaining details determined by the concept of reasonableness or by law. Section 8 of the Sale of Goods Act states in the absence of the parties to settle the issue as to price, a reasonable price must be paid. Since the petrol is 'goods' the Sale of Goods Act will apply to it, with the result that the agreement will be enforceable.

Additionally, the contract provides for arbitration in the event of any dispute which would inevitably cover 'price', as in **Foley v. Classique Coaches Ltd (1934).** So the terms can be rendered complete and certain without the need for further negotiations.

(d) Acceptance requires some positive act by the offeree. The offeror cannot insist that silence shall amount to acceptance (**Felthouse v. Bindley (1863)**). This rule is intended for the protection of the offeree, not the offeror. So there is no binding contract here. Moreover, if the seller is a dealer, he will be committing a criminal offence under the Unsolicited Goods and Services Act 1971 to sell goods on these terms.

Question 3: Dullard an elderly man with weak sight, has two cars for sale. Smart agrees to buy one and by pretending to be a well known local business man, is allowed to drive it away in return for a cheque. The cheque is dishonoured. Alec asks if he may hire the second car for a week and persuades Dullard to allow him to draw up a hire agreement which Dullard signs. The agreement in fact transfers the ownership of the car to Alec. Both Smart and Alec have now sold the cars and disappeared.

Advise Dullard as to his right to recover the cars from the subsequent purchasers.

(CIMA)

Answer: Dullard is the victim of a mistake induced by fraudulent misrepresentations from Smart and Alec. He parted with the two cars he had for sale after Smart induced him to accept a cheque for one by pretending to be a well-known local business man and Alec persuaded him to sign a document transferring ownership of the second by deceiving him that it was only a hire agreement.

As between Dullard and the two rogues, the contracts are voidable for misrepresentation but Dullard would have to rescind them before the rogues resell the cars to subsequent purchasers (**Car & Universal Finance Co v. Caldwell (1965)**). It is probably too late to rescind the contracts with Smart and Alec because they have already resold the cars. Nevertheless, if Dullard can show that the subsequent purchasers bought the cars with knowledge of the fraud, the courts may still order rescission, thus enabling Dullard to recover the cars or their value.

Dullard's best bet may be to rely on mistake because if his contracts with Smart and Alec are affected by mistake, the contracts will be void and title to the cars would not have passed from him.

The contract with Smart can be declared void for mistake as to identity but Dullard must prove that there were two separate entities in existence, one being mistaken for the other (i.e. Smart and the well known local business man), the mistake was known to Smart, and the mistake was fundamental. The first two conditions are satisfied, but Dullard may find it very difficult to convince the courts that he intended to contract with some person other than Smart. A plea of mistake as to the identity of the other party has rarely succeeded with face to face contracts. In **Ingram v. Little (1961),** a rogue induced the plaintiffs to accept a cheque for their car by pretending to be 'P.G.M. Hutchinson of Stanstead House, Stanstead Road, Caterham.' But in two other face to face contracts, **Phillips v. Brooks (1919)** and **Lewis v. Averay (1972),** the courts refused to declare the contract void , holding that the mistake was only as to the name and credit-worthiness of the other party and not as to identity.

The contract with Alec can be declared void for mistake as to the nature of the document signed if the doctrine of *non est factum* applies. This doctrine is generally only available to persons with limited capabilities and persons induced by fraud. Dullard is within the class of persons who can rely on it. But to plead it successfully, Dullard must prove that the document he signed was fundamentally different from what he thought it was, and that he was not careless in signing it (**Sanders v. Anglia Building Society (1971)**). While the first condition appears to have been satisfied, it will be difficult for Dullard to prove that he was not careless. In **Saunders,** a householder with weak sight signed a document without reading it because she had misplaced her spectacles. The court held that she had been careless and her plea of *non est factum* failed. In the question, therefore, Dullard may not be able to recover the second car by pleading mistake.

Question 4: (a) (*i*) Explain the difference between specific , ascertained and unascertained goods in a contract for the sale of goods. (*ii*) When does property in unascertained goods pass to the purchaser under such a contract?

(b) **J** owned a garage and agreed to sell cars to two customers.

(i) The car **K** had agreed to buy required minor repairs before it could be delivered to him.

(ii) The car **L** wished to buy had to be ordered by **J** from the manufacturer.

When both cars were in **J**'s garage it and the contents were destroyed by fire.

Advise **J.**

(ACCA)

Answer: (a): (i) Specific goods are defined by the Sale of Goods Act section 61 as 'goods identified and agreed upon at the time a contract of sale is made.' Thus, if a buyer goes into a showroom which has on display a particular car for sale, and agrees to buy it, that is a sale of specific goods. If goods are not specific, then they are said to be unascertained. Thus unascertained goods are either generic goods (e.g. a Ford Escort) or goods forming part of a larger consignment (e.g. 5 gallons of petrol from a tank containing 200 gallons). Ascertained goods are not defined by the Act but probably means goods which are identified and agreed upon after the making of the contract (**Re Wait (1927)**). Thus, if a car dealer agrees to sell a Ford Escort, this is a contract for unascertained goods; but if the buyer later chooses one from the seller's stock, the goods will then become ascertained.

(ii) Section 16 of the Sale of Goods Act provides that property in unascertained goods cannot pass to the buyer until the goods become ascertained (i.e. are agreed on and in a deliverable state) after which the parties' intention becomes relevant. If their intention cannot be determined then section 18 rule 5 provides that property will pass once the goods are unconditionally appropriated to the contract with the express or implied assent of the parties.

(b) J's contracts with **K** and **L** respectively are governed by the Sale of Goods Act. Section 20 provides that in the absence of a contrary intention, risk of accidental loss or damage to goods must be borne by the party with title at the time.

(i) The car that **K** agreed to buy from **J** is specific goods but it is not in a deliverable state since **J** has to carry out some minor repairs before the car can be delivered to him. Property in the car will pass to **K** when the repairs are carried out and **K** receives notice that it is ready for collection. **J** must, therefore, bear the risk of accidental loss of the car. By section 7, the contract is automatically terminated and neither party will have rights under it.

(ii) The car that **L** has agreed to buy from **J** is future specific goods. Property in such goods passes to the buyer as soon as the seller obtains title to them. Thus, title to the car was vested in **L** at the time of the fire, so **L** must bear the loss.

Question 5: **G** goes to see a delivery van which has been advertised by **H** as 'a 1983 model in good condition able to carry large loads, £3,500.' **G** specifically asks **H** about the carrying capacity of the van because he has heavy equipment to deliver. **H** assures **G** the van is suitable. Although **G** inspects the van he fails to notice it is a 1982 model. **G** buys the van and one week later **I** visits **G** and claims the van belongs to him and **H** had no right to sell it. Some weeks later, while still contesting ownership, **G** is delivering heavy equipment when the van breaks down and **G** is told it requires new suspension and a new gear box.

Advise **G.**

(ACCA)

Answer: **H** has made pre-contractual statements to **G** about the van and these statements have turned out to be inaccurate. He stated in the advertisement that the van was a '1983 model' whereas it was an earlier model; he assured **G** that the van was suitable to carry heavy equipment whereas it broke down when heavy equipment was put in it. Such statements constitute a misrepresentation and **G** is entitled to damages (in the tort of deceit if the statements were made fraudulently, or under the Misrepresentation Act 1967 if they were made carelessly) in addition to his right to rescind the contract. Alternatively, the courts may decide that the statements constitute a collateral contract between **G** and **H,** thus giving **G** a right to damages (**Andrews v. Hopkins (1939)**).

The Sale of Goods Act also applies since the contract between **G** and **H** is 'a contract of sale of goods...by which the seller transfers or agrees to transfer the property in goods to the buyer for a money consideration called price.' The Act imposes obligations on the seller of goods and gives the buyer various remedies where these obligations are not fulfilled.

Under the Act certain implied terms are implied in favour of the buyer and several of these terms affect **H**'s contract with **G.** Section 12 (1) implies a condition that the seller has a right to sell the goods and section 12 (2) implies a warranty that the buyer will enjoy quiet possession of the goods if the rights of another are not made known to him at the time of the sale. If **I**'s rights to the van are indeed confirmed and **G** has to give up the van, both implied terms would have been broken. **G** will have a right to terminate the contract with **H** and recover the full purchase price from him (**Rowland v. Divall (1923)**).

Section 13 of the Act which implies a condition that where goods are sold by description they will correspond with the description, also appears to have been breached because **G** was relying on the description 'a 1983 model' to buy the van and the van turned out to be a 1982 model. The courts may feel that despite **G**'s inspection of the van before the sale, no reasonable purchaser would have notice the difference and may give **G** the appropriate remedy (**Beale v. Taylor (1967)**).

It is unclear whether the sale of the van to **G** was a private sale or whether **H** was selling it in the course of a business. If the former, then the rule *caveat emptor* (let the buyer beware) will apply and **G** will have to bear any loss resulting from a bad bargain. If the latter, then the Act implies conditions that the goods will be of satisfactory quality except for defects which the buyer ought to have discovered **(s.14(2))**, and that the goods will be fit for the purpose for which the buyer has bought them **(s.14(3))**. The van was not of satisfactory quality because it broke down with major defects shortly after the purchase; and although **G** carried out an inspection at the date of purchase it is unlikely to have revealed the extent of the defects of the gearbox and suspension shaft. Section 14 (3) is also breached because **G** informed **H** of the purpose for which he intended to use the van and was assured that it was suitable for that purpose.

For breach of sections 13 and 14 **G** is entitled to damages **(s.53)**. The measure of damages will include the cost of repairs to the van and the loss of ordinary profits which he might have obtained from its use. It is unlikely that he can terminate the contract for breach of sections 13 and 14 because he has accepted the goods under section 11(4)

Question 6: Mrs. Dicey bought a freezer from Arctic Freezers Ltd and signed a hire purchase agreement at the shop. She now feels that she cannot afford the freezer.

(a) Explain to Mrs. Dicey her rights of cancellation, the way in which she can exercise these rights and the effects of such action.

(b) Would it make any difference:

(i) if she signed the agreement at home?
(ii) if she had paid the first instalment?

(ACCA)

Answer: A hire purchase agreement is an agreement of the owner of goods (the creditor) to hire out the goods to a hirer (debtor) and to give him the option to purchase the goods after payment of a stated number of instalments. If the hirer is not a company and the credit does not exceed a statutory limit (at present £25,000), the Consumer Credit Act 1974 will regulate it.

The Act requires the debtor to be given certain information in a prescribed form (e.g. the cash price and credit charges) before the agreement is made. The agreement itself must be in writing and must give the debtor notice of his rights to cancel it (if it is a cancellable agreement), and it must be signed by both the debtor and the creditor (or his agent). Moreover, the debtor must be given copies of the agreement. He is always entitled to a copy as soon as he signs the agreement. If the creditor does not sign the agreement at the same time as the debtor, the debtor must be given a second copy of the agreement within seven days after the creditor signs it. In the case of a cancellable agreement, the second copy must be sent by post and contain details of the debtor's rights of cancellation.

A cancellable agreement is an agreement which the debtor signs off the trading premises of the person (the creditor or dealer) with whom he originally negotiated **(s.67).** The debtor has a right to cancel the agreement within five days after receiving the second copy. If notice of cancellation is sent by post, it takes effect as soon as it is posted. The debtor is then entitled to a refund of all moneys paid by him prior to cancellation but must allow the creditor to recover the goods unless they were perishable goods or were consumed.

In the problem, if Mrs. Dicey signed the agreement at the shop she does not have a right to cancel it; but if she signed it elsewhere she can send notice of cancellation within five days of receiving the second copy of the agreement. Notice of cancellation must be sent to Arctic Freezer or the finance company but she is under a duty to take reasonable care of the freezer for up to 21 days after cancellation.

Even if she cannot cancel the agreement, Mrs. Dicey has a statutory right to terminate the agreement at any time before the final instalment becomes payable **(s.99).** Notice of termination must be in writing and it take effect when the notice is received by Arctic Freezer or the finance company. She must then return the freezer and pay all instalments due before termination. She may also have to pay an additional amount to bring the total payments up to half the hire purchase price if the agreement contained a minimum payment clause.

Question 7: Devious buys second hand cars, repairs them and re-sells them at a cheap price. He always displays a notice at the entrance of his business premises stating that they are second-hand and they are bought at the purchaser's risk with no liability on Devious's part. Some are sold to second- hand car dealers and others directly to the public.

In repairing many of the cars, Devious uses faulty reconditioned car engines. Andy buys one of Devious's cars from a second- hand car dealer. He pays for the car by credit card supplied by Financing Ltd. Two days after purchasing the car, the engine ignites and starts a fire. Andy suffers burns when he tries to put out the fire and his suit is badly damaged. Andy hears that the second-hand car dealer from whom he bought the car is in financial difficulties and may cease trading.

Advise the car dealer and Andy.

Answer: As between Devious and the car dealer, the Sale of Goods Act implies terms that where goods are sold in the course of a business, the goods will be of satisfactory quality and fit for their purpose **(s.14).** 'Satisfactory quality' means that the goods will be of a good quality; and among the factors that will determine whether the goods reach the standard that a person can reasonably expect as good include the safety of the goods. Clearly, the car is not of an acceptable standard so Devious will be liable to the trader for breach of both conditions. However, as the dealer is not a consumer, Devious may be able to avoid liability to him by relying on the exemption clause. But he must prove that the exemption clause is reasonable **(Unfair Contract Terms Act 1977).** He may be able to do so since the parties were dealing on equal footing and the dealer bought the radios at a reduced price.

As between Devious and Andy, there is no contractual relationship between them and so the Sale of Goods Act will not apply. Devious's only liability will be in tort. Andy may be able to claim damages
in the tort of negligence if he can establish that Devious was in breach of duty of care towards him.
Manufacturers have a duty of care to ensure that their products are reasonably safe when used by members of the public (**Donoghue v. Stevenson (1932)**). Devious may also be liable to Andy under the Consumer Protection Act 1987. This Act imposes strict liability (i.e. liability not based on carelessness) on a producer who includes a person who manufactures or processes a defective product which causes injury to a consumer while the product is in consumers use. Liability under the Act does not depend on there being a contract between the producer and the consumer. The Act does not allow for the recovery of defective product economic loss; and where the defective product causes damage to other property, such loss is only recoverable if it exceeds £275. So under the Act, Devious may be liable to Andy for personal injuries and for the damage to his suit as long as damage to the suit is in excess of £275.

As between the car dealer and Andy, the car dealer will be liable both in contract for breach of the implied conditions as to 'satsifactory quality, and 'fitness for purpose'and in the tort of negligence. It remains more advantageous to bring an action in contract since all types of economic loss are recoverable in a contract action. Thus Andy may recover damages for personal injuries, damages because the car sold to him was defective, and damages for damage to his suit. Financing Ltd may also be sued under section 75 of the Consumer Credit Act 1973. This section provides that in a three party debtor-creditor- supplier agreement, the creditor is jointly and severally liable with the dealer for breach of contract by the dealer. Since the financial position of the dealer is in question, Andy is advised to sue Financing Ltd for breach of contract by the dealer.

Question 8: **(a)** Explain the various forms which the authority of an agent can take. How can this authority be terminated?

(b) **K** and **L** are partners in a business. What is the legal position if:

(i) They appoint **M** to buy goods on behalf of the business. They later become dissatisfied with **M**'s work and write to him on 1 September telling him he is to cease acting on their behalf. On 7 September **M** purchases goods from **N**, and **N** invoices **K** and **L** for the goods?

(ii) **K** pretending to act on behalf of the business, borrows a large sum of money from the bank and disappears with the money?

(ACCA)

Answer: **(a)** The authority of an agent will determine the liability of the principal to third parties for the agent's acts. If the agent exceed this authority, the agent alone is liable to the third party unless the principal ratifies his act and thus becomes liable. In the main, there are five types of authority (actual, ostensible, usual , authority of necessity and authority by ratification); each depending on the type of agency and how it is created.

An agent will have actual authority under an express agency. The agreement appointing him will set out his instructions. These instructions constitute the express authority of the agent. If the instructions are insufficient to enable the agent to carry out his task, it may be necessary to imply powers to enable him to do acts incidental to his express authority. Such powers may be implied by the courts or by custom and constitute the implied authority of the agent. An agent who is employed to act for his princpal in a market place is deemed to have authority to act in accordance with a custom of the market unless the custom is inconsistent with the instructions given to the agent.

An agent will have ostensible (or apparent) authority under an agency created by estoppel. This agency relationship arises because the principal represents (by word or conduct) to a third party that he has authorised another to act on his behalf and that the latter has authority to act. As against the third party, the principal is prevented from denying the truth of the representation (**Rama Corp Ltd v. Proved Tin & General Investments Ltd (1952)**).

An agent will have usual authority even if he has no actual or ostensible authority where the principal employs him to represent him in the course of his business. If the agent is of a class of agent who acts for another and the act is of a type which it is customary for the agent to perform, the principal will be liable to the third party even though he expressly prohibited the act in question and the third party was unaware that the agent was not acting for himself (**Watteau v. Fenwick (1893)**).

An agent will have authority of necessity where he is in possession of another's property and acts in an emergency to protect the property. The law will confer authority on him to act as he did so as to enable him to recover reasonable expenses from the owner of the property (**Great Northern Rail Co v. Swaffield (1874)**).

An agent who has no authority or who exceeds his authority may acquire authority if the act is ratified by the principal. However, the agent must have purported to act for the principal and the principal must have capacity to enter into the transaction.

An agent's authority can terminate in the same way as the agency can terminate. Thus, actual authority can terminate by agreement, performance, revocation, death or on insanity of either principal or agent, bankruptcy of the principal, and cessation of the principal's business. Ostensible authority is terminated in similar circumstances except that notice of revocation of authority and the principal's insanity must be notified to third parties. Authority of necessity terminates once the emergency ceases.

(b) (i) M has been appointed agent expressly by **K** and **L** who will be liable for any contracts made on their behalf. If **M** is of a class of agents who can act for others and the contract with **N** is of a type that someone in **M**'s position can make on behalf of the business, **M** will have usual authority and **K** and **L** as joint principals will be both liable **(Watteau v. Fenwick).** **M** also appears to have ostensible authority to act for **K** and **L**.

To avoid liability, **K** and **L** must establish that they had notified **N** of the withdrawal of **M's** authority.

(ii) Every partner is deemed to be an agent for the firm and for his fellow partners except if restrictions are placed on his power to act and such restrictions are known to third parties or he is a 'sleeping partner' with limited liability. The borrowing of money, ostensibly for the firm's business, is an action which **K** is expected to undertake, so that **L** can be made liable for the full loan. The fact that **K** used the money for his private use is irrelevant (**Tower Cabinet Co v. Ingram (1949)**).

Question 9: **F** asks his agent **G** to sell 10 typewriters for him. He instructed him that they are not to be sold for less than £500. What is the legal position if:

(i) **G** sells the typewriters for £450?

(ii) **G** buys the typewriters for £500 without informing **F** and later sells them to **H** for £550?

(iii) **G** sells the typewriters to **J** for £550 and also receives 'commission' from **J** of £50?

(ACCA)

Answer: **G** is **F**'s agent under an express agency. The contract governing the relationship between **G** and **H** is called the contract of agency proper. In addition to the express provisions of the contract which will include the agent's express authority, certain duties are implied in the contract on the parties. This question is concerned with the agent's authority and some of his implied duties.

(i) **G** is given express authority to sell his principal's typewriters for not less than £500. By selling for £450, **G** has clearly exceeded this authority and unless the purchaser of the typewriters can show that **F** represented that **G** had authority to sell for less than £500, the contract for the typewriters is *prima facie* void and **F** can recover the typewriters. However, the purchaser is not without a remedy. He can sue **G** damages for breach of warranty of authority (**Yonge v. Toynbee (1910)**) and in the tort of deceit (**Polhill v. Walters (1832)**).

If **G** is not an ordinary agent but a mercantile agent (i.e. a professional selling agent), he can pass a good title to the typewriters notwithstanding that he has exceeded his authority and **F** will be unable to recover them from the purchaser on **G**'s authority. **F**'s only claim will be against **G** for breach of the agency contract (**Eastern Distributors v. Goldring (1957)**).

(ii) An agent owes duties of good faith towards his principal. These include the duty not to personally buy from or sell to his principal without making a full disclosure. **G** is clearly in breach of his duty because he bought his principal's typewriters himself without disclosing this information to **F.** Had **G** still been in possession of the typewriters, **F** could have rescinded the transaction (**Armstrong v. Jackson (1917)**). However, this course of action is not available to **F** because **G** had resold them to **H**.

F may recover the secret profit of £50 which **G** made from the resale. In addition, he can terminate **G**'s agency and, if he can establish fraud on **G**'s part, he can refuse to pay **G** his commission.

(iii) An agent occupies a position of trust as between the principal and himself and as such he should not make secret profits or accept bribes or benefit from his position in any other way.

The 'commission' of £50 is a secret profit and **G** must hand it over to **F** unless the latter allows him to keep it. In **Hippesley v. Knee Bros (1905)**, an advertising agent who obtained discounts from printers with whom he dealt regularly had to pass on the discounts to his principal but was still entitled to his commission as he had not acted fraudulently.

If **G** accepted the commission as an inducement to make the contract with **J**, then the commission is a 'bribe' and the contract between **G** and **J** is fraudulent. **F** may dismiss the agent and recover the amount of the bribe from him (**Boston Deep Sea Fishing & Ice Co v. Ansell (1888)**) and also refuse to pay him his commission. As against **J**, **F** may repudiate the contract that **G** made on his behalf but he will have to return to **J** his £550. Alternatively, **F** may recover the bribe from **J** in an action for deceit. In **Salford Corp v. Lever (1891)**, it was held that a third party who had paid a secret commission to an agent could be sued by the principal for its recovery, even though the principal had already recovered it from the agent. The reason given was that the payment and receipt of a bribe are separate frauds and are actionable separately even though this can result in the principal receiving more than the proper price for the goods.

Question 8: Linda and Susan have run a partnership business for several years. The major activity of the firm has been to operate a wine bar and restaurant. Business has been very good and the partners now wish to extend their business interests by acquiring new premises and opening a leisure complex. They have decided to form a private limited company with themselves as major shareholders and sole directors of the company. Linda and Susan seek your advice upon the issues listed below.

(a) The new company requires a long-term injection beyond the capital which Linda and Susan can subscribe.

What methods may the company use to invite investment and what types of capital may the company raise?

(b) The company is keen to minimise its expenditure in the early years of trading by keeping fixed, long-term, assets to the minimum.

What are the advantages and disadvantages for the company in raising mush of its capital requirement by debentures, particularly those secured by way of a floating charge?

(c) Assume that the company decides to issue ordinary shares to investors.

Discuss the position of minority shareholders and their power to dictate corporate policy to Linda and Susan or to challenge their right to be directors.

(d) Assume the business fails and the company proceeds into an insolvent liquidation.

What personal liability might Linda and Susan incur?

(e) What is the position if Linda or Susan should, during the lifetime of the company, decide to leave the business?

How might the departing shareholder realise her investment in the company?

(CIMA)

Answer: (a) As the company is a private company it is restricted in the ways in which it can raise capital. It cannot apply for a stock exchange listing of its shares or debentures or advertise such securities for sale **(s.170 Financial Services Act 1986).** However, the Secretary of State may exempt any advertisement offering securities if it is of a private nature (e.g. aimed at a few friends or a bank) or if it is aimed primarily at experts (e.g. those involved in the Eurobond market).

Investors may be invited to provide either share or loan capital. The former is raised by an issue of shares. The latter is raised by the issue of debentures. Both shares and debentures are long-term investments in the company but shares, unless issued as redeemable, are only realised when the company goes into solvent liquidation or on their resale. The provision of share capital by an investor makes him a member of the company and, unless such capital carries restricted voting rights, he has a say in the democratic process of the company.

Loan capital makes the holder a creditor of the company and is repayable regardless of the company's assets so that failure to repay may result in foreclosure and resale of those assets.

(b) A debenture is a document acknowledging a debt and it may be secured by a charge over property. A legal charge of land by a company is a debenture (**Kinghtbridge Estates Trust Ltd. v. Byrne (1940)**).

A debenture is a safer investment than shares since interest is payable out of capital; and, if the company defaults with its payments, the investor has a right to appoint a receiver or liquidator. However, since the loan capital is not treated in law as part of the company's share capital, a debenture-holder is not a shareholder and so has no say in the management of the company. Debentures are usually secured by a floating charge which is a charge on general (as opposed to specific) assets which change from time to time.

The main advantage of issuing debentures secured by a floating charge is that the company can use the assets charged until the charge crystallises. As debentures carry a fixed rate of interest the company can calculate its liability early. The company is also able to avoid shareholders' pressure for a good dividend by issuing debentures rather than shares. Debenture interest is a charge on income for tax purposes, but dividend is not.

The main disadvantages of debentures are that as interest is payable regardless of the company's financial position the company is constantly under threat of receivership or liquidation. Also a floating charge may not be a good security for investors if the company's future prospects seem uncertain. So a higher level of interest may be required to attract investors.

(c) The rights attached to shares are usually found in the memorandum or articles. Such rights include the right to vote, right to a dividend when one is declared, right to a return of capital if the company goes into insolvent liquidation. These rights are enforced by a shareholder against the company and against other shareholders in the same company by virtue of section 14 of the Companies Act. But there are also membership obligations including the obligation to be bound by majority decisions taken at properly constituted shareholders' meetings. The majority have the right to formulate company policy, and to remove the directors by ordinary resoluti9on **(s.303),** at such meetings. Only if the majority act fraudulently can the minority challenge their act. Minority protection exists at common law in an action for fraud on the minority and under various statutory provisions (e.g. section 459 for unfair prejudicial conduct; section 127 for variation of class rights; and section 122(g) of the Insolvency Act 1986 for oppression justifying a compulsory winding up of the company).

As long as Linda and Susan retain their controlling interest in the company the minority cannot influence company policy or remove them as directors.

(d) The liability of a member of a company limited by shares is limited to the amount unpaid on his shares in a winding up. So, as long as the shares held by Linda and Susan are fully paid up they do not have to contribute to the assets, unless they gave personal guarantees. Nevertheless, if it appears to the courts that the company's business was being carried on to defraud its creditors, the courts may make any person trading on behalf of the company liable for any or all of its debts **(s.213 IA)**. Linda and Susan may be liable on this basis. The courts also have power to make officers of the company liable for the company's debts if such officers were engaged in wrongful trading **(s.214 IA).** To be liable for wrongful trading it must be proved that the officers could have foreseen insolvent liquidation of their company and took no reasonable steps to minimise the company's liability (such as by ceasing to trade). Linda and Susan can also be liable on this basis.

It is standard practice for a private company to include a pre-emption clause in its articles. Such a clause gives members a ready-made market for their shares when they wish to leave the company. This is particularly important for members since the shares of a private company cannot be offered to the public at large. Alternatively, the company itself may purchase the shares under section 171 out of capital provided that its articles authorise it and the directors make a statutory declaration of solvency backed by an auditor's report. Another solution is for the company to give financial assistance for the purchase of the shares bnut this assistance should not reduce the company's net assets or if it does, then to the extent that the assistance is provided out of distributable profits **(s.155).**

Question 9: You are the financial adviser of Apeel plc. The board of directors is concerned at the low profits achieved in the current trading period, which will substantially affect the dividend received by shareholders. The board seeks your advice as to whether other funds might be utilised to give shareholders a satisfactory dividend return and how preference shareholders could be bought out, to achieve a uniform capital structure in future years. Write a report for the board, concentrating on the following specific issues:

(a) statutory restrictions upon the company's freedom to distribute funds as dividends;

(b) the feasibility of distributing to shareholders any surplus arising from a revaluation of the company's land and buildings;

(c) the possibility of using funds in the company's share premium account for the shareholders' benefit;

(d) the methods available to the company to carry out a restructuring of capital to repay the preference shareholders.

(CIMA)

Answer : **(a)** Dividends can be declared only out of profits available for distribution **(s.263).** Profits means the amount by which the company 's realised profits exceed its accumulated realised losses. Any provision in the accounts for depreciation or renewal of assets will be treated as a realised loss. A public company is further restricted from making a distribution if the effect would be to reduce the company's net assets to less than the aggregate of its called up capital and its undistributable reserves **(s.264).** Thus a public company will have to make good both its accumulated realised and unrealised losses.

Apeel plc will have to comply with the above provisions before it can distribute any of its funds by way of dividend.

(b) Since unrealised profits are treated as a capital reserve, they cannot be distributed or applied in paying up debentures or amounts payable on issued shares; but if the articles permit it, fully paid bonus shares may be issued to members out of the revaluation reserve. Only if the surplus arising from the revaluation of Apeel's land and buildings is realised could it be distributed to members.

(c) The share premium account is treated as a capital account and is subject to the statutory rules regarding the reduction of capital **(s.135).** However, this account may be used to write off discounts on debentures and to pay for bonus shares issued to members **(s.130).**

(d) Section 135 allows a company to redeem its shares with the courts' consent; and section 159 allows it to do the same, but without resort to the courts as long as certain conditions are satisfied. Under section 159 the shares must be issued as redeemable shares, there must be in existence non-redeemable shares, the shares must be fully paid up before they can be redeemed and the redemption must be effected on the terms set out in the articles. If the shares were not issued as redeemable, then they can be redeemed under section 162 but here the members' consent must be obtained. Such consent is given by resolution and it may be an ordinary resolution (for a market purchase) or a special resolution (for an off-market purchase).

A redemption under sections 159 or 162 must be financed out of distributable profits or the proceeds of a fresh issue of replacement shares; and there are provisions to ensure that the capital of the company remains intact. A redemption under section 135 will invariably result in a reduction of capital.

Table of Cases

Table of Statutes

Index